Aquaculture Industry - Recent Advances and Applications

Edited by Yusuf Bozkurt

Published in London, United Kingdom

Aquaculture Industry - Recent Advances and Applications
http://dx.doi.org/10.5772/intechopen.107800
Edited by Yusuf Bozkurt

Contributors
Abebe Getahun, Akewake Geremew, Amha Belay, Argwings Omondi, Denis Worlanyo Aheto, Edward Adzesiwor Obodai, Isaac Kofi Osei, James Barasa Echessa, Job O. Omweno, Michael Chebanov, Norma Estrada, Seyoum Mengistou, Solomon Melaku, Yusuf Bozkurt

First published in London, United Kingdom, 2024 by IntechOpen
IntechOpen is the global imprint of INTECHOPEN LIMITED, registered in England and Wales, registration number: 11086078, 167-169 Great Portland Street, London, W1W 5PF, United Kingdom

British Library Cataloguing-in-Publication Data
A catalogue record for this book is available from the British Library

Additional hard and PDF copies can be obtained from orders@intechopen.com

Aquaculture Industry - Recent Advances and Applications
Edited by Yusuf Bozkurt
p. cm.

This title is part of the Agricultural Sciences Book Series, Volume 7
Topic: Animal Farming
Series Editor: W. James Grichar
Topic Editor: Vasileios Papatsiros

Print ISBN 978-1-83769-198-2
Online ISBN 978-1-83769-199-9
eBook (PDF) ISBN 978-1-83769-200-2
ISSN 3029-052X

For EU product safety concerns:
IN TECH d.o.o., Prolaz Marije Krucifikse Kozulić 3, 51000 Rijeka, Croatia,
info@intechopen.com or visit our website at intechopen.com.

IntechOpen Book Series

Agricultural Sciences

Volume 7

Aims and Scope of the Series

The importance of agriculture cannot be overstated. It helps sustain life, as it gives us the food we need to survive and provides opportunities for economic well-being. Agriculture helps people prosper around the world and combines the creativity, imagination, and skill involved in planting crops and raising animals with modern production methods and new technologies. This series includes two main topics: Agronomy and Horticulture, and Animal Farming. This series will help readers better understand the intricacies of production agriculture and provide the new knowledge that is required to be successful. The success of a farmer in modern agriculture requires knowledge of events happening locally as well as globally that impact input decisions and ultimately determine net profit.

Meet the Series Editor

W. James Grichar has been employed with Texas A&M AgriLife Research for over 45 years with an emphasis on research in agronomy, plant pathology, and weed science. He obtained his BS from Texas A&M in 1972 and his Masters of Plant Protection in 1975. He has published 195 journal articles, over 330 research reports and briefs, 11 book chapters, and over 300 abstracts of profession meetings. He also directs research in many crops including corn, grain sorghum, peanuts, and sesame. He has held various positions in different professional societies including the American Peanut Research and Education Society, Southern Weed Science Society, and Texas Plant Protection Conference in addition to being Associate Editor for Peanut Science and Weed Technology. Significant accomplishments have included spearheading efforts to determine the optimum planting time for soybean production along the upper Texas Gulf Coast. These efforts have shown growers that soybean yields can be improved by 10 to 20% by following a late March to early April plant date. He also has been instrumental in developing a herbicide program for peanut production in the south Texas growing region. Through the development and use of herbicides that are effective against major weed problems in the south Texas region, peanut yields have increased by 25 to 30%.

Meet the Volume Editor

Prof. Dr. Yusuf Bozkurt, who graduated from Ankara University with a Certificate of Honour, also received his MSc and Ph.D. degrees from the same university. Furthermore, he empowered his academic background by studying in different universities and institutions abroad. He has a strong background in the field of reproductive biology and biotechnology, with an emphasis on cryoconservation. His current academic research focuses on the conservation of aquatic genetic resources.

Contents

Preface **XIII**

Section 1
Overview of Biotechnology in Aquaculture **1**

Chapter 1 **3**
Introductory Chapter: Biotechnological Applications in the Aquaculture Industry
by Yusuf Bozkurt

Section 2
Conservation of Aquatic Genetic Resources **11**

Chapter 2 **13**
Action before the Extinction of Endangered Sturgeon Species: With Emphasis on Stock Enhancement and Conservation
by Yusuf Bozkurt and Michael Chebanov

Section 3
Aquaculture Profiles of Countries **29**

Chapter 3 **31**
Fish Seed Production for National Development in Kenya: Current Status, Challenges, Quality Control and Innovative Strategies for Commercialization
by James Barasa Echessa

Chapter 4 **57**
Recent Developments in Fish Nutrition and Culture Technologies in Kenya
by Job O. Omweno and Argwings Omondi

Section 4
Technology Usage in Aquaculture **71**

Chapter 5 **73**
Bioflocs Technology in Freshwater Aquaculture: Variations in Carbon Sources and Carbon-to-Nitrogen Ratios
by Solomon Melaku, Abebe Getahun, Seyoum Mengestou, Akewake Geremew and Amha Belay

Section 5
Bivalve Culture **97**

Chapter 6 **99**
Perspective Chapter: Health and Safety in Oyster Aquaculture
by Norma Estrada

Chapter 7 **135**
Biofouling of the Mangrove Oyster (*Crassostrea tulipa*, Lamarck, 1819) Cultivation: The West African Perspective
by Isaac Kofi Osei, Edward Adzesiwor Obodai and Denis Worlanyo Aheto

Preface

Aquaculture can be defined as the controlled production of aquatic organisms such as fish, crustaceans, mollusks, algae, and other organisms. Today, aquaculture is not only the fastest-growing industry but also the only way to supply safe and sustainable seafood production. However, this industry is experiencing some challenges due to several environmental, economic, and social concerns in recent years. For that reason, the aquaculture industry needs novel technologies, which may provide solutions to increase sustainable and profitable aquaculture production.

In this regard, the *Aquaculture Industry – Recent Advances and Applications* book highlights important implementations in terms of the conservation of aquatic genetic resources globally but also describes the current situation and applied technologies regionally.

This book is divided into five sections including seven chapters written by experts in their specialized fields.

Section 1, "Overview of Biotechnology in Aquaculture", provides information on significant biotechnologies applied in aquaculture.

Section 2, "Conservation of Aquatic Genetic Resources", includes one chapter entitled "Action before the Extinction of Endangered Sturgeon Species: With Emphasis on Stock Enhancement and Conservation", which describes the importance of cryopreservation biotechnology in terms of the conservation of aquatic animal biodiversity and aquaculture as well.

Section 3, "Aquaculture Profiles of Countries" includes two chapters. The first chapter entitled "Fish Seed Production for National Development in Kenya: Current Status, Challenges, Quality Control and Innovative Strategies for Commercialization" describes the current situation of aquaculture in Kenya. The second chapter entitled "Recent Developments in Fish Nutrition and Culture Technologies in Kenya" reviews the use of re-circulatory aquaculture system in tilapia hatchery to conserve limited water supplies and guarantee 95% success in mono-sex production of all male tilapia fingerlings.

Section 4, "Technology Usage in Aquaculture" includes one chapter entitled "Bioflocs Technology in Freshwater Aquaculture: Variations in Carbon Sources and Carbon-to-Nitrogen Ratios" which describes the biofloc technology applied in aquaculture.

Finally the last section "Bivalve Culture" includes 2 chapters. "Perspective Chapter: Health and Safety in Oyster Aquaculture" and "Biofouling of the Mangrove Oyster (*Crassostrea tulipa*, Lamarck, 1819) Cultivation: The West African Perspective".

This book addresses different topics regarding aquaculture. It is a useful resource for researchers studying in this field. We would like to thank all the authors for their distinguished contributions, as well as Author Service Manager Ms. Karmen Daleta at IntechOpen for her cooperation at various phases of the publication process.

Dr. Yusuf Bozkurt
Professor,
Faculty of Marine Sciences and Technology,
Department of Aquaculture,
İskenderun Technical University,
İskenderun, Hatay, Turkey

Section 1

Overview of Biotechnology in Aquaculture

Chapter 1

Introductory Chapter: Biotechnological Applications in the Aquaculture Industry

Yusuf Bozkurt

1. Introduction

Aquaculture has important roles for human beings, especially in meeting the need for animal protein, and creates important opportunities such as healthy nutrition for people, supply of raw materials to the industrial sector, creation of employment, contribution to rural development, and conservation of biological diversity. As a matter of fact, aquaculture has been identified as the fastest growing food sector in the world by the FAO.

Biotechnology is a technique that uses living organisms and their building blocks, and it is widely employed in different areas such as health, agriculture, food, and industry. The importance of biotechnology, which has great potential in terms of contribution to agricultural production, in aquaculture has been increasing, especially in recent years. Today, biotechnology is a tool that contributes significantly to aquaculture development. The excessive demand for aquatic foods, whose importance as an animal protein source increases daily, causes biotechnology to become widely used in aquaculture.

Modern biotechnology holds great potential not only to meet demand for aquatic food but also to improve aquaculture. In this regard, biotechnology holds tremendous potential to improve the quality and quantity of aquatic organisms reared in aquaculture. Today, biotechnology continues to develop rapidly, and its applications in aquaculture are increasing day by day [1].

2. Application fields of biotechnology in aquaculture

Effective use of biotechnological methods in aquaculture contributes not only to the improvement of this sector but also to the economic development of countries [2]. Biotechnology can be used for many purposes in aquaculture. In this regard, biotechnological applications in this field mainly focus on gender control, chromosome manipulations, gene transfer, and cryopreservation-related issues.

2.1 Gender control

Because of the early maturation of one or both sexes and, as a result, negative changes in growth, feed evaluation rate, behavior, health, body, and meat color, gender control practices are carried out [3]. Various techniques are used in breeding to produce single-breed or sterile populations. Gender control in fish is implemented by three different methods, such as feminization, masculinization, and sterilization.

2.1.1 Feminization

Usually, feminization is implemented by the administration of 17β – estradiol application at the first feeding of offspring. Other estrogens (ethyl-estradiol) are also used for feminization, but estradiol and estrone are not preferred because they are naturally found in fish. In this regard, the critical point in this application is that the fry receives a sufficient level of hormones during the sexual differentiation period, starting from the first feeding.

In many aquacultured species, females grow faster than males and are less aggressive. For this reason, the female population is less stressed, hence healthier and more resistant to diseases. Because of these features, all-female populations are preferred in the breeding of many species. However, the fact that all female populations spend most of the energy they get during sexual maturation on gonad development leads to a decrease in meat yield.

2.1.2 Masculinization

Since functional male (XX) individuals are needed to obtain all-female individuals in the indirect sex change method, androgen hormones such as 17α-methyltestosterone must be introduced into the bloodstream of fish that have hatched and consumed the yolk sac. In this method, the hormone should be added to the feed in certain ratios to ensure that the fish larvae that have consumed the yolk sac consume this feed, or to add this hormone to the aquatic environment to ensure that the larvae are bathed [4].

2.1.3 Sterilization

The production of sterile fish in aquaculture is possible by changing the chromosome numbers. For this purpose, it is necessary to apply one of the environmental shocks to the eggs shortly after fertilization. The aim of sterilization is to ensure that metabolic energy is spent on growth instead of gamete development. As a result, the negative effects of reproductive activity on growth, survival, and meat quality in fish can be prevented [5].

2.2 Chromosome manipulations

Creatures that reproduce with male and female develop from fertilized eggs formed by the union of their parents' sex cells. Sex cells provide the connection between parents and the next generation. The most important asset of a sex cell is the chromosomes that carry heredity factors from generation to generation. One of the homologous chromosomes, which are the same shape and size, comes from the mother and the other from the father, are separated from each other when gametes are formed, and one from each partner goes to each gamete [6].

With the merger of male and female gametes, the spouses come together again and the chromosome numbers remain constant between generations. There are various manipulations performed for different purposes against meiotic and mitotic events during chromosome division. These manipulation processes gynogenesis, androgenesis, triploidization, and tetraploidization techniques. There are various environmental shocks and chemicals used to alter chromosome numbers. These are heat shock, pressure shock, and chemicals such as colchicine, cytochalasin B, and N_2O [3].

2.2.1 Triploidy

The final division of chromosomes within the egg occurs immediately after sperm penetration during fertilization. In this process, the pole cell in the egg is prevented from being expelled from the egg after fertilization by the environmental shock effect.

In this way, the offspring obtained from a triploid egg, if they carry XXX chromosome, sterile females, if they carry XXY chromosomes, fertile male individuals are formed. Many of the studies on triploidy are based on the rule that the triploid homogametic sex is sterile and grows better [7]. Providing triploidy can be acquired by blocking the second meiosis division and keeping the second pole cell after fertilization [5]. Additionally, hot or cold shock, hydrostatic pressure, and chemicals such as colchicine, cytochalasin B, and N_2O are used for the shock performed during triploid application [3].

2.2.2 Tetraploidy

The aim of tetraploidization is to produce fish with four chromosomes. In this process, individuals with 4 N chromosomes are obtained by applying shock during the first mitotic division after a normal egg is fertilized by an active spermatozoa.

2.2.3 Gynogenesis

Gynogenesis is a technique occurring between inactivated sperm and normal egg. As a result of fertilization, all individuals have XX chromosomes, allowing obtain a female individual. In the process of gynogenesis, the male germ cell nucleus is an inactive structure in the egg plasma and the embryo's development is controlled only by maternal heredity [8].

Mature eggs of gynogenetic species do not take action to form the embryo when there are no male sex cells in the environment. Therefore, for success in gynogenetic reproduction, there must be male sex cells that will activate mature eggs. Sperm cells, which have destroyed genetic material, are used in the fertilization of eggs during gynogenesis. γ-rays, X-rays, and ultraviolet (UV) are used to neutralize the genetic material of sperm cells [9]. Since the inheritance material of the sperm is destroyed, the sperm taken from different fish species can also be used for fertilization of the eggs. To activate the eggs, artificial reproduction using sperm with UV radiation is required, and then, physical or chemical shocks are required to restore the embryo's diploid state. These shocks prevent nuclear division by destroying microtubules.

Two different methods, myogenesis and mitogenesis, are used in such studies. Myogenesis occurs by inhibition of the outflow of the second polar cell. The egg is fertilized by spermatozoa whose chromosome material has been eliminated. After a while, it is subjected to shock to prevent the outbreak of the second polar cell, and thus, meiotic gynogenetic embryos with two sets of chromosomes are formed [10]. Mitogenesis produces completely homozygous progeny because it is carried out by inhibition of the first mitotic division after genome duplication. By using this breeding method, after two generations, homozygous-related lines of genetically similar fish can be obtained [4].

2.2.4 Androgenesis

Androgenesis, unlike gynogenesis, is a technique in which the genetic material of the egg is eliminated and fertilization and embryo development continue from the chromosome set of the spermatozoa [6]. In other words, androgenesis is a technique that allows all individuals to carry XY chromosomes, that is, to obtain a male individual, as a result of fertilization of inactivated eggs with normal sperm cells [11].

2.3 Gene transfer

The process of transferring special gene sequences of a certain length to the deoxyribonucleic acid (DNA) structure, which is known as the basis of genetic material, using genetic engineering techniques is called gene transfer [12]. Transgenic creatures are obtained by transferring a foreign gene to the genome using gene transfer techniques. Transgenic organisms are defined as organisms that carry a recombinant gene from another organism in their genome [13]. Rapid developments in recombinant DNA technology increase the importance of gene transfer technologies day by day.

2.4 Gamete cryopreservation and cryoinjuries

Success in aquaculture depends on many technical factors applied in hatcheries. In this regard, induced breeding is considered viable to obtain the required quantity of larvae in hatcheries. On the other hand, apart from induced breeding, new biotechnological techniques such as cryopreservation should be considered in aquaculture programs to provide continuous gamete and larvae production. In this context, FAO has endorsed cryopreservation as a major strategy for the conservation of fish resources [14]. Cryopreservation boosts the viability of gametes for several years without any severe change in the fertilizing capacity of the gametes by lowering the temperature, usually to −196°C [15]. Almost all biological activities are suspended at this temperature, including biochemical reactions that lead to cell death and DNA degradation [16].

Preservation of gametes is of great importance in selection programs applied in aquaculture. Because rearing the same fish species in the same environment and conditions throughout generations causes rare genes to be lost in the current population and heterozygosity to decrease. This reduction in genetic variation limits the potential of existing fish stock to be used in future selection programs, which manifests itself in low survival rates, low growth rates, reduced feed conversion efficiency, increased risk of disease, and increased mortality in juvenile fish [17].

Currently, the cryopreservation technique is routinely applied to the conservation of sperm, embryos, tissues, and cells. Researchers involved in aquaculture are especially working on the cryopreservation of fish sperm [18]. The cryopreservation technique was first used in the field of aquaculture in 1953 to fertilize herring (*Clupea harengeus*) eggs with frozen semen and is now used successfully in many fish species [19].

The most important purpose of cryobiology for use in aquaculture is to create a sperm bank or gene pool belonging to the cultured species. Creating a gene pool by applying cryobiological methods not only allows the preservation of genes but is also a necessity in hybridization, genetic manipulation, and stock enrichment programs [20].

During the cryopreservation of sperm, cryoinjury is practically inevitable. In general, cryoinjuries occur regarding freezing and thawing processes during conventional cryopreservation protocols. Most of the cryoinjuries take place when the temperature is between 0 and −40°C due to heat removal, cryoprotectant toxicity, cold shock, pH fluctuation, osmometric effects, and ice crystal formation [21]. Major cryoinjury can disrupt and damage cellular structures like DNA, the acrosome, and the plasma membrane by oxidizing cellular compounds and causing oxidative stress [22]. It is important to note that permeability plays a critical role in the formation of cryoinjury in the cells. Cells that are permeable demonstrate more tolerance to the cooling and freezing stages of the cryopreservation process [23].

3. Conclusion

Thanks to the biotechnological methods applied in aquaculture, the growth and reproduction rates of aquatic organisms increase, the existence of conditions such as diseases and DNA damage decreases, healthier, more productive individuals with desirable characteristics can be obtained, and the genes of endangered species can be conserved for years. The fact that modern biotechnological methods are effectively used in the field of aquaculture, as well as in farm animals, will allow the sector to develop significantly and will make an important contribution to the national economy.

Author details

Yusuf Bozkurt
Faculty of Marine Sciences and Technology, İskenderun Technical University, Türkiye

*Address all correspondence to: yusuf.bozkurt@iste.edu.tr

References

[1] Arat S. Biotechnology and its applications on aquaculture. In: 3rd National/1st International Workshop on Gamete Biology in Aquaculture, September 19-21, 2018. İskenderun/Hatay. 2018. pp. 19-20 Abstract Book, ISBN: 978-605-256-001-3

[2] Gupta V, Sengupta M, Prakash J, Tripathy BC. An introduction to biotechnology. In: Basic and Applied aspects of Biotechnology. 2016. pp. 1-21

[3] Okumuş İ. Deniz Balıkları Yetiştiriciliği Ders Notları. Trabzon: KTÜ Deniz Bilimleri Fakültesi; 2008

[4] Özden O, Güner Y, Kızak V. Tatlısu balık kültüründe uygulanan bazı biyoteknolojik yöntemler. Ege Üniversitesi Su Ürünleri Dergisi. 2003;**20**(3-4):563-574

[5] Yeşilayer N, Doğan G, Karslı Z, Aral O. Triploid alabalık üretimi. I. In: Ulusal Alabalık Sempozyumu. 2008, 14-16 Ekim, Isparta, Türkiye. 2008

[6] Purdom CE. Genetics and Fish Breeding. Chapman and Hall, Fish and Fisheries Series; 1993. p. 8

[7] Emre Y, Kürüm V. Havuz ve Kafeslerde Alabalık Yetiştiriciliği Teknikleri. Ankara, Türkiye: MİNPA Matbaacılık; 2007

[8] Palti Y, Li JJ, Thorgaard GH. Improved efficiency of heat and pressure shocks for producing gynogenetic rainbow trout. Progressive Fish Culturist. 1997;**59**(1):1-13

[9] Chourrout D. Gynogenesis caused by ultraviolet irradiation of salmonid sperm. The Journal of Experimental Zoology. 1982;**223**:175-181

[10] Galbusera P, Volckaert FAM, Ollevier F. Gynogenesis in the African catfish *Claris gariepinus* (Burchell, 1822) III. Induction of endomitosis and the presence of residual genetic variation. Aquaculture. 2000;**185**:25-42

[11] Devlin RH, Nagahama Y. Sex determination and sex differentiation in fish: an overview of genetic, physiological and environmental influences. Aquaculture. 2002;**208**(3-4):191-364

[12] Babaoğlu M. Bitkilerde gen transferi teknikleri. Ziraat Yüksek Mühendisleri Birliği Dergisi. 1999;**322**:24-26

[13] Gordon JW, Scangos GA, Plotkin DJ, Barbosa JA, Ruddle FH. Genetic transformation of mouse embryos by microinjection of purified DNA. Proc Natl Acad Sci. 1980;**77**:7380-7384

[14] Khoshoo TN. Conservation of India's endangered mega animals: Tiger and lion. Current Science. 1997;**73**(10):830-842

[15] Diwan AD, Ayyappan S, Lal KK, Lakra WS. Cryopreservation of fish gametes and embryos. The Indian Journal of Animal Sciences. 2010;**80**(4):109-124

[16] Agarwal NK. Cryopreservation of fish semen. In: Himalayan Aquatic Biodiversity Conservation & New Tools in Biotechnology. Srinagar (Garhawal) Uttarakhand, India: Transmedia Publication; 2011. pp. 104-127

[17] Bozkurt Y. Cryopreservation and aquaculture. 8th Global Conference on the Conservation of Animal Genetic Resources Proceedings. 04-08 October 2011, Tekirdağ: Türkiye; 2011. p. 389-392

[18] Bozkurt Y. Introductory chapter: Application fields of Cryopreservation biotechnology. In: Bozkurt Y, editor. Cryopreservation Biotechnology in Biomedical and Biological Sciences. London, UK: IntechOpen Publications; 2018. pp. 1-4. ISBN 978-1-78984-680-5

[19] Bozkurt Y. Balık yetiştiriciliğinde gamet kalitesinin önemi. Ziraat Mühendisliği Dergisi. 2010;**355**:28-33

[20] Bozkurt Y, Yavaş İ, Karaca F. Section IV. In: Katkov I, editor. Cryopreservation of Brown Trout (*Salmo trutta Macrostigma*) and Ornamental Koi Carp (*Cyprinus carpio*) Sperm. London, UK: IntechOpen Publications; 2012. pp. 293-304, ISBN: 978-953-51-0302-8

[21] Bozkurt Y. In: Ankara BY, editor. Gamete and Embryo Cryopreservation in Aquatic Species. In: Modern Reproductive Biotechnologies in the Conservation of Aquatic Genetic Resources. Türkiye: Türkiye Klinikleri Publications; 2023. pp. 6-11

[22] Xin M, Niksirat H, Shaliutina-Kolešová A, Siddique MAM, Sterba J, Boryshpolets S, et al. Molecular and subcellular cryoinjury of fish spermatozoa and approaches to improve cryopreservation. Reviews in Aquaculture. 2020;**12**:909-924

[23] Chao NH, Liao IC. Cryopreservation of finfish and shellfish gametes and embryos. Aquaculture. 2001;**197**(1-4):161-189

Section 2

Conservation of Aquatic Genetic Resources

Chapter 2

Action before the Extinction of Endangered Sturgeon Species: With Emphasis on Stock Enhancement and Conservation

Yusuf Bozkurt and Michael Chebanov

Abstract

Sturgeons are one of the most valuable fish species in the world due to their pleasant meat, famous black caviar, and isinglass. Sturgeons are believed to be among primitive groups of vertebrates in the world and have been described as "living fossils". It is assumed that they have been living in the natural waters of the northern hemisphere of the world for 200 million years. Their natural populations are now highly endangered because of overfishing for their black caviar and delicate flesh, destruction of spawning habitat, pollution of freshwater, and human-constructed barriers to access spawning migration. Nowadays, living populations have little chance of survival without stock enhancement and sustainable conservation programs. This review document presents general features of current restoration programs and describes how stock enhancement and conservation strategies can be used to recover Eurasian-based sturgeon resources in peril.

Keywords: sturgeon, stock enhancement, *ex situ* conservation, live gene banks, cryobanks

1. Introduction

Sturgeon is a common name for the 27 fish species belonging to the families of *Acipenseridae* and *Polyodontidae* which are some of the most important aquacultured freshwater fish. Their evolutionary history dates back to the Triassic period some 208–245 million years ago [1].

These fishes are highly appreciated not only because of their quality meat but also for their caviar and isinglass, a kind of gelatin used for various industrial aims derived from sturgeon's swim bladder. In terms of aquaculture, sturgeons are the most promising temperate freshwater species. Today, sturgeons are thought to be the perfect candidate species for aquaculture because of their high commercial value. Furthermore, the enormous financial gains of sturgeon farming are the main impulse for sturgeon aquaculture [2].

Today, sturgeons are described as 'living fossils' and are threatened with extinction due to some reasons such as habitat loss and overharvest according to the Red List compiled by the International Union for Conservation of Nature [3]. It has become clear that conventional measures such as decreasing pollution and protecting habitats to maintain and restore these populations did not reach their aim. Thus, biotechnological tools should be implemented as soon as possible in terms of *ex-situ* conservation programs. This review is aimed at describing the ways of stock enhancement and conservation strategies can aid the protection of endangered Eurasian-based sturgeon species.

2. Taxonomy

Sturgeons are classified within the *Acipenseridae* and *Polyodontidae* families include 27 species in four genera, which are *Acipenser* with 19 species, *Huso* with 2 species, *Scaphirhynchus* with 3 species, and *Pseudoscaphirhynchus* with three species [1, 4, 5].

3. Morphological characteristics

Sturgeons have been known as "primitive fishes" or "relict species" because their morphological characteristics have remained relatively unchanged since the earliest fossil record, which evolved some 200–250 million years ago [6].

Sturgeons are distinguished generally by their cartilaginous skeleton from other bony fish species. They are recognized by their flattened rostra, elongated bodies, heterocercal tail lobes, and distinctive barbels. Additionally, their body is covered by bony dermal plates. The notochord is surrounded by a perichord supporting the cartilaginous structure. The spinal cord is located above the notochord. The caudal fin is typically heterocercal, with the continuation of the spinal cord into the upper body. The sturgeons have an intestinal spiral valve that increases the surface availability for nutrient intake and the time required for food digestion. The swimbladder is simple and physostomous, connected with the gut [7].

4. Biological characteristics

The sturgeons are an anadromous and migratory fish species. Most sturgeon species return from marine systems to the rivers, where they were born when sexually mature. Some species spend their whole life in fresh waters while others migrate into the brackish or seawater after a certain size (e.g. Russian sturgeon (*Acipenser gueldenstaedtii*), Siberian sturgeon (*Acipenser baerii*), sterlet (*Acipenser ruthenus*), and beluga (*Huso huso*) [5]. River currents carry the larvae from the upstream areas to downstream towards backwater areas. During their first year of growth, they reach 18–20 cm in length and begin to migrate to the salt waters [8].

Sturgeons exhibit a very long life cycle their first spawn does not occur until they reach around 7–12 years old. A female sturgeon may release 100,000–3 million eggs. They can grow to very large sizes (up to 6–7 m long). Most of the sturgeon species are anadromous. There are also potamodromous (landlocked) species and forms that spend their entire life cycle in freshwater [9].

Furthermore, hybrids between the beluga (Huso huso) and the sterlet (Acipenser ruthenus) obtained artificially are widely used in aquaculture in the Soviet Union [10], Germany [11], and Japan [12]. It is known that the intraspecific or intergenetic crosses (2n × 2n or 4n × 4n) are fertile, while the interploid hybrids (2n × 4n) are triploid and usually sterile (with a chromosome number of approximately 160–180) in sturgeons [6]. This situation is important in case the escaping of hybrids into the wild from sturgeon farms can lead to genetic contamination of sturgeon populations in the natural waters.

5. Distribution

Sturgeons are especially distributed throughout the Northern Hemisphere where living in lakes, large rivers, coastal waters, and interior seas in Russia, Turkey, Azerbaijan, Iran, Kazakhstan, Turkmenistan, Ukraine, Romania, Bulgaria, China, and Western Europe countries as well as North America (**Figure 1**) [13].

The sturgeons reaching sexual maturity, migrate to the larger rivers in the Northern Hemisphere such as Volga, Kuban, Don, Ural, Danube, Terek, Kura, Sefidroud, Tajan, Gorgan, Atrak, Kızılırmak and Yeşilırmak [14]. Furthermore, most of the natural sturgeon stocks inhabit the basins of the Sea of Azov, the Black Sea, and the Caspian Sea where 90% of the world's supply of caviar and flesh comes from these areas.

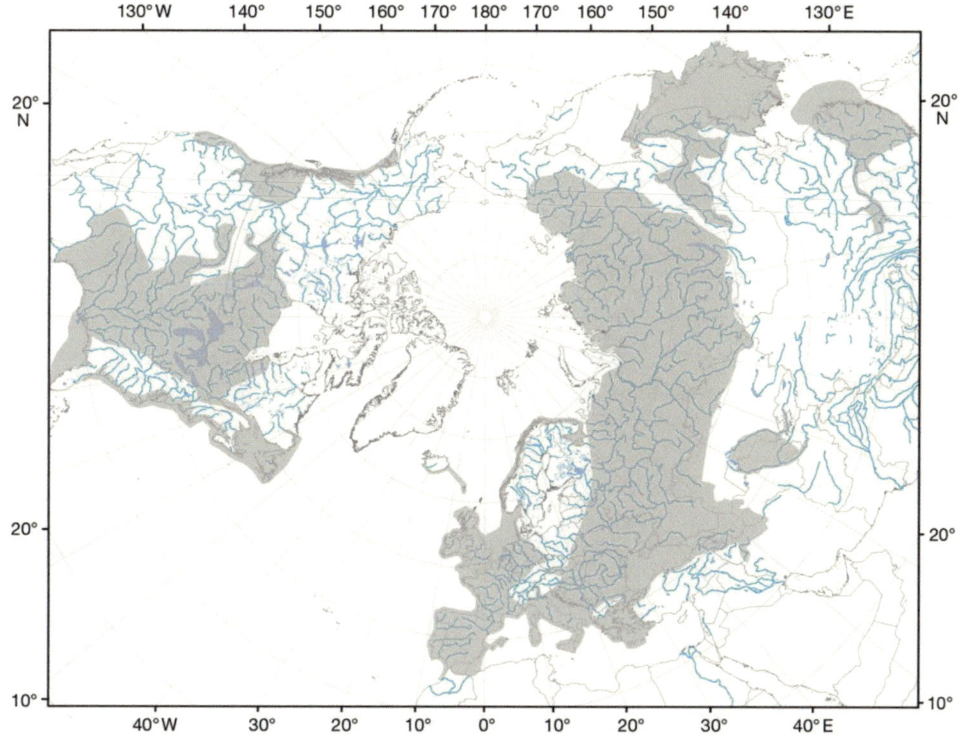

Figure 1.
Global distribution of the 27 Acipenseriformes species (depicted in gray) [3].

6. Current situation

In spite of their long history and abundance until 200–250 years ago, and also their adaptation ability to different habitats such as from the cold waters of Canada and Siberia to the warm waters of northern Italy and Spain, almost all sturgeon species are in danger of extinction (**Table 1**). Sturgeon species have experienced a significant decrease in abundance, as they are sought for their valuable flesh and caviar, by primarily human-constructed barriers to blocking spawning migrations, overfishing, and poaching, as well as due to impacts to their natural habitats such as reductions in river flow, and environmental pollution especially throughout the past century [15].

The decrease in sturgeon populations has prompted some international restrictions on fishing and trade of sturgeons and their valuable products. Currently, existing measures to protect sturgeon focus on holding live breeders in captivity through aquaculture. These attempts have demonstrated the possibility of maintaining a broodstock and showed potential for the conservation of endangered species through management under controlled conditions. For these reasons, those interested in sturgeon aquaculture have started to grow rapidly throughout the world and nowadays almost all sturgeon products such as caviar are the result of aquaculture production [15].

Species	Authority	Continent	Red List status	Year assessed
Acipenser baerii	Brandt, 1869	Eurasia	EN	2010
Acipenser brevirostrum	Lesueur, 1818	North America	VU	2004
Acipenser brevirostrum	Lesueur, 1818	North America	VU	2004
Acipenser dabryanus	Duméril, 1869	Eurasia	CR	2010
Acipenser fulvescens	Rafinesque, 1817	North America	LC	2004
Acipenser gueldenstaedtii	Brandt & Ratzeburg, 1833	Eurasia	CR	2010
Acipenser medirostris	Ayres, 1854	North America	NT	2006
Acipenser medirostris	Ayres, 1854	North America	NT	2006
Acipenser mikadoi	Hilgendorf, 1892	Eurasia	CR	2010
Acipenser naccarii	Bonaparte, 1836	Eurasia	CR	2013
Acipenser nadiventris	Lovetsky, 1828	Eurasia	CR	2010
Acipenser oxyrinchus	Mitchill, 1815	North America	NT	2006
Acipenser persicus	Borodin, 1897	Eurasia	CR	2010
Acipenser ruthenus	Linnaeus, 1758	Eurasia	VU	2010
Acipenser schrenckii	Brandt, 1869	Eurasia	CR	2010
Acipenser sinensis	Gray, 1835	Eurasia	CR	2010
Acipenser stellatus	Pallas, 1771	Eurasia	CR	2010

Species	Authority	Continent	Red List status	Year assessed
Acipenser sturio	Linnaeus, 1758	North America	CR	2010
Acipenser transmontanus	Richardson, 1836	North America	LC	2004
Huso dauricus	Georgi, 1775	Eurasia	CR	2010
Huso huso	Linnaeus, 1758	Eurasia	CR	2010
Pseudoscaphirhynchus fedtschenkoi	Kessler, 1872	Eurasia	CR	2010
Pseudoscaphirhynchus hermanni	Kessler, 1877	Eurasia	CR	2010
Pseudoscaphirhynchus kaufmanni	Kessler, 1877	Eurasia	CR	2010
Scaphirhynchus albus	Forbes & Richardson, 1905	North America	EN	2004
Scaphirhynchus platorynchus	Rafinesque, 1820	North America	VU	2004
Scaphirhynchus suttkusi	Williams & Clemmer, 1991	North America	CR	2004
Polyodon spathula	Walbaum, 1792	North America	VU	2004
Psephurus gladius	Martens, 1862	Eurasia	CR	2010

CR: critically endangered; EN: endangered; VU: vulnerable; NT: near threatened; and LC: least concern.
Source: [3].

Table 1.
IUCN red list status of sturgeon and paddlefish by continent in 2016.

The first sturgeon farming trials were performed almost simultaneously in the mid-nineteenth century in Russia, Germany, and North America to produce juveniles as stock material to prevent population declines in the wild. As a result of the investigations in artificial reproduction, the commercial production of a hybrid between *Huso huso* and *Acipenser ruthenus*, the 'bester', started in the 1960s in Russia [16]. Currently, sturgeon aquaculture has been developing in three directions: (a) to conserve and enhance natural populations via controlled propagation; (b) to generate farmed sturgeon broodstocks for artificial reproduction and commercial aquaculture (including meat and caviar production); and (c) to promote recreational farming such as for aquarium fish and garden ponds [17, 18].

7. Stock enhancement in the wild

In the past, a large number of sturgeon juveniles produced by hatcheries, located in the basins of the Azov, Black, and Caspian Seas (Russia, Turkey, Iran, etc.), were released into the natural water bodies to enhance sturgeon stocks. According to observations, it was seen that such traditional releasing of a large number of juveniles (weighing 2–3 g) from sturgeon hatcheries leads to strong food competition and inefficient use of food resources in natural waters. However, different age and size-graded juveniles that have different spawning ecotypes migrated into the river mouth at different seasons, which reduced competition among the juveniles and optimized the use of food resources in the wild [19].

Resultingly, it is well understood that expanded (from May to September) release of different size- and age-graded juveniles into different sections of rivers will contribute to an elevated survival rate of released juveniles and also to the conservation of biodiversity of established sturgeon populations and rational use of food organisms in different water bodies [19]. From this point of view, long-standing research on the seasonal dynamics of food organisms in the river and estuary, combined with monitoring of growth and survival of different sturgeon juveniles led to supporting of new strategies regarding stocking of sturgeon species to the water bodies. This novel approach implies the importance of optimization of the seasonality of reproduction, the releasing of different size- and age-graded juveniles, depending on the site, season of juvenile releasing, and climate variations (wet or dry years) [20–22].

Additionally, the implementation of controlled reproduction, breeding methods, and rearing systems made it possible to achieve significant success in restoring these species that have not been observed for several decades in the wild. As a result, the number of sexually mature adult beluga and stellate sturgeon in the Krasnodar Center's genetic collection significantly exceeds their current number in the Sea of Azov [6].

8. Stock enhancement in the hatcheries

A logical mitigation strategy to be carried out to reduce the fishing pressure on natural stocks facilitates the sustainable development of sturgeon aquaculture [6]. It is obvious that a genetically heterogeneous broodstock population, comprising from 40 to 200–300 individuals of the same species, should be ensured for the formation of a biologically valuable sturgeon population in the sturgeon hatcheries to back up for gene maintenance. On the other hand, it should be noted that another broodstock population should be provided at another hatchery within the same region as "safety precaution" [23].

By providing fertilized eggs for the growing of fish in aquafarms and also the formation of captive broodstock in wild breeders, the hatcheries contribute to the improvement of sturgeon farming effectively. From this point of view, the installation of a sturgeon broodstock based on hatcheries had to be made in view of the properly prepared breeding plans, considering the optimal species and age structure of the broodstocks. At present, technological feasibilities exist to apply these kinds of programs to provide control of the environmental conditions at the sturgeon hatcheries. Breeding technologies such as artificial spawning, egg incubation, and initial larvae rearing have been used over the last 50–70 years in sturgeon hatcheries [24].

Efforts have been made to broaden the reproduction period in order to provide more effective usage of the hatcheries [21]. It is known that expansion of the reproduction period also allows the insertion of the winter spawning stock into the stocking programs. In this regard, controlling the sexual cycle and spreading the spawning period over the year is possible by using captive broodstocks in the hatcheries. In this way, the combination of thermal and hormonal manipulations, ovulation, and spermiation can be possible earlier or later than the normal spawning period [25]. Additionally, hatchery technologies to collect ovulated eggs in place of performing cesarean surgery, have increased female survival following spawning [26].

9. Monitoring of the farmed broodstock

It is known that captive breeding is an important measure to conserve endangered sturgeon species and also serves as the prime strategy to overcome the challenges in the near future [27, 28]. Monitoring programs should record the biological characteristics of juveniles, including physiological-biochemical indices, teratology, melanophore adaptive response, and resistance to the extreme values of environmental factors (temperature, salt resistance, and oxygen deficiency).

Also, morphological, biological, genetical, and reproductive properties of the mature broodstock should be monitored frequently to ensure its quality and fitness in the hatcheries. Genetic monitoring should be used as a tool in each of the programs to assess whether genetic variation is being maintained and measure the efficiency of conservation programs for endangered sturgeon species [29].

Additionally, behavioral experiments including assessment of the background reactivity to the effect of low/high-frequency sounds and light of long/short duration, swimming capacity of larvae, and fry should be observed [6].

Resulting monitoring of the broodstock at the hatcheries can help avoid inbreeding depression (e.g. late maturation, reduction of reproductive properties, and disease resistance) and also will help to provide broodstock quality and proper health conditions.

10. Monitoring of sexual structure of the broodstock

One of the main problems of the management of sturgeons is their late sexual maturation and long reproduction period between spawnings. But in captivity, males reach maturity in from 3 to 4 years (Russian, Siberian, stellate sturgeon) to 8–15 years (beluga, kaluga). Moreover, in captivity, males can reproduce each year and females every 1–3 years [30].

The gonadal status as an important component of the sexual structure of the sturgeon broodstock requires exact determination and should be monitored throughout the lifetime of the broodstock. Taking into account the lack of external signs of sexual dimorphism in the sturgeon, the sex ratio of the stock should be monitored with the help of a specific ultrasound technique of sexing and staging at the early age of the sturgeon (1–2 years) [31]. For this aim, echograms are used to determine the stages of gonadal maturity in both male and female sturgeons.

The maturity stage is species-dependent and can be attained at different body weights and ages. When analyzing the sexual structure of the domestic broodstock several factors should be considered as follows:

- sexual differences in gametosomatic properties and age of maturity for each species,
- different ages of maturity for females and males,
- intervals between successive spawnings for females and males,
- maximum time of spawning observed for females.

When programs reach the optimum restocking targets, sufficient juveniles and non-mature fish at different age groups should be kept in the hatcheries to establish and maintain a continuously efficient reproductive stock. Thus, the sexual ratio of the broodstock should be under regular control. Consequently, all the broodstock data should be recorded according to their reproductive characteristics, and the variations observed during the monitoring should be recorded as well. In view of these data and results of ultrasound monitoring (gonads, liver, heart) the specimens that do not match the requirements for the brood fish destined for reproduction should be discarded.

11. Solution with the *ex-situ* conservation

When considering the future biodiversity status of sturgeon in nature, conservation of its gene pool is important to maintain for these species to keep from becoming threatened. It is therefore important to take immediate measures to safeguard the genetic diversity of this species. There are several ways to conserve endangered sturgeon species, yet long-term preservation of its genetic structure is an inevitable need. From this point of view, *ex-situ* conservation is one of the effective preservation ways with the aid of cryopreservation biotechnology.

Ex-situ conservation can be described as the "conservation of components of biological diversity outside of their natural habitats". This could be in the form of captive broodstock held in "live banks" like aquaria or aquafarm and also in the form of a frozen state in "gene banks". There is a growing concern for *ex-situ* conservation programs worldwide. *Ex-situ* conservation indicates an integral component of whole conservation programs in many countries [32]. The main purpose of *ex-situ* conservation is to maintain the same genetic structure as the source of the original population. It should be noted that cryopreservation deals with cryobiology which is related preservation of biological materials at ultra-low temperatures such as −196°C. Cellular viability can be preserved in a genetically stable form at this low temperature [33, 34].

In this regard, cryopreservation biotechnology provides the availability of genetic resources (sperm, egg, and embryo) for later use such as propagation material for the (re)stocking or base population for selective breeding programs [32]. Therefore, cryopreservation of genetic material, mostly sperm cells is preferred, and can be used for genetic management programs and also for genetic resource banking of those endangered species [35]. From this point of view, *ex-situ* conservation of genetic material via cryopreservation is an important strategy to preserve genetic diversity. Moreover, the original strain can be reconstructed of the population or variety after required environmental restoration with the help of this biotechnology. On the other hand, these efforts must be done simultaneously with *in-situ* conservation of habitats and the identification of the specific population structures, because only by recognizing the importance of distribution, environmental factors, and mechanisms that have conditioned the adaptive process can conservation of fish biological diversity be achieved.

Growing interest in cryopreservation biotechnology has enhanced the scientific studies in this research field [36, 37]. It is possible to use cryopreserved semen in routine reproduction implementations in aquaculture [38]. To date, more than 200 fish species reproducing with external fertilization, have been tested for sperm cryopreservation [39]. In terms of aquaculture, cryopreserved sperm can be used in breeding programs to produce developed lines and to form genetic resources for aquaculture. Additionally, cryopreserved sperm cells can be used to fertilize viable mature eggs during the off-season and even during the breeding season if the maturity of male and female fishes does not synchronize [40].

At the same time, it is necessary to find ways to protect endangered species. Cryopreserved sperm makes possible the establishment of gene banks and also allows genetic combinations for the endangered species. In spite of the successful application of cryopreservation of sperm in many fish species, it is not possible for the eggs and embryos to exclude oysters. The main reasons are the large size of eggs, penetration of cryoprotectants, and uniform cooling and freezing during the cryopreservation process [40]. Investigations regarding the cryopreservation of teleost eggs and embryos are going on because of difficulties regarding storing and reanimating the following freezing process [41].

Thus, more research is needed to increase membrane permeability in terms of cryosolutions, microinjections of cryoprotectants, and antifreeze proteins In order to overcome this problem. Recent studies have focussed on the cryopreservation of primordial germ cells and tissues for the cryopreservation of both paternal and maternal genomes [40].

12. Establishment of cryobanks

One of the largest areas of interest in the field of cryopreservation biotechnology is in the creation of biodiversity sperm cryobanks [42]. With this biotechnology, it is possible to preserve semen samples for many species and cryopreserved sperm banks can serve as insurance against unforeseen events or outcomes [43]. The creation of sperm banks for the selected stock is necessary to establish genetic selection programs in commercial aquaculture. It is also necessary for the conservation of aquatic species in danger of extinction until the environmental conditions recovered [40].

Furthermore, sperm cryobanking has several significant advantages in terms of cost, security, and labor [44]. Additionally, the management and transportation of frozen samples are relatively simple which allows flexibility to design recovery programs. Also, cryogenic gene banks are less costly than the establishment of live gene banks. Consequently, the use of cryopreserved semen could support conservation efforts for the endangered species through stock enhancement [43].

There are some examples of cryogenic sperm banks in Russia [24], Europe, and North and South America established for aquaculture and conservation purposes [45]. To the best of our knowledge, the oldest fish cryobank in Europe was established in the former USSR. The second was at the Ukrainian Institute in Kharkiv. Other cryobanks were established in the Research Institute of Fish Culture and Hydrobiology (RIFCH-Vodnany) in Czechia and all Russian Research Institute of Freshwater Fisheries [46].

13. Establishment of live gene banks

It is well known that key elements of a biodiversity conservation strategy are not only the creation of controlled conditions but also the reserving of the gene pool of species that are on the verge of extinction. For this reason, the establishment of live gene banks is important to restore the diversity of target species and to increase the efficiency of their control in reproduction. The first live gene bank center of the Azov was established in 1994 in Krasnodar to overcome the challenges as follows [47]:

- collection of all sturgeon species (and seasonal biological forms) presented in the basin,
- capture of suitable brood fish as a source of the necessary material, using available technology and storing technological information in a data bank,
- rehabilitation of endangered sturgeon species,
- domestication of wild specimens of different age groups,
- construction of pilot facilities with a variety of conditions for holding individuals (in cold and warm water),
- monitoring of genetic and physiological peculiarities in the course of selection and building of the broodstock,
- revealing proper conditions and requirements for different seasonal forms.

This Center possesses a heterogeneous broodstock of five sturgeon species (beluga, stellate, Russian, sterlet, and ship sturgeons), all listed in the Red Book of the Krasnodar Region, with a total number of over 11,000 individuals. It is one of the largest living genetic banks of sturgeons in the World [47].

14. Conclusion

Since most sturgeon stocks in Eurasia are considered highly endangered, conservation and restoration of this valuable species are needed urgently. From this point of view, in order to conserve and replenish sturgeons stocks, it is necessary to:

- Conduct more research to improve cryopreservation techniques and embryo banking in conservation programs.
- Implement urgent measures to prevent sea and river pollution from any sources such as the petroleum industry, agricultural pesticide runoff, and domestic sewage outfalls.
- Establish natural refuges and restrict human activities within refuge boundaries.
- Implement urgent measures to maintain natural reproduction by rebuilding adequate spawning stock sizes
- Increase hatchery production in the stocking of juvenile fish per year for restoration and management purposes.
- Implement urgent strict measures against illegal fishing of sturgeon species.

Acknowledgements

There is no conflict of interest in this manuscript.

Data availability statement

The data that support the findings of this study are available on request from the corresponding author.

Author details

Yusuf Bozkurt[1*] and Michael Chebanov[2]

1 Department of Aquaculture, Faculty of Marine Sciences and Technology, İskenderun Technical University, İskenderun, Hatay, Turkey

2 Department of Aquatic Bioresources and Aquaculture, Kuban State University, Kuban, Russia

*Address all correspondence to: yusuf.bozkurt@iste.edu.tr

References

[1] Birstein VJ, Hanner R, De Salle R. Phylogeny of the acipenseriformes: Cytogenic and molecular approaches. In: Birstein VJ, Waldman JR, Bemis WE, editors. Sturgeon Biodiversity and Conservation: Developments in Environmental Biology of Fishes. Vol. 17. 1997. pp. 127-155. DOI: 10.1007/0-306-46854-9-6

[2] Wei QW, Zou Y, Li P, Li L. Sturgeon aquaculture in China: Progress, strategies, and prospects assessed on the basis of nation-wide surveys (2007-2009). Journal of Applied Ichthyology. 2013;**27**:162-168

[3] Haxton T, Cano T. A global perspective of fragmentation on a declining taxon-the sturgeon (Acipenseriformes). Endangered Species Research. 2016;**31**(1):203-210

[4] Bemis WE, Kynard B. Sturgeon rivers: An introduction to Acipenseriform biogeography and life history. Environmental Biology of Fishes. 1997;**48**:167-183

[5] Billard R, Lecointre G. Biology and conservation of sturgeon and paddlefish. Reviews in Fish Biology and Fisheries. 2001;**10**:355-392

[6] Chebanov M, Galich EV. Sturgeon Hatchery Manual. FAO: Ankara; 2013. p. 303. FAO Fisheries and Aquaculture Technical Paper No. 558

[7] Hochleithner M, Gessner I. The Sturgeons and Paddlefishes of the World: Biology and Aquaculture. Kitzbuehel: Aquatech; 1999. p. 165

[8] Alpbaz A. Su ürünleri yetiştiriciliği. İzmir (in Turkish): Rotifler Su Ürünleri Publications; 2009

[9] Friedrich T. Danube Sturgeons: Past and Future. In: Schmutz S, Sendzimir J, editors. Riverine Ecosystem Management. Aquatic Ecology Series. Vol. 8. Cham: Springer; 2018. DOI: 10.1007/978-3-319-73250-3_26

[10] Krylova VD. Use of morphological test characteristics in diagnosis of selected forms of bester. In: Burtzev IA, editor. Genetic Analysis of Marine Hydrobionts. Moscow, Russia (in Russian): VNIRO; 1988. pp. 119-137

[11] Steffens W, Janichen H, Fredrich F. Erffolgreche Vermehrung von Hausen-Sterlet-Hybriden (Huso huso × Acipenser ruthenus) (Pisces, Acipenseridae). Zoologischer Anzeiger. 1983;**211**:55-64

[12] Kijima T, Maryama T. Histological research for the development of the gonad of hybrid sturgeon, bester (*Acipenser ruthenus* (L.), male × *Huso huso* (L.), female). Bulletin of the National Institute of Aquaculture. 1985;**8**:377-381

[13] Haxton TJ, Cano TC. A global perspective of fragmentation on a declining taxon – The sturgeon (Acipenseriformes). Endangered Species Research. 2016;**31**:203-210

[14] Ovissipour M, Rasco B. Sturgeon: Conservation of Caspian Sea Stocks. Journal of Aquaculture Research and Development. 2012;**3**:7. DOI: 10.4172/2155-9546.1000e104

[15] Birstein VJ. Sturgeons and paddlefishes: Threatened fishes in need of conservation. Conservation Biology. 1993;**7**:773-787

[16] Burtzev IA. The history of global sturgeon aquaculture. Journal of Applied Ichthyology. 1999;**15**:325

[17] Williot P, Sabeau L, Gessner J, Arlati G, Bronzi P, Gulyas T, et al. Sturgeon farming in Western Europe: Recent developments and perspectives. Aquatic Living Resources. 2001;**14**(6):367-374

[18] Tyapugin VV, Vasilieva LM, Yusupova AZ. Interspawning periods of domesticated females of Beluga and Russian sturgeon reared in the cages of fish farm LLC "Beluga" in the astrakhan region. Journal of Natural Sciences. 2013;**1**(42):81-86. (in Russian)

[19] Chebanov M, Billard R. The culture of sturgeons in Russia: Production of juveniles for stocking and meat for human consumption. Aquatic Living Resources. 2001;**14**:375-381

[20] Chebanov MS. Ecological foundations of the optimal artificial reproduction of sturgeons. Rybolovstvo I Rybolovstvo. 1996;**2**:9-12. (in Russian)

[21] Chebanov MS, Savelyeva EA. New strategies for broodstock management of sturgeon in the sea of Azov basin in response to changes in patterns of spawning migration. Journal of Applied Ichthyology. 1999;**15**:183-190

[22] Chebanov MS, Karnaukhov GI, Galich EV, Chmir YN. Hatchery stock enhancement and conservation of sturgeon, with an emphasis on the Azov Sea populations. Journal of Applied Ichthyology. 2002;**18**:463-469

[23] Bronzi P, Rosenthal H, Gessner J. Global sturgeon aquaculture production: An overview. Journal of Applied Ichthyology. 2011;**27**:169-175

[24] Chebanov M, Rosenthal H, Gessner J, Van Anrooy R, Doukakis P, Pourkazemi M, et al. Sturgeon Hatchery Practices and Management for Release–Guidelines. Ankara: FAO; 2011. p. 110. FAO Fisheries and Aquaculture Technical Paper. No. 570

[25] Ananiev VI. Research results and perspectives of the program: Low-temperature gene bank of marketable, rare and endangered fish and aquatic invertebrate species. In: Proceedings of the International Workshop, Action before Extinction, Vancouver, Canada. 16-18 Feb 1998. pp. 147-161

[26] Chebanov MS. Conservation of sturgeon genetic diversity: Enhancement and living gene banks. In: Proceedings of the International Conference, Action before Extinction, Vancouver, Canada. 16-18 Feb 1998. pp. 163-173

[27] Podushka SB. Egg Obtaining in Sturgeon with Life Preservation in Brood Fishes. Nauchno-technicheskiy Bull. Lab. Ichtiol., St-Petersburg; 1999. pp. 4-19

[28] Meffe GK. Conservation genetics and the management of endangered fishes. Fisheries. 1986;**11**:14-23

[29] Osborne MJ, Dowling TE, Scribner KT, Turner TF. Wild at heart: Programs to diminish negative ecological and evolutionary effects of conservation hatcheries. Biological Conservation. 2020;**251**:108768

[30] Akimova NV. Gametogenez i polovaya tsiklichnost sibirskogo osetra v estestvennykh i eksperimentalnykh usloviyakh (Gametogenesis and reproductive cyclicity of the Siberian sturgeon in natural and experimental conditions). In: Osobennosti Reproduktivnykh Tsiklov u Ryb v Vodoemakh Raznykh Shirot (Characteristics of Reproductive Cycles of Fish in Water Bodies at Different Latitudes). Moscow: Nauka; 1985. pp. 111-122. (in Russian)

[31] Chebanov MS, Galich EV. Diagnostic capabilities of non-invasive

ultrasonic monitoring for assessing of reproductive welfare and conducting of breeding programmes in large sturgeon broodstock in aquaculture. In: Abstracts of 8th International Symposium. Austria: Vienna; 10-15 Sep 2017. pp. 2-16

[32] Bozkurt Y. The Role of Cryobiology in Conservation of Aquatic Genetic Resources. Saarbrücken, Germany: Lambert Academic Publications; 2017. p. 94

[33] Ashwood-Smith MJ. Low-temperature preservation of cells, tissues, and organs. In: Ashwood-Smith MJ, Farrant J, editors. Low-Temperature Preservation in Medicine and Biology. Tunbridge Wells: Pitman Medical; 1980. pp. 19-45

[34] Bozkurt Y. Introductory chapter: Application fields of cryopreservation biotechnology. In: Bozkurt Y, editor. Cryopreservation Biotechnology in Biomedical and Biological Sciences. London, United Kingdom: IntechOpen Publications; 2018. pp. 1-4

[35] Holt WV, Bennett PM, Volobouev V, Watwon PF. Genetic resource banks in wildlife conservation. Journal of Zoology. 1996;**1996**:531-544

[36] Carolsfeld J, Harvey B, Godinho HP, Zaniboni-Filho E. Cryopreservation of sperm in Brazilian migratory fish conservation. Journal of Fish Biology. 2003;**63**:472-481

[37] Tiersch TR. Introduction. In: Tiersch TR, Green CC, editors. Cryopreservation in Aquatic Species. 2nd ed. Baton Rouge, Louisiana: World Aquaculture Society; 2011. pp. 1-17

[38] Maria A, Carneiro P. Fish semen cryopreservation in Brazil: State of the art and future perspectives. Ciencia Animal. 2012;**22**(1):124-131

[39] Blesbois E, Labbe C. Main improvements in semen and embryo cryopreservation for fish and fowl. In: Planchenault D, editor. Workshop of Cryopreservation of Animal Genetic Resources in Europe. Paris; 2003. pp. 55-65

[40] Bozkurt Y. Introductory chapter: Cryopreservation biotechnology in aquatic science. In: Bozkurt Y, editor. Biological Research in Aquatic Science. London, UK, London, United Kingdom: IntechOpen Publications; 2019. pp. 3-8

[41] Bart A. New approaches in cryopreservation of fish embryos. In: Terrence TR, Mazik PM, editors. Cryopreservation in Aquatic Species. Vol. 8. Baton Rouge: World Aquaculture Society; 2000. pp. 179-187. DOI: 10.1006/cryo.1997.2014

[42] Wildt DE, Rall WF, Crister JK, Monfort SL, Seal US. Genome resource banks: 'Living collections' for biodiversity conservation. Bioscience. 1997;**47**:689-698

[43] Chew PC, Abd-Rashid Z, Hassan R, Asmuni M, Chuah HP. Semen cryobank of the Malaysian mahseer (Tor Tambroides and T. Douronensis). Journal of Applied Ichthyology. 2010;**26**:726-731

[44] Martínez-Páramo S, Pérez-Cerezales S, Gómez-Romano F, Blanco G, Sánchez J, Herráez M. Cryobanking as tool for conservation of biodiversity: Effect of brown trout sperm cryopreservation on the male genetic potential. Theriogenology. 2009;**71**:594-604

[45] Harvey B, Ross C, Greer D, Carolsfeld J. Action before extinction: An international conference on conservation of fish genetic diversity. In: Harvey B, Ross C, Greer D, Carolsfeld J, editors. World Fisheries Trust, Victoria, Canada. 1998. 259 p

[46] Kovalev KV, Pronina ND, Dokina OB, Milenko VA. Opportunities of the largest fish sperm cryobank in Russia. Cryobiology. 2018;**85**:176

[47] Chebanov MS. Sturgeon culture in the Sea of Azov basin: Problems and prospects of a new biotechnology. In: Dunont H, Wilson S, Wazniewicz B, editors. Caspian Environment Programme. Proceedings from the First Bio-Network Workshop. Bordeaux: World Bank; 1997. pp. 29-42

Section 3

Aquaculture Profiles of Countries

Chapter 3

Fish Seed Production for National Development in Kenya: Current Status, Challenges, Quality Control and Innovative Strategies for Commercialization

James Barasa Echessa

Abstract

From only two fish hatcheries at independence to the current number of more than 50, Kenya has achieved a milestone in aquaculture production and development. Investments in sustainable exploitation of Blue economy for national economic growth provide further impetus for seed production. Cage culture of tilapia in Lake Victoria requires use of all-male seed, whose achievement is still a challenge, and demands more innovative strategies. Therefore, production of adequate and high quality fish seed in Kenya is vital as it provides livelihood and incomes to farmers, reduces exploitation pressure on natural fisheries, and facilitates expansion and commercialization of aquaculture for food and nutrition security. This chapter reviews current seed production strategies and systems in Kenya, including quality control measures and some of the strategies that could help improve production, availability and quality of fish seed for the main cultured species in Kenya for commercialization of aquaculture. Improved practices at hatcheries, strict control of importation of live fish in to the country as well as better husbandry practices at fry nurseries and farms could help improve the quality and quantity of fish seed for expanded aquaculture in Kenya.

Keywords: fingerlings, hatching jars, spawning, brood stock, incubation

1. Introduction

It is well recognized that aquaculture, the fastest growing animal food producing sector globally, is poised to make an important contribution to fish food supply in the world. This is because fish supply from major fisheries in the world are either over-exploited, dwindling or collapsed. Global farmed tilapia production averaged 6 million metric tons in 2019 [1], while total farmed catfishes was 5,518,878 metric tons in 2017 [2]. Tilapias and catfishes are often the main freshwater farmed species in many African countries. A total of 1,356,370 metric tons of farmed tilapias was produced on the continent in 2019 [1]. Of this total, Egypt produced almost 80%, with 1,081,202 metric tons [1]. In 2017, 1,324,530 metric tons of Clariid catfishes were produced on the continent [2]. In 2022, total aquaculture production in Kenya was 27,939 metric tons [3], comprising of fish production from ponds, cages (in Lake Victoria) and mariculture [3]. This total was valued at US$ 57,718 [3]. Farmed sea weed production along the Kenyan coast produced 106 metric tons, valued at US$ 17,601. In the same year, the country produced a total of 136,247 metric tons of fish from inland fisheries valued at US$ 254,054,054, while 37,494 metric tons were landed from marine fishery, valued at US$ 69,716 [3]. Depending on the inland fishery, the main landed fish species is tilapia, while clariid catfishes, the African lungfish, *Protopterus aethiopicus*, *Labeo* and Haplochromine cichlids are landed. The Nile perch, *Lates niloticus* and silver cyprinid, *Rastrineobola argentae* dominate Lake Victoria. Tilapias constitute 70% of freshwater farmed finfishes, the rest being mainly *Clarias gariepinus* [3]. The vibrant cage culture industry in Lake Victoria is entirely for tilapias (*Oreochromis niloticus*), with average landings of 14,000 metric tons in 2022 [3].

However, for aquaculture to continue making a significant contribution to fish supply, especially in the tropical areas, critical improvements are required in the areas of impediment. One area that is critically important to successful expansion of aquaculture is fish seed production. Fish seed production ensures availability of stocking material for new aquaculture farmers and businesses, supports augmentation of depleted or declining fisheries to boost the fortunes of fishermen, and for the hatchery operators, it is an important source of income and livelihood. Despite this importance, fish seed production remains a challenge to farmers, both in terms of quantity and quality. This challenge seems to affect many parts of the world [4], including Asia [5], but is especially serious in sub-Saharan Africa [6]. In many of these regions, there is an overall trend of intensification of aquaculture due to high demand for fish, therefore availability of high-quality fish seed is essential, to support this growth in fish production.

In Kenya, for instance, growth in aquaculture has been boosted over the years by several factors. Between 2009 and 2012, the Government implemented the National Fish Farming Enterprise Productivity Program (NFFEPP) under the Economic stimulus program, in which farmers were supported to venture in to fish farming in a total of 140 constituencies country wide. This created an interest in fish farming nationally, and spurred farmed tilapia production to 14,738 metric tons in 2015 from about 3000 metric tons in 2008 [7]. Following the promulgation of the new constitution of Kenya 2010, implementation of the new order was initiated as from 2014, in which new devolved units of governance, county governments, took over the management of aquaculture in the country. This was previously a function of the national government.

A number of county governments have since invested substantial resources in revamping aquaculture in their jurisdictions, to boost fish production for their people. In this regard, such county governments have recruited more staff for extension services, bought vehicles and motor bikes to support staff mobility for extension service, and a few have invested in establishing new hatcheries, as well as fish feed formulation and manufacturing. For instance, Machakos, Uasin Gishu and Vihiga counties have invested in new hatcheries (**Table 1**), an effort that is paying off substantially by increasing availability of quality fish seed for farmers at a fair price. For sustainability, such hatcheries need to adopt innovative strategies for producing high quality seed while safeguarding the environment.

County	Name of Hatchery	Year Started	Fish species	Annual Production
Nairobi	Kiamumbi Fish Farm	2016	Tilapia	480,000
			Catfish	360,000
	Paradise Fish Farm	2005	Tilapia	6, 000,000
			Catfish	6, 000,000
	Quarry Lane Fish Farm	2012	Tilapia	180,000
			Catfish	180,000
Kakamega	Labed Cash Marine Enterprises	2012	Tilapia	840,000
			Catfish	120,000
	Jafi Fish Farm	2010	Tilapia	480,000
Vihiga	Tigoi Fish Farm	2011	Tilapia	600,000
	Mwitoko Fish farm	2020	Tilapia	500,000
Bungoma	Chwele Fish Farm	1991	Tilapia	480,000
Busia	Wakhungu Fish Farm	2020	Tilapia	1,500,000
Kisumu	Apondo Fish Hatchery	2015	Tilapia	500,000
	Vicnaqua Hatchery	2018	Tilapia	300,000
	KEMFRI Sangoro station	1982	Tilapia	8,400,000
			Catfish	6,000,000
Homa Bay	Victory Farms	2016	Tilapia	72,000,000
	Jewlett Enterprises	2007	Tilapia	9, 600, 000
	George Muga	2013	Tilapia	500, 000
			Catfish	200, 000
	Kiba Fish Hatcheries	2017	Tilapia	1, 200,000
	Lake View Fisheries	2014	Tilapia	3, 600,000
	Homa Bay Multipurpose Farm	2010	Tilapia	500,000
	Phillip Agwanda Fish Farm	2018	Tilapia	200,000
Kisii	County Fish Multiplication and Training Centre	1987	Tilapia	500,000
	KEMFRI Kegati station	1985	Tilapia	1, 200,000
Machakos	Kamuthanga Fish farm	2011	Tilapia	3,000,000
			Catfish	960,000
	ATC	2014	Tilapia	100,000
Meru	Vision Hatchery	2010	Tilapia	1, 200,000
			Catfish	720,000
	Nchiru Children's Home Hatchery	2012	Catfish	240,000
	Muthuri Hatchery	2014	Catfish	225,000
	Kithima Hatchery	1991	Tilapia	60,000
Kiambu	Pegi Fish Farm	2013	Tilapia	1, 200,000

County	Name of Hatchery	Year Started	Fish species	Annual Production
			Catfish	1, 200,000
	Samaki Tu Farm	2010	Tilapia	1, 200,000
			Catfish	600,000
	Bariki Fish Farm	2014	Tilapia	360,000
			Catfish	600,000
Murang'a	Makindi Fish Farm	2016	Tilapia	1, 200,000
Nyeri	Kiganjo Trout Hatchery	1948	Trout	60,000
Kirinyaga	Mwea AquaFish Farm	2009	Tilapia	1, 500,000
			Catfish	1,000,000
	Green Algae Highlands Farm	1998	Tilapia	1, 200,000
			Catfish	1,000,000
	Emmick Farm	2011	Tilapia	1, 500,000
			Catfish	1, 500,000
	National Aquaculture Research and Training Center Sagana	1948	Tilapia	1, 560,000
			Catfish	180, 000
Nyandarua	Geta Trout Hatchery	2009	Trout	120,000
	Malewa Gorge Trout Hatchery (North Kinangop)	2013	Trout	1, 200,000
	Avil Fish Farm	2011	Tilapia	360,000
			Catfish	360,000
	Kenya Agriculture and Livestock Research Organization (Kalro)-Ol Jororok	2011	Tilapia	360,000
	Kentalo Farm	2012	Tilapia	360,000
Nakuru	Lake Naivasha Hatchery	2011	Tilapia	1, 200,000
			Catfish	250,000
	Egerton University Hatchery	2015	Tilapia	100,000
			Catfish	50,000
Uasin Gishu	University of Eldoret	2017	Tilapia	3, 600,000
			Catfish	600,000
LBDA Farms	Kibos Fish Farm (Kisumu)	1984	Tilapia	700,000
			Catfish	100,000
	Yala Fish Farm (Siaya)	1989	Tilapia	600,000
			Catfish	240,000

Table 1.
Fish hatcheries in different counties of Kenya, including number of fingerlings produced annually and year of establishment of the hatcheries. Figures for catfish seed production represent capacity, as this seeds for this species are produced on order.

1.1 Historical development of fish hatcheries in Kenya

The first hatcheries in Kenya were established during the colonial era in 1948, with Sagana Fish Culture Farm for warm water fish species and Kiganjo Trout hatchery for the cold water fish species. These were designed to provide seeds and mature fish, to boost aquaculture which had been started in the 1920s. In the 1970s, mariculture was initiated, and with it came the establishment of the Ngomeni Mariculture Prawn Farm. These hatcheries did not perform well in post-independence Kenya, mostly due to limited expertise and budgetary support by Government. In 1993, however, Sagana fish Culture farm was renovated, and the hatchery revamped, through the technical support of the Royal government of Belgium. In 1994, the Aquaculture research project Collaborative Research Support Programme/Pond Dynamics Aquaculture (CRSP/PDA) funded by the United States Agency for International Development (USAID) was relocated from Rwanda because of ethnic strife, to Sagana Fish farm. This boosted the farm's activities and capacity to produce fish seeds and mature fish through scientific research. Since this project involved collaboration between The Kenya Fisheries Department, Moi University and Auburn University, USA, it enabled the training of graduate students of Aquaculture from Moi University, both locally and at Auburn. Similarly, the project supported the training of Fisheries Officers and other cadres of the Kenya Department of Fisheries on a variety of topics, as a way of building capacity for the Department. By the year 2000, Moi University, which had started the Department of Fisheries in 1990 constructed a fish farm and a small fabricated hatchery, which became operational in 2002, under the support of the World Bank/GEF funded Lake Victoria Environmental Management Programme (LVEMP). This facility also boosted production and supply of fish seed to farmers in the region [8, 9].

Between the late 1980s and early 1990s, when the Department of Fisheries was housed by the Ministry of Regional Development, several fish farms were set up in the country, supported by the Rural Development Fund. These included Murang'a Fish farm, Kisii Multipurpose Fish Multiplication center, and the Kithima Fish Hatchery in Meru (**Table 1**). At around the same time, the Norwegian Agency for International Development (NORAD) helped establish Chwele Fish Farm in Bungoma. With the establishment of the Lake Basin Development Authority (LBDA) in the 1980s, the Authority established several fish farms and hatcheries around the Lake Victoria basin, and these have been actively involved in fish seed multiplication and distribution over the years. However, many of these farms and hatcheries rely on financial support from the Exchequer, which is often unreliable and inadequate. Therefore, their activities often fluctuate, based on financial flows, and so, at times they have very low activity. Also, most of these farms have inadequate staff strength with limited technical know-how in modern fish seed production technology.

With the onset of the National Fish Farming Enterprise Productivity Program under the Economic Stimulus Program of 2009, several hatcheries were established, because of the impetus created by the Government support nation-wide. Many serious farmers were motivated and took up the opportunity, many have since established their own hatcheries (**Table 1**), in different parts of the country, and doing fairly well. However, and especially for the western Kenya region, many hatcheries have been established over the last seven or so years, to take advantage of the cage culture of tilapia in Lake Victoria, an industry that requires a large and steady supply of all-male tilapia fish seed. Those hatcheries established slightly earlier than this time were also motivated by the demand for catfish fry for use as bait fish to catch Nile perch,

Lates niloticus in Lake Victoria using long lines. This is heavily driven by the impact of the water hyacinth in the lake, which renders the use of traditional filament nets ineffective.

As envisaged in the National Oceans and Fisheries policy of 2008, government has established a hatchery for marine fisheries under the National Mariculture Centre/ Hatchery in Shimoni, Kwale county, through the National Infrastructure support Programme. The hatchery is set to start operations in the multiplication and distribution of affordable, adequate and high quality seed for marine fish species. This will support investments in aquaculture by providing relevant infrastructure for production, demonstration and research activities for development of ocean resources, and sustainable exploitation of the Blue economy [10].

2. Spawning of fish

In the natural environment, the breeding behavior of tilapias begins with sexually mature males putting on bright colors, such as blueish, red, and yellow on different parts of the body. Such males constitute the ready to spawn males, and as such, they construct nests (leks) [11, 12], which is basically a "home", where breeding will take place. The construction of the lek is called lekking, and once complete, the brightly colored male stays in the lek, guarding it against any intruding males (territoriality), while simultaneously attracting ready to spawn female tilapias. A ready to spawn female (abdomen swollen with eggs) is attracted to the lek, enters and after acquaintance with the male, the pair performs a courtship dance. The breeding pair is in an elevated energy level, and the female spawns her eggs, while the male sheds millions of milt (sperms) over the eggs simultaneously, completely covering the batch of eggs in milt to increase the chance of most of the eggs getting fertilized. It is important to note that optimal environmental temperature is necessary for this process, and so spawning by tilapias occurs on a sunny afternoon. On a cloudy afternoon therefore, the ready to spawn female will have eggs in the ovary being resorbed in to the body, and so will not spawn until the next ovulation cycle. The female picks all the fertilized eggs in to her buccal cavity [12] (**Figure 1**), leaves the lek, and moves to a quiet area in the water, to begin incubation of the eggs (**Figure 1**). Another ready to spawn female enters the lek, and the spawning process is repeated. Meanwhile, a female that is incubating the eggs frequently churns the eggs, i.e. opens the mouth a bit, to allow entry of fresh water (and oxygen), which are necessary for incubation, and also allows the eggs to change position, so that each egg is uniformly exposed to water, air and warmth, for successful development of the zygote and therefore hatching.

The African catfish, *Clarias gariepinus*, the main farmed species, breeds in the natural environment at the onset of rains, usually in inundated conditions. Therefore, catfishes move to the flood plains, either from the lake, or from upstream the river. Since the floodplains are usually flooded in the rainy seasons, there is an abundant supply of food materials that come with the waters. The food materials are exploited by catfishes with active feeding, and subsequently get energized in the inundated conditions. The sexually mature males and females pair up, perform a courtship dance around the inundated marginal areas, and the females spawn the eggs. Males release millions of milt simultaneously over the eggs, and fertilization occurs. Fertilized eggs attach on inundated marginal vegetation, where they undergo incubation. The incubation period is dependent on the ambient temperature, and hatchlings are released in to the environment, where they learn how to survive on their own.

Figure 1.
A mouth brooding female tilapia with eggs in her buccal cavity. Eggs are harvested periodical from such mouth brooding females and taken to the hatchery for incubation at optimal temperature and aeration conditions to fasten the egg hatching process. A breeding pair is normal introduced in to a net hapa, where spawning occurs naturally under optimal sunshine conditions.

2.1 Artificial production of tilapias

Whether in the natural waters (lakes, rivers), or in ponds at fish farms, tilapias construct leks in the shallow areas and pond dykes of the lake and ponds respectively. Hatchery operators therefore try to simulate the process of natural spawning, by pairing up ready to spawn male and female fish in net hapas in ponds or tanks, where after spawning, the female similarly picks eggs in to her buccal cavity (**Figure 1**). Eggs are therefore harvested from the mouth of the female the following morning after pairing up the fish in net hapas the previous afternoon. The harvested eggs are taken for incubation in McDonald's jars (**Figure 2**) in the hatchery (often a greenhouse that creates higher temperatures naturally, or a hatchery where incubation units are fitted with thermostats to regulate temperature to the desired optimum). Due to lower temperatures in the natural environment, eggs hatch in about 14 days. However, incubating the eggs at optimal temperatures (25–28°C) in the hatchery substantially reduces the incubation period to about 5 days, enabling the farmer to do more cycles of egg incubation in unit time. Artificial incubation of eggs at the hatchery also releases the females earlier, so that they can begin the recovery process in readiness for the next spawning.

2.2 Artificial production of African catfish, *Clarias gariepinus*

In culture facilities, *C. gariepinus* does not breed freely, and has therefore to be induced or artificially propagated. Artificial propagation of catfishes is a well perfected procedure, and is routinely practiced at most hatcheries in Africa [13]. The process involves injection of a sexually mature female with a hormone (from the pituitary extract of fish or a synthetic hormone), which induces maturation of eggs in the ovary [14]. The process involves the following steps:

1. A ready to spawn pair that is good looking is selected for the exercise. Ready to spawn female will have a swollen abdomen (because of eggs), while a male of

Figure 2.
McDonald jars used to incubate tilapia eggs at the hatchery for hatching. Water supply to the jars is from the bottom, so that the pressure of the water causes the eggs to be in constant motion upwards. This ensures the eggs do not stick on the bottom of the jar (fertilized eggs become sticky), but remain in constant motion, so that they are exposed to uniform aeration and heat, which are necessary for the development of the zygote.

suitable size will generally be able to breed. Both brooders should be good looking: uniform in body shape, not deformed, free from parasites, or injuries.

2. The brood pair is taken to the hatchery, and the female injected with a pituitary extract (containing a gonadotropic hormone) from another catfish or any other fish species like carps, to induce maturation of eggs in the ovary. This is done in the evenings (around 16.00–17.00 hours), and left overnight in separate holding tanks. The female is injected in the abdomen, with about 1 ml of pituitary extract at a dosage of 3 mg/kg of female [14]. The pituitary is taken from the head of a catfish that has been sacrificed, and stored in a saline solution.

In the absence of the pituitary hormone from fish, a synthetic hormone is used: an example is deoxy-corticosterone acetate (DOCA, 50 mg/kg of female), or human chorionic gonadotropin (HCG, 2500 IU/kg of female) which are purchased from authorized commercial dealers.

3. In the morning (about 8 hours), the ready to spawn female is stripped of the eggs, by gently pressing on the abdomen (**Figure 3**), so that the eggs ooze out through the genital papilla, into a clean bowl.

4. A male catfish is sacrificed immediately, and the testes (**Figure 4**) slit open, so that the milt pours over the eggs in the bowl. Note: The stucture and location of the testes cannot allow the milt to be removed by pressing the abdomen of the male fish, so each time artificial propagation is done, a male has to be sacrificed, to provide the milt.

Figure 3.
A gravid female Catfish being stripped of her eggs in to a bowl, in readiness for fertilization by milt from a sacrificed male.

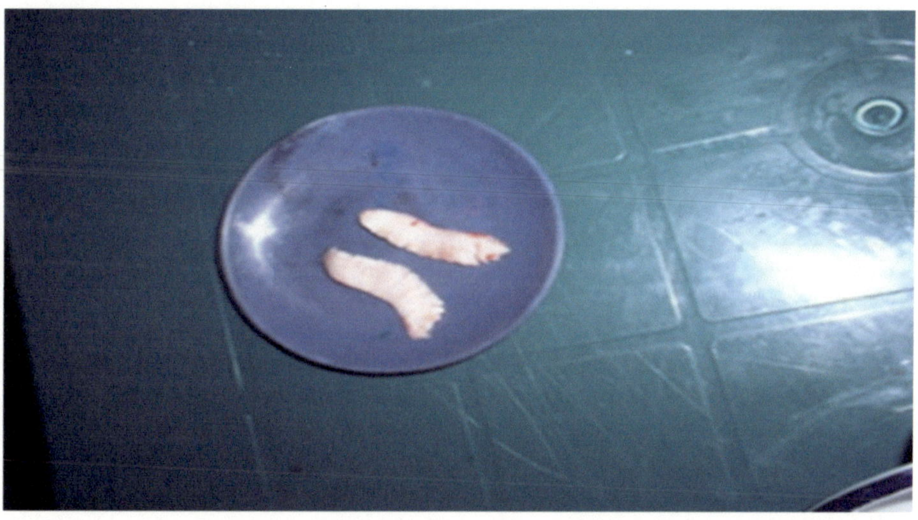

Figure 4.
A pair of gonads (testes) from a male catfish. These are cut open and the resultant milt mixed with eggs in the bowl, for fertilization of eggs.

5. A clean feather is used to mix the eggs and the sperms (milt) gently, to ensure complete mixing, so that as many eggs as possible are fertilized.

6. Fertilized eggs are then transferred on to an egg tray (**Figure 5**) (fish eggs become adhesive immediately they are fertilized). They therefore attach on to the mesh of the egg tray or any other suitable substrate or kakaban material.

Figure 5.
Glass tank (Aquarium) for incubating Clarias eggs during artificial propagation at the hatchery. Fertilized eggs are spread on the egg tray (see the board in the tank stretching from top right to bottom left corner of the tank, with brownish stuff), and immersed in the water in the tank. Any newly hatched fry drops to the bottom of the tank, and can be sucked out of the tank. Water supply to the tank is from up the tank (see the yellow-black stripped horse pipe), and the thermostat for temperature regulation is inserted in to the tank. Aeration of the eggs in water is via the white tubes in the tank, connected to the blower.

7. The egg tray is transferred in to the aquarium or the incubation tank (**Figure 5**), and the incubation process started. The incubation tank should be supplied with clean fresh water continuously for the 24 or so hours over which eggs will hatch, as well as ample supply of oxygen (aeration of the water), and optimal temperature (25–28°C). This temperature will be obtained by use of a thermostat fixed in to the tank.

8. Complete hatching of the eggs will be accomplished in 12–24 h, depending on the temperature of the water. It is important to note that catfish hatchlings drop down into the tank bottom from the egg shells, and eggs that do not hatch turn white, either because they were not fertilized, or they are infested with bacteria and fungi.

Therefore, during this process of artificial propagation, it is critical to ensure complete mixing of eggs and milt for complete fertilization. Also, incubation process must be done under very clean or hygienic conditions, to avoid contamination of eggs with fungi and bacteria that will prevent hatching, even if the eggs are fertilized.

In the absence of egg trays, diverse materials can be used as kakabans, substrates on which fertilized eggs attach for incubation. Such simple substrates include sisal threads from sacks or gunny bags, and in the Lake Victoria basin where water hyacinth is abundant, roots of the hyacinth are also used as kakabans [14, 15]. Eggs attach on to the roots, and the plants introduced in to incubation tanks where leaves float on the water, while the roots are inside the water to allow ample incubation of eggs.

2.3 Nursery of tilapia and catfish seed

After full absorption of yolk sac, fry should be transferred to nursery units (**Figure 6**) for good management. At this stage, fry require optimal temperature and feeding, because this is also the stage of fast development and growth. For species like *C. gariepinus* that have high mortality at the fry stage, optimal rearing temperature

DOI: http://dx.doi.org/10.5772/intechopen.114064

Figure 6.
Tanks for rearing fry at the nursery unit. Each tank is supplied with aerator and water supply, in a green house, where high temperatures prevail naturally, to support fast growth.

and feeding regimes of fry are critical. Ideally, it is desirable to develop a fish nursery under a green house, for ease of achieving the requisite high temperatures cost effectively. Also, in the green house, it is easier to maintain a higher standard of hygiene, to reduce on fry mortality due to parasites and pathogens, as well as control of predators, and unnecessary human traffic around fish holding facilities that cause stress to fry. However, because of the high cost of green house facilities and related installations, only resource endowed hatchery operators are able to acquire these facilities and develop the fish nursery unit in a green house. Farmers who must establish fry nursery units outside the green house need to devise ways to address the need for optimal rearing temperature.

2.4 Feeding of tilapia and catfish fry in the nursery unit

In the nursery, fry are fed on live feeds because the digestive system is not yet well formed, and so fry survival increases by application of live feeds that are easy to digest and absorb. Main live feeds are zooplankton and phytoplankton that are easily harvested from an enriched pond on the farm or at the hatchery. This means that the farmer or hatchery operator has to invest in fertilization of a pond with organic manure, to make it green, or boost primary productivity in the pond. Alternatively, the brine shrimp, *Artemia* may be acquired and used as a live feed by periodical hatching of Artemia cysts.

The feeding frequency for the fry should be high, depending on the species, to ensure satiation always that helps to reduce cannibalism and hampered growth of the fry. For instance, catfish may be fed 6 times daily, while tilapia fry should be fed 3 or 4 times daily and gold fish 4 times per day.

After a period of about 1 month, when the digestive system of the fry is fully developed, the fry should be introduced to dry feeds, i.e. formulated or commercial diets. Such diets should be of high quality, i.e. be of the required crude protein content. Diets of about 45% crude protein would be ideal for fry. An appropriate feeding frequency should be maintained on this diet, depending on the species. The feeding ration should be adequate, of about 3% body weight daily, to ensure satiation of the fry. Higher feeding ration should be avoided, as it leads to wastage of feed, causes a deterioration of water quality leading to fish mortality, and unnecessarily increases production costs while reducing profitability of the enterprise. Also, fry should be fed at certain times of the day, without delayed or earlier application of the feed, to get the fish accustomed to the schedule, which increases the response of the fish to feeds, and maximizes feed utilization. The particle size of the feed should be the right for the fry, so that it is ingested with ease.

2.5 Challenges in fish seed production

Quality of fish seed, the ability of the seed to serve its purpose, by ensuring fast growth rates, high survival and high fecundity of fish being grown by the farmer, is dependent on genetic characteristics of brood stock, and husbandry practices under which the brood stock are kept. Fish seed are generally obtained from two sources: hatcheries owned by individual farmers or institutions and the natural habits (what is commonly called the wild). In each of these two sources, fish can and do lose their genetic quality (the vigor or strength to grow, survive and reproduce at a fast rate or in sufficient quantity), and therefore, when such fish are collected for use as brood stock or as seed in aquaculture enterprises, the fish exhibit stunted growth. The growth rate, survival and fecundity of fish is generally low, leading to small sizes of individual fish at harvest after a reasonable grow-out period, occasioning loses to the farmer.

The problem of stunted growth in cultured fish results from genetic drift, the change in the frequency of alleles or genes of the fish due to random processes [16, 17]. This way an allele, for instance responsible for growth rate or survival or fecundity can be lost from the population of the fish, in which case the allele becomes rarer in members of the population, and individual fishes lose the ability to grow, survive or reproduce in desirable quantities in aquaculture. On the other hand, an allele for any of these traits can increase in frequency in the population, and become fixed in members of the population, so that many individual fishes of the population harbor the allele. However, whether an allele is being fixed in the population (fixation) or is lost from the population (loss), the overall effect of genetic drift in fish is always negative [18], in so far as it reduces genetic variability at a locus for the desirable trait of the cultured fish. Similarly, since genetic drift occurs mostly in small populations, or a fish population with fewer members, it is invariably accompanied by inbreeding [18], another process that exacerbates loss of quality in fish. In small populations, the actual number of fish individuals that breed to form the next generation is small. Therefore, the possibility of repeated use of same breeders to create the next generation is higher. This increases the chances of using related parental stock to create the next generation, a practice that indirectly favors fixation of some alleles in the population, as well as loss of other valuable alleles from the population. If fish suffering these effects is reared in a poor environment or under poor husbandry, stunting is exacerbated, and performance in culture declines substantially.

In natural fish populations, loss of genetic quality occurs through several processes. For instance, natural aquatic habits can undergo fragmentation through damming, which disconnects the fish upstream from those downstream. This structures the fish population, interferes with the biology of the fish species, which eventually reduces the size of the population and reduces its genetic variation. Introduction of exotic fish species to aquatic habitats seriously affects native fish populations, either through predation [19], hybridization [20, 21], competition for feeding, breeding and nursery grounds [22] or through introduction of parasites and or disease pathogens for the native fish species. The overall effect of these factors is the reduction of population sizes of native fish species, which reduces the genetic variation of the species and consequently, loss of genetic quality or vigor to grow, survive and reproduce. Therefore, farmers collecting native fish species from such habitats for use as brood stock, or directly as fish seed for stocking in ponds invariably end up with stunted fish and poor harvests [20]. For instance, the native tilapias of Lake Victoria, *Oreochromis esculentus* and *O. variabilis* declined under the effects of predation from the exotic Nile perch [23, 24], as well as hybridization [25, 26] and competition [26] by the exotic Nile tilapias, *O. niloticus* and *Oreochromis leucostictus*. If the populations of the native tilapias ever recover and begin to appear in fishermen's landings, they will be suffering from low genetic variation due to population bottleneck induced by predation, hybridization and competition.

While hybridization may lead to genetic drift in a fish population by creating genotypes whose fitness in the wild is low, prejudicing recruitment of the fishery, it also creates fish individuals of impure genetic make-up. Therefore, what farmers collect from natural sources for use as brood stock at the hatchery is not pure stock, whose performance at the hatchery and in ponds declines [20]. Hybridization has been reported in sympatric *O. esculentus* and *O. niloticus* of Lake Kanyaboli [27], as well as other satellite lakes of East Africa [28, 29]. Hybridization is also reported between *O. niloticus* and *O. leucostictus* of Lake Baringo [30], and, together with changes in genetic diversity in *O. niloticus* [31], as well as water quality variability, is thought to have affected the growth of *O. niloticus* in the lake. Other examples include hybridization of *O. niloticus* and *O. urolepis* in the Great Ruaha-Rufiji rivers system [32], as well as between *O. niloticus* and *O. mossambicus* in South Africa [33], and *O. niloticus* and the native *O. macrochir* and *O. andersonii* of Kafue River [21]. Hybridization between farmed *O. niloticus* and *O. mossambicus* in Asia, with both species established from imported stocks suffering from founder effects, caused widespread stunting and poor growth of *O. niloticus* [20], occasioning the need for developing improved strains to boost farmed production of the species [34].

For small water bodies such as satellite lakes, genetic drift in natural fish populations could result from overfishing, which creates a population bottleneck due to fishing mortality. Examples include tilapias of Lake Kanyaboli, and other satellite lakes where the size of native tilapas *O. esculentus* has since dropped from a maximum size of 50 cm to about 17–20 cm length per piece of fish [35, 36], and also the numbers have gone down in the lake. This invariably reduces genetic variation of the fish, which makes the fish unsuitable for use as brood stock for aquaculture enterprises. Coupled with this is periodical desiccation of small lakes and reservoirs due to recurrent drought in arid and semi- arid areas, leading to massive mortality of fish species. When the lakes fill up again during the rainy season, the fish populations increase through natural recruitment, but suffer population bottlenecks which reduce genetic diversity of the fish. Examples of such lakes include Kamnarok in the Elgeyo Marakwet county and Kenyatta in Lamu county, Kenya, which are also isolated, and so suffer high levels of genetic drift. Furthermore, fish stocks of these lakes have been boosted by re-stocking or fishery augmentation by conservationists, using germplasm from the Lake Victoria region. This augmentation with fish from different drainage basins merely exacerbates the loss of quality by respective fish species, because of mixture of different genotypes. Fish populations in such lakes are unsuitable for use as brood stock for aquaculture enterprises.

Farmed fish also undergo genetic drift and inbreeding [16, 37], leading to loss of quality, and therefore poor performance in ponds expressed as poor growth, survival and low fecundity of the fish. This is mainly because aquaculture enterprises naturally start with a small number of brooders. Therefore, even before the start of aquaculture activities, the fish is already suffering from founder effects, where population bottleneck induces genetic drift. This is compounded by selection of good-looking brooders from the pool of brood stock available on the farm, since not all the brooders available on the farm can be used for propagation to generate seed. Because of selection of brooders and the smaller numbers of brood stock on the farm, aquaculture practices therefore commonly involve fish of imbalanced sex ratios. Also, the actual number of breeders that give rise to the next generation is low, and the fish used to create the next generation have different reproductive success, i.e. the fish give different number of eggs or fry during spawning [37]. Differences in reproductive success among brooders arise from differences in fecundity, fertility, viability or longevity [37], so that different brooders will contribute different numbers of fry to the next generation.

Furthermore, viability of the fry is quite critical. In *Clarias gariepinus* for instance, poor survival of fry is a key challenge in seed supply for aquaculture. Therefore, genetic drift is likely to seriously affect the stocks available for the enterprise. Different environmental conditions on the spawning grounds or presence of predators on nursery grounds, as well as contamination of egg incubation facilities with parasites and pathogens may affect reproductive success of individual fishes [37]. Brooders with lower viability will have a higher number of their fry die early, before they reach sexual maturity and reproduce, and so their overall contribution to the pool of the next generation decreases. This means that the fish in this generation that will grow to sexual maturity and reproduce will be from only a few parents, a factor that increases inbreeding in subsequent generations, and poor performance of the fish.

Sex ratio of the breeding pairs is another crucial factor that influences inbreeding and genetic drift, and therefore loss of genetic variation in farmed fish [37]. While in the propagation of catfishes at the hatchery milt from a single male is used to fertilize eggs from a single female, sex ratio of the breeding pairs in tilapias is often skewed towards more females per male. Some studies recommend a sex ratio of 1 male to 2 females [38], while [39] recommends 1 male to 3 females. Ideally, the correct stocking ratio for tilapia breeding pairs in net hapas should be 1:1, to reduce chances of inbreeding and therefore increase the genetic vigor of the resultant fry to grow, survive and reproduce. Furthermore, using imbalanced sex ratios of breeding pairs of tilapias in net hapas increases fight for mates, which injure the brooders in the net hapas and affect spawning.

3. Measures for producing high quality fish seed

3.1 Genetic approaches of producing high quality fish seed

Fish hatcheries keen on producing high quality fish seed need to focus on both genetic and managerial practices in their operations. To start with, however, there is need to ensure genetic principles are applied in the brood stock acquired and maintained at the hatchery, as well as the breeding techniques and designs used to generate the next cohort of fingerlings. This should be followed by appropriate fish husbandry practices, to ensure that the farm reaps from the investment made from the application of genetic principles. This is because some of the measures will require substantial investment in facilities and expertise. In this regard, therefore, the most important factor in fish seed quality is to ensure the starting stock has a very high genetic variation [9, 40]). This means minimizing on factors that reduce genetic diversity in populations of fish, or factors that increase genetic drift and inbreeding in fish.

In the development of the Genetically Improved Farmed Tilapia (GIFT) strain, for instance, genetic variation of the base population of GIFT was boosted by a complete diallele cross of the 8 founding strains (4 natural and 4 farmed) [34]. Due to this, the GIFT strain had a very high growth rate, helping tilapia farmers in the Philippines increase their farmed tilapia production by 186% between 1990 and 2007 [41]. Similarly, the use of GIFT strain helped farmers increase availability of quality tilapia seed in the Philippines [41], as well as China and Thailand. Since its development in 1997 and subsequent distribution to farmers in Asia and lately to most parts of the world for culture, the GIFT strain still performs very well in culture, as long as it is reared under good management practices.

Therefore, the first step in ensuring high genetic variation of the brood stock at the hatchery is to source the fish from natural habitats that are large. While large aquatic habitats do not automatically imply the extant fish population is large, there is high possibility that a large water mass will host a large population of a given fish species. For instance, sourcing fish brood stock from Lake Kanyaboli may be less desirable than Lake Victoria, since Lake Kanyaboli, a satellite and therefore a fragment of the main Lake Victoria, is much smaller, and its fish populations are likely to have been affected further by higher fishing pressure. Therefore, it will comparatively have less genetic variation and less vigor to grow and survive in culture facilities. Related to the size of the fish population is the fact that in a large population, the fish will also have random mating, with less severe competition for mates, since the pool of mates will be larger. Therefore, as many fish individuals as possible will be able to contribute their genes to create the next generation. Brood stock obtained from such an ecosystem will have a high genetic variation. However, even if the aquatic ecosystem is large, habitats whose fish are known to have undergone interspecific hybridization, or have received additional fish from different drainage basins should be avoided, since the stock will be impure, or homogenized, and so negatively impact growth and survival of the seed.

Furthermore, after identifying a habitat that meets these criteria on genetic variation, a large number of brooders should be collected [18], in order to avoid founder effects in the fish that the hatchery will use to start the aquaculture enterprise. Many hatcheries naturally collect a small number of brood stock from the wild during expeditions to collect fish brooders from the wild, in order to minimize costs [42]. This is because of limited facilities at the hatchery to hold a large number of brooders, limited finances to support collection of more fish during the expedition, and limited capacity to transport a large number of live fish at once, especially if the natural habitat is far away from the hatchery. Also feeding cost of a large number of brooders would be high. However, it is always desirable that hatcheries collect and maintain a high number of brood stock at the hatchery for their aquaculture enterprises [42], in order to benefit from the higher genetic diversity and vigor of the fish to grow and survive. Most of the tilapia brood stock imported in to Asia in the 1980s were composed of few founders, with some as few as 30 or much less [43, 44], and because of founder effects, most were highly inbred and introgressed [45], and therefore had stunted growth in ponds [34].

For farmers collecting fish seed from other hatcheries, care is still needed, so that the fish is purchased only from reputable hatcheries, i.e. those with a good name from their good practices on fish breeding, rearing and fish brood stock management.

Good hatcheries are those that practice good husbandry for their brood stock, and understand the genetic principles of fish hatchery operations. Such hatcheries should also have been certified by professionals, and so use best management practices in their operations. Many hatcheries in Kenya may not be managing their brood stock well, and so the quality of their fingerlings is probably poor. The poor quality of seed is often manifested in poor survival. For tilapia, poor survival of seed is especially noted in cages in Lake Victoria. Poor quality seed therefore occasions losses to farmers and hampers expansion of commercial aquaculture in the country.

3.2 Fish breeding designs that reduce genetic drift and inbreeding

An important technique of increasing genetic variation by reducing inbreeding and genetic drift among brooders is to increase the spawning stock. Here, several suitable mating pairs are chosen, allowed to breed and an equal number of hatchlings from each mating pair or family is chosen and pooled, to form the next breeding stock at the hatchery. If the breeding pairs are taken from families, it is often desirable to use half-sib rather than full-sib families. Full-sib family is one in which the offspring have the same parents (mother and father, dam and sire), while Half-sib family is one in which the offspring have the same one parent but not both [18]. Fish seed from half-sib family have a higher genetic variation, and increasing the spawning stock similarly increases genetic variation of the breeders, which give high quality fingerlings.

Genetic quality of fish seed is also attained at the hatchery by operators practicing pedigree mating rather than random mating schemes for breeders. In pedigree mating scheme, each breeding pair of known productivity or performance in culture contributes an equal number of offspring to the next generation. A farmer is able to know the productivity of the fish on his farm or hatchery by accurate record keeping, and tagging of individual fishes. Only high performing fish (high growth rates, survival and fecundity) are allowed to breed, and the population of the spawning stock is increased by allowing the chosen breeders to contribute an equal number of fry to the next generation.

Hatchery operators should also avoid overlapping generations in their fish culture enterprises, or even in the rearing of fry or brood stock. Overlapping generations involve mixing of different generations of fish, which, by extension, will be of different ages and sizes. During fish harvests at grow-out, farmers should harvest all the fish in ponds or tanks for sale or consumption. Partial harvest of the fish should be avoided, so that at the time of restocking ponds with a new crop of seeds, the younger generation should not mix with older generation of fish. This reduces the chances of breeding of related fish, which will increase inbreeding and genetic drift in the stock. This is especially critical for quality of tilapias, which mature precociously [46] and breed with ease in culture facilities [47, 48], so that at the end of the grow out period, the farmer has many but small sized fish of low market value.

The sex ratio of the breeding pairs should as much as possible be kept equal, at 1:1, and the frequency of re-use of any given brooder minimized as much as possible. This ensures that the offspring are generated from diverse fish individuals, and so minimizes inbreeding and genetic drift in the seeds.

3.3 Fish husbandry practices for maintaining quality in fish seed

These are husbandry practices at the hatchery that ensure the number of brood stock kept does not reduce and create a bottleneck that would induce genetic drift and inbreeding in the fish. Also, they ensure the fish are in a good health and nutritional state as to be able to grow, survive and reproduce adequately in culture facilities, to give the desired quality and quantity of the end product. Healthy- and good-looking fish of uniform shape are often appealing to sight, and can attract steady market and value.

One of the most important husbandry practices for maintaining the quality of brooders so that they produce high quality fingerlings is feeding. Fish should be fed on a high-quality diet, often measured as crude protein content (CP%). Brood stock should be fed on diets of crude protein content of 20–30%, which should preferably be formulated on the farm. This assures the quality of the feed. Similarly, the fish should be fed daily on recommended feeding ration (3% body weight). This ration is administered in several portions, the feeding frequency. The feeding frequency will vary according to fish species, but the brooders should be fed at least twice daily. At each of these intervals, the feed should be applied when it is sunny (morning and afternoon), and at each feeding exercise, the feed should be applied until the fish is satiated.

In order to reduce mortality from parasites and diseases, the hatchery environment should always be kept clean, with a good flow of waste water so that it does not accumulate on the floor, but drain out smoothly. All facilities at the hatchery should be cleaned, disinfected and kept at the right places. In particular, the egg incubation and larval rearing facilities should be thoroughly cleaned, before egg incubation and new batch of fry are introduced. This ensures that eggs do not get contaminated with bacteria and fungi, which limit fertilization of eggs and interfere with the hatching process [49]. In the fry nursery unit, these pathogens and parasites attack the fry leading to mortalities and deformities [50]. Mortality of brooders reduces the total number of brooders, which lowers the effective number of breeders, and consequently reduces genetic variation. This should be accompanied by cleaning and slashing around the ponds, hatchery and larval rearing units, including draining pools of water that may be stagnant around these facilities that may harbor predators, parasites and other pathogens.

The control of predators at the farm or brood stock ponds is very critical in maintaining a high number of brooders. Common predators include birds such as the king fisher and cormorants, snakes, and otters, as well as theft by humans. All these reduce the number of fish, and so should be controlled effectively.

Similarly, water quality monitoring should be undertaken regularly. This ensures that sudden declines in water quality do not occur in the ponds or the hatchery, which would otherwise suddenly kill the fish. Such mortalities will reduce the number of brood stock at the hatchery and lead to genetic drift, inbreeding and lose of genetic variation.

In order to preserve the quality and quantity of brood stock for production of quality seed, it is important that all inlets for water supply to the brood stock ponds and the hatchery are screened with fine mesh. This prevents entry of feral fish to the ponds and hatchery facilities. Feral fish are fish of unknown origin, identity and therefore quality, which enter aquaculture facilities with the water supply, especially if the source is a river or stream. Entry of feral fish into brood stock ponds and hatchery facilities creates competition for space, feeds and mates with the brooders, affecting the growth rates of the brooders as well as breeding to produce hybrids or fry of inferior quality, or creating an impure stock. Similarly, feral fish could introduce parasites and disease-causing pathogens to the brood stock and eggs in the hatchery and fry in the nursery units, leading to stress and mortality of the fish. Additionally, some of the feral fish could be cannibalistic, and therefore predate on the brood stock, eggs or fry, which will reduce the numbers, leading to genetic drift and inbreeding.

Hatchery operators should also routinely seine the brood stock ponds to remove any newly hatched fry, especially with tilapias that are highly prolific in culture. Such fry should then be kept in a separate pond. This ensures that offspring do not continue staying with their parents, as this will bring challenges of breeding. When the offspring reach sexual maturity in just 2–3 months of age, they will start breeding with their parents, and any other older generation in the holding pond or tank, leading to inbreeding. Also, the number of fish in the pond increases exponentially due to prolific breeding, overshooting the carrying capacity, which easily leads to stunted growth of fish. Therefore, separating fry from brood stock ponds is a good management strategy because it helps avoid inbreeding and keep the fish at suitable carrying capacity, for faster growth with reduced stress levels. It improves management of the different stages of fish, especially on feeding and management of feeding costs, since different stages of fish require feeds of different quality (crude protein content). It is also an easier way of managing seeds, for a farm that also deals in sale of fingerlings, since it will take a very short time to get the number of seeds required when a customer comes to buy seeds.

4. Perspectives on seed production for commercial aquaculture in Kenya

Countries that are global leaders in aquaculture production, such as China, Indonesia, Thailand and Egypt have invested heavily in fish seed production, for sustainable supply to farmers. For instance, Bangladesh has over 400 hatcheries that produce over 5 billion monosex male tilapia fry annually [51]. In Vietnam, up to 93 hatcheries produce 813 million fry of the striped catfish, *Pangasianodon hypophthalmus* annually [52], for uptake by farmers.

Kenya's aquaculture industry is dominated by two species: *O. niloticus* and *C. gariepinus*, although many farmers are focused on producing *O. niloticus*. This is because the species commands a higher market. Similarly, landings of the species from inland fisheries has declined due to overfishing, habitat degradation and impacts of invasive species. As a result, cage culture of tilapias is now practiced in Lake Victoria, and offers new frontiers for intensification of farmed tilapia production. Additionally, devolution of aquaculture extension services to county governments in the new constitution of Kenya 2010 provided new impetus for investment in aquaculture ventures. As a result, new hatcheries have been constructed. County governments now support augmentation of inland fisheries by purchasing tilapia seed from existing hatcheries for stock augmentation. Although this practice is largely undocumented, initial observations show that this exercise does not substantially increase fish stock abundance and landings in the lake, even with closed seasons that should encourage growth and survival of the introduced seed.

These require special focus on the quality of the seed produced by hatcheries. In order to minimize the impact of tilapia cage culture on natural tilapias in the open waters of the lake for instance, seed stocked in cages need to be all-male tilapia. However, current methods used by hatcheries to produce all-male tilapia seed (manual sorting, heat treatment, hormonal, hybridization, and YY super male tilapia technology) are inefficient, and even technically complex. Sex reversal by hormonal steroids [53], for instance, achieves sex inversion rates of only 70–90%. Therefore, the batch of such seed that is assumed to be all-male will have some females, and so breeding will occur in cages when the stocked seed reach sexual maturity. Fry so spawned in cages escape through the mesh to the open waters, and interact with the natural tilapias in the open waters of the lake in ways that are often negative, including hybridization. Similarly, the use of hormonal substances at the hatchery is environmentally unfriendly, and unhealthy for the workers.

In view of these challenges, there is need for developing more innovative methods of producing all-male tilapia seed for commercial and intensive farmed tilapia production in Kenya. One possible method is the use of molecular markers and genomic selection [54, 55] in combination with hormonal sex reversal as well as sex inversion by heat treatment [56] to identify and map the sex determining loci in strains of *O. niloticus*. This will enable development of highly inbred lines whose crossing will yield 100% all-male progeny for commercial use. Developing such a strain requires large financial resources, and as well as a strong collaborative team of scientists with a clear focus on the work, similar to the efforts that produced the GIFT strain of tilapia.

Despite a proliferation of hatcheries along the beaches of Lake Victoria to supply all-male tilapia fingerlings to cage culture farmers, there is still a challenge of adequacy, as well as quality of the seed so produced. High mortality of seed in cages is currently experienced by most cage culture farmers. These deaths may be attributed to environmental impacts from the high concentration of cages especially in shallower areas [57], as well as pollution of the water from nutrient loading by feeds, parasiticides and antibiotics used in managing diseases of caged fish [58]. However, mortality of fish in cages could be also be attributed to poor quality of seed stocked in the cages, especially with regard to survival. Poor quality of seed from hatcheries could result from use of impure brood stock for spawning, inadvertent use of different tilapia species as brood stock at the hatchery, while thinking it is *O. niloticus*, often due to poor taxonomic skills among hatchery operators and extension personnel at counties around the lake.

Use of different tilapia species is possible and may be already happening at many of the hatcheries, through collection from the natural waters of Lake Victoria. The native tilapiine species of the lake (*O. esculentus* and *O. variabilis*) are recovering due to changed dynamics in the lake, and these could be caught by fishermen or hatchery operators for use as brood stock at the hatcheries. Similarly, it is suspected that different tilapia species are also be imported in to the country by well-endowed hatchery owners, especially due to porous borders and weak enforcement of existing laws against importation of live fish in to the country. Apart from the possibility of the imported tilapia not being *O. niloticus*, it could also be the improved variety, suitable for culture only under certain husbandry conditions. This mix of tilapia species potentially reduces the vigor of the seed for growth, survival and fecundity, especially in a natural ecosystem like Lake Victoria, even if the seed is caged. Similarly, if a different species is used to breed for the seed, then if the batch stocked in cages is not 100% all-male, then spawning in cages will release a different species in to the open waters of the lake, potentially creating negative impacts on the *O. niloticus* of the lake. This will threaten tilapia biodiversity, persistence in the environment and performance in culture, should such impacted tilapias in the natural habitats be collected for use as brood stock at hatcheries. All these threats are so far not studied, and therefore are less documented and little understood. In order to improve the quality of seed supplied by hatcheries, and conserve existing tilapia biodiversity in the Lake Victoria basin while improving sustainable utilization, these challenges need to be tested in well-structured scientific studies.

5. Conclusion

In conclusion, hatchery operators need to improve practices used in seed propagation, and inparticular incorporate genetic principles in seed production. Maintaining optimal conditions at fry nursery units is also critical to improve survival of seed. In general, government needs to strictly enforce laws against importation of live fish in to the country, and hatchery opearators and farmers need to be encouraged to source their seed from reputable hatcheries, and as much as possible, avoid harvesting of natural fish populations for use as seed or broodstock at hatcheries and fish farms. In order to improve the quality and quantity of fish seed available for aquaculture, farmers also need to improve husbandry practices at their farmes, especially feeding, as well as the control of diseases and predators.

Author details

James Barasa Echessa
Department of Fisheries and Aquatic Sciences, University of Eldoret, Eldoret, Kenya

*Address all correspondence to: jbarasa@uoeld.ac.ke

References

[1] FAO (Food and Agriculture Organization). Global Aquaculture Production 1950-2019. 2021. Available from: http://www.fao.org/fishery/statistics/globalaquaculture-production/query/en

[2] Food and Agriculture Organization of the United Nations (FAO). Global Fishery and Aquaculture Production 1950-2017. FAO Fisheries & Aquaculture - Global production by production source Quantity (1950-2021). 2019

[3] State Department of Fisheries (SDF). Annual Fisheries Statistical Bulletin, 2022. State Department of Blue Economy and Fisheries. Nairobi, Kenya: Ministry of Mining, Blue Economy and Maritime Affairs; 2022. p. 49

[4] Little DC, Satapornvanit A, Edwards P. Freshwater fish seed quality in Asia. In: Edwards P, Little DC, Demaine H, editors. Rural Aquaculture. UK: CABI Publishing; 2002. pp. 185-195

[5] Kongkeo H. Current status and development trends of aquaculture in the Asian Region. In: Subasinghe RP, Bueno P, Phillips MJ, Hough C, McGladdery SE, Arthur JR, editors. Aquaculture in the Third Millenium. Technical Proceedings of the Conference on Aquaculture in the Third Millenium, Bangkok, Thailand, 20-25 February 2000. Bangkok: NACA and Rome, FAO; 2001. pp. 267-293

[6] Machena C, Moehl J. African Aquaculture: A regional summary with emphasis on Sub-Saharan Africa. In: Subasinghe RP, Bueno P, Phillips MJ, Hough C, McGladdery SE, Arthur JR, editors. Aquaculture in the Third Millenium. Technical Proceedings of the Conference on Aquaculture in the Third Millenium, Bangkok, Thailand, 20-25 February 2000. Bangkok: NACA Rome, FAO; 2001. pp. 341-356

[7] Fisheries. The Kenya Fisheries Statistical Bulletin 2016. Nairobi, Kenya: Ministry of Agriculture, Livestock and Fisheries Development; 2016. 65 pages

[8] Ngugi CC, Amadiva J, Veverica KL, Bowman J, Imende S, Nyandat B, Matolla G. On-farm trials in Kenya change attitudes of fish farmers and extensionists. Samaki News I. 2003

[9] Barasa JE, Mdyogolo S, Abila R, Grobler JP, Skilton RA, Bindeman H, et al. Genetic diversity and population structure of the African catfish, *Clarias gariepinus* (Burchell, 1822) in Kenya: Implication for conservation and aquaculture. Belgian Journal of Zoology. 2017;**147**(2):105-127. DOI: 10.26496/bjz.2017.9

[10] Fisheries. National Oceans and Fisheries Policy. Nairobi, Kenya: Ministry of Fisheries Development; 2008. 41 pages

[11] Fryer G, Iles TD. The Cichlid Fishes of the Great Lakes of Africa. Ediburgh, UK: Oliver and Boyd; 1972

[12] Turner GF, Robinson RL. Reproductive biology, mating systems and parental care. In: Beveridge MCM, McAndrew BJ, editors. Tilapias: Biology and Exploitation. Kluwer Academic Publishers; 2000. pp. 33-58

[13] Hogendoorn H, Vismans MM. Controlled propagation of the African catfish, *Clarias lazera* (C & V) II. Artificial reproduction. Aquaculture. 1980;**21**(1):39-53

[14] de Graaf GJ, Galemoni F, Banzoussi B. Artificial reproduction

and fingerling production of the African catfish, *Clarias gariepinus* (Burchell 1822), in protected and unprotected ponds. Aquaculture Research. 1995;**26**:233-242

[15] Macharia SK, Ngugi CC, Rasowo J. Comparative study of hatching Rates of African catfish, *Clarias gariepinus*, eggs on different substrates. NAGA, World Fish Center Quarterly. 2005;**28** (3 and 4):23-26

[16] Romana-Eguia MRR, Ikeda M, Basiao ZU, Taniguchi N. Genetic changes during mass selection for growth in Nile tilapia, *Oreochromis niloticus*, assessed by microsatellites. Aquaculture Research. 2005;**36**:69-78. DOI: 10.1111/j.1365-2109.2004.01185.x

[17] McKinna EM, Nandlal S, Mather PB, Hurwood DA. An investigation of the possible causes for the loss of productivity in genetically inproved farmed tilapia in Fiji: Inbreeding versus wild stock introgression. Aquaculture Research. 2010;**41**:730-742

[18] Tave D. Inbreeding and Brood Stock Management. FAO Fisheries Technical Paper 392. Rome, Italy: FAO; 1999. 134 pages

[19] Goudswaard PC, Witte F. The catfish fauna of Lake Victoria after Nile perch upsurge. Environmental Biology of Fishes. 1997;**49**:21-43

[20] Taniguchi N, Macaranas JM, Pullin RSV. Introgressive hybridization in cultured Tilapia stocks in the Philippines. Bulletin of the Japanese Society of Scientific Fisheries. 1985;**51**(8):1219-1224

[21] Deines AM, Bbole I, Katongo C, Feder JL, Lodge DM. Hybridisation between native *Oreochromis* species and introduced Nile tilapia *O. niloticus* in the Kafue River, Zambia. African Journal of Aquatic Science. 2014;**39**(1):23-34. Available from: https://www.tandfonline.com/loi/taas20

[22] Njiru M, Kazungu J, Ngugi CC, Gichuki J, Muhoozi L. Management of Lake Victoria fishery: An overview of the current status of Lake Victoria fishery: Opportunities, challenges and management strategies. Lakes & Reservoirs: Research and Management. 2008;**13**:1-12. DOI: 10.1111/j.1440-1770.2007.00358.x

[23] Ogutu-Ohwayo R. The decline of native fish species of Lake Victoria and Kyoga (East Africa) and the impact of introduced species, especially the Nile perch, *Lates niloticus* and Nile tilapia, *Oreochromis niloticus*. Environmental Biology of Fishes. 1990;**27**:81-96

[24] Goudswaard K, Witte F, Katunzi EFB. The tilapiine fish stock of Lake Victoria before and after the Nile perch upsurge. Journal of Fish Biology. 2002;**60**:838-856

[25] Lowe-McConnell RH. Observations on the biology of Tilapia nilotica (Pisces: Cichlidae) in East African waters. Revue Zoologie et de Botanique Africaines. 1958;**57**:129-170

[26] Lowe-McConnell RH. The roles of tilapias in ecosystems. In: Beveridge MCM, Andrews BJ, editors. Tilapias: Biology and Exploitation. Dordrecht (The Netherlands): Kluwer; 2000. pp. 129-162

[27] Angienda PO, Lee HJ, Elmer KR, Abila R, Waindi EN, Meyer A. Genetic structure and gene flow in an endangered native tilapia fish (*Oreochromis esculentus*) compared to invasive Nile tilapia (*Oreochromis niloticus*) in Yala swamp, East Africa. Conservation Genetics. 2011;**12**:243-255

[28] Mwanja W, Kaufman L. A note on recent advances in the genetic

characterization of tilapia stocks in Lake Victoria region. African Journal of Tropical Hydrobiology and Fisheries. 1995;**6**:51-53

[29] Mwanja WW, Fuerst PA, Kaufman L. Reduction of the "ngege", *Oreochromis esculentus* (Teleostei: Cichlidae) populations, and resultant population genetic status in the Lake Victoria region. Uganda Journal of Agricultural Sciences. 2012;**13**(2):65-82

[30] Nyingi DW, Agnese J-F. Recent introgressive hybridization revealed by exclusive mtDNA transfer from *Oreochromis leucostictus* (Trewavas, 1933) to *Oreochromis niloticus* (Linnaeus, 1758) in Lake Baringo, Kenya. Journal of Fish Biology. 2007;**70**(Supplement A):148-154

[31] Chuhila Y. Assessment of Changes in Genetic Diversity of Nile tilapia, *Oreochromis niloticus* (Linnaeus, 1758), of Lake Baringo. [MSc Thesis]. Nairobi: University of Nairobi; 2015. 133 pages

[32] Shechunge A, Ngatunga BP, Bradbeer SJ, Day JJ, Freer JJ, Ford AGP, et al. Losing cichlid fish biodiversity: Genetic and morphological homogenization of tilapia following colonization by introduced species. Conservation Genetics. 2018;**19**:1199-1209

[33] D'Amato ME, Esterhuyse MM, van der Waal BCW, Brink D, Volckaert FAM. Hybridization and Phylogeography of the Mozambique tilapia, *Oreochromis mossambicus* in southern Africa evidenced by mitochondrial and microsatellite DNA genotyping. Conservation Genetics. 2007;**8**:475-488

[34] Eknath AE, Tayamen MM, Palada-de Vera MS, Danting JC, Reyes RA, Dionisio EE, et al. Genetic improvement of farmed tilapias: The growth performance of eight strains of *Oreochromis niloticus* tested in different farm environments. Aquaculture. 1993;**111**:171-188

[35] Opiyo SV, Dadzie S. Diet and food utilization in *Oreochromis esculentus* (Graham) in Lake Kanyaboli, Kenya. Fisheries Management and Ecology. 1994;**1**:79-90

[36] Nagayi-Yawe JK, Ogutu-Ohwayo R, Kizito YS, Balirwa JS. Population characteristics of *Oreochromis esculentus* in the Victoria and Kyoga lake basins. Implications for conservation and improvement of the stocks. African Journal of Ecology. 2006;**44**:423-430. DOI: 10.1111/j.1365-2028.2006.00645.x

[37] Kapuscinski AR, Miller LM. Genetic Guidelines for Fisheries Management. Second ed. Minnesota, Duluth, USA: University of Minnesota Sea Grant Program; 2007. 116 pages. Available from: Genetic+guidelines+for+Fisheries+Management&rlz=1C1GCEA_enKE1095KE1095&oq=Genetic+guidelines+for+Fisheries+Management&gs_lcrp=EgZjaHJvbWUyBggAEEUYOTIKCAEQABiABBiiBDIKCAIQABiiBBiJBdIBCTI2MjYzajBqN6gCALACAA&sourceid=chrome&ie=UTF-8

[38] Bhujel RC. A review of strategies for the management of Nile tilapia, *Oreochromis niloticus* broodfish in seed production systems, especially hapa-based systems. Aquaculture. 2000;**181**:37-59. DOI: 10.1016/S0044-8486(99)00217-3

[39] FAO (Food and Agriculture Organization of the United Nations). Outline Research Program for the African Regional Aquaculture Centre ADCP/REP/80/12. Rome, Italy; 1980. Available from: Outline+Research+Program+for+the+African+Regional+Aquaculture+Centre+ADCP%2F+REP%2F80%2F12.+Rome+Italy%3B+1980&rlz=1C1GCEA_enKE1095KE1095&oq=Outline+Research+Pro

gram+for+the+African+Regional+Aquaculture+Centre+ADCP%2F+REP%2F80%2F12.+Rome+Italy%3B+1980&gs_lcrp=EgZjaHJvbWUyBggAEEUYOdIBCDI0NTVqMGo3qAIAsAIA&sourceid=chrome&ie=UTF-8

[40] Rutten MJM, Bovenhuis H, Komen H. Modeling fillet traits based on body measurements in three Nile tilapia strains (*Oreochromis niloticus* L.). Aquaculture. 2004;**231**(1-4):113-122. DOI: 10.1016/j.aquaculture.2003.11.002

[41] ADB (Asian Development Bank). Impact Evaluation Study on the Development of Genetically Improved Farmed Tilapia and Their Dissemination in Selected Countries. 90 pages. Thailand. Manila, Philippines: Asian Development Bank; 2004

[42] De Silva SS, Ingram BA, Wilkinson S, editors. Perspectives on Culture-Based Fisheries Developments in Asia. Bangkok, Thailand: Network of Aquaculture Centres in Asia (NACA); 2015. NACA Monograph Series No. 3, 126 pages

[43] Tangtrongpiros M. The status of wild and cultured tilapia genetic resources in various countries: Thailand. In: Pullin RSV, editor. Tilapia Genetic Resources for Aquaculture. ICLARM: Manila, Philippines; 1988. pp. 45-48

[44] Pullin RSV, Capili JB. Genetic improvement of tilapias: Problems and prospects. In: Pullin RSV, Bhukaswan T, Tonguthai K, MacLean JI, editors. The Second International Symposium on Tilapia in Aquaculture. ICLARM Conference Proceedings. Vol. 15. Manilla, Philippines: Department of Fisheries, Thailand and ICLARM; 1988, pages 259 to 266

[45] Macaranas JM, Taniguchi N, Pande MJR, Capili J, Pullin RSV. Electrophoretic evidence for extensive hybrid gene introgression in to commercial *Oreochromis niloticus* stocks in the Philippines. Aquaculture and Fisheries Management. 1986;**17**:249-258

[46] Mair GC, Little DC. Population control in farmed tilapias. NAGA. 1991;**14**:8-13

[47] Mair GC, Abucay JS, Skibinski DOF, Abella TA, Beardmore JA. Genetic manipulation of sex ratio for the large scale production of all-male tilapia *Oreochromis niloticus* L. Canadian Journal of Fisheries and Aquatic Sciences. 1997;**54**(2):396-404. DOI: 10.1139/cjfas-54-2-396

[48] Beardmore JA, Mair GC, Lewis RI. Monosex male production in finfish as exemplified by tilapia: Applications, problems, and prospects. Aquaculture. 2001;**197**:283-301. DOI: 10.1016/S0044-8486(01)00590-7

[49] Rasowo J, Oyoo EO, Ngugi CC. Effects of formaldehyde, sodium chloride, potassium permanganate and hydrogen peroxide on hatch rate of African catfish *Clarias gariepinus* eggs. Aquaculture. 2007;**269**:271-277. DOI: 10.1016/j.aquaculture.2007.04.087

[50] Magondu EW, Rasowo J, Oyoo-Okoth E, Charo-Karisa H. Evaluation of sodium chloride (NaCl) for potential prophylactic treatment and its short-term toxicity to African catfish *Clarias gariepinus* (Burchell 1822) yolk-sac and swim-up fry. Aquaculture. 2011;**319**:307-310. DOI: 10.1016/j.aquaculture.2011.06.038

[51] Hussain G, Kohinoor A, Rahman M, Rahman Z, Nguyen NH. Bangladesh's Tilapia Aquaculture Industry Shows Resilience Global Aquaculture Advocate. 2017. Available from: https://www.aquaculturealliance.org/advocate/bangladesh-tilapia/?headlessPrint=AAAAAPIA9c8r7gs82oWZBA

[52] Bui TM, Phan LT, Ingram BA, et al. Seed production practices of striped catfish, *Pangasianodon hypophthalmus* in the Mekong Delta region, Vietnam. Aquaculture. 2010;**306**:92-100. DOI: 10.1016/j.aquaculture.2010.06.016

[53] Popma T, Green B. Sex Reversal of Tilapia in Earthen Ponds. Publications from USDA-ARS/UNL Faculty. 2559. 1990. Available from: https://digitalcommons.unl.edu/usdaarsfacpub/2559

[54] Palaiokostas C, Bekaert M, Khan MGQ, Taggart JB, Gharbi K, McAndrew BJ, et al. Mapping and validation of the major sex-determining region in Nile tilapia (*Oreochromis niloticus* L.) using RAD sequencing. PLoS One. 2013;**8**(7):e68389. DOI: 10.1371/journal.pone.0068389

[55] Palaiokostas C, Bekaert M, Khan MGQ, Taggart JB, Gharbi K, McAndrew BJ, et al. A novel sex-determining QTL in Nile tilapia (*Oreochromis niloticus*). BMC Genomics. 2015;**16**:171. DOI: 10.1186/s12864-015-1383-x

[56] Wessels S, Krause I, Floren C, Schütz E, Beck J, Knorr C. ddRADseq reveals determinants for temperature-dependent sex reversal in Nile tilapia on LG23. BMC Genomics. 2017;**18**:531. DOI: 10.1186/s12864-017-3930-0

[57] Musinguzi L, Lugya J, Rwezawala P, Kamya A, Nuwahereza C, Halafo J, et al. The extent of cage aqua- culture, adherence to best practices and reflections for sustainable aquaculture on African inland waters. Journal of Great Lakes Research. 2019;**45**(6):1340-1347. DOI: 10.1016/j.jglr.2019-09.011

[58] Njiru JM, Aura CM, Okechi JK. Cage fish culture in Lake Victoria: A boon or a disaster in waiting? Fisheries Management and Ecology. 2019;**26**(5):426-434. DOI: 10.1111/fme.12283

Chapter 4

Recent Developments in Fish Nutrition and Culture Technologies in Kenya

Job O. Omweno and Argwings Omondi

Abstract

Kenya has immense potential for aquaculture growth and development due to recent decline of capture fisheries production from Lake Victoria, which accounts for over 80% of the national production. However, lack of subsidies and slow adoption of aquaculture nutrition and culture technologies have slowed aquaculture growth and development nationally. There is need to explore innovative aquaculture production technologies and alternative protein sources that can replace fish meal to yield optimal returns in the foreseeable future. The study reviews the use of re-circulatory aquaculture system in tilapia hatchery to conserve limited water supplies and guarantee 95% success in mono-sex production of all male tilapia fingerlings. In Kenya, Freshwater shrimps, *Caridina niloticus* is the most common fish meal in aquafeed formulations. Although readily affordable, plant-based protein sources contain low crude protein levels and lack essential micronutrients. More sustainable animal protein sources such as black solder fly (BSF) *Hermetia illucens* pre-pupae and Redworms *Eisenia foetida* have shown the potential to yield optimal returns in a commercial scale, and can solve environmental problems associated with aquaculture. This study further recommends the use of recirculatory aquaculture in water scarce areas and those faced with intermittent interruptions due to prolonged droughts and pollution of surface waters.

Keywords: black soldier fly prepupae, *Caridina niloticus*, biofloc, redworms, recirculatory aquaculture system

1. Introduction

The dwindling nature of capture fisheries production in Lake Victoria and other inland lakes, accounting for ~ over 80% of the total national catch has been attributed to many anthropogenic interventions [1, 2]. This has contributed to lower national catch. For instance, the country's annual fish production declined from ~150,000 tons in 2013 to 102,000 tons in 2020 [3]. Whereas this decline contributes to an annual per capita fish consumption of 4.5 kg, which is comparatively lower than the global average per capita of 20 kg [4], aquaculture has still the great potential of bridging the deficit in affordable animal protein supply among developing countries [5]. While some fish mongers have taken an entrepreneurial advantage to import frozen tilapia from China, there have been inconclusive discussions among various stakeholders as to whether the current fish importation can sustainably bridge the existing demand-supply gap [3]. Currently, the Kenyan aquaculture sector is facing many critical challenges. These could be attributed to lack of bilateral and multilateral subsidies as well as weak adoption of the existing aquaculture technologies. For instance, during the 2009–2012, Kenya reported significant aquaculture growth due to marginal subsidies injected into the subsector by the inter-sectorial economic stimulus program (ESP) [3, 6]. Nevertheless, aquaculture subsector has continued to grow steadily with a high potential to improve food and nutrition in Kenya. The period 2016–2023 was characterized by the radical shift from extensive to semi-intensive pond management and culture systems, which constitute of 90% of fish farming systems in Kenya. Despite these milestones, there has been low adoption of sustainable aquaculture technologies. This can be attributed to such factors as low levels of education, high cost of inputs, limited awareness on the available technologies, limited appropriate financing mechanisms and limited extension services.

The most pertinent challenges include lack of accessibility to affordable and high-quality fingerlings and fish feed [7]. These challenges have been compounded by inadequate sharing of information, extension services, training and capacity building on best aquaculture production and management practices [8]. With the projected growth in fish supply gap to about 350,000 tons annually, it is highly expected that aquaculture growth will create hundreds of job and business opportunities for many actors within the expanded value chain and contribute to improved food and nutrition security in Kenya [7, 9]. Furthermore, Kenya has many unexploited small water bodies (SWBs), which can be utilized to promote aquaculture growth and development. Due to the foregoing developments, there is need to review the recent developments in fish feeding and culture technologies to assess development needs for future sustainability [8, 10].

2. Development of aquaculture technologies

Various studies have posited that Kenya has an immense potential for aquaculture growth and development. However, the country is yet to report significant global aquaculture contribution because of slow adoption of the recent aquaculture technologies [11]. According to Munguti et al. [7], there is need to explore various technological interventions that have been employed to boost aquaculture growth and development in many parts of the world. Recent aquaculture technologies include biofloc technology, genetic engineering, selection and breeding and hybridization [11, 12]. These aquaculture technologies seek to increase protein utilization for improved growth performance and reduce the cost of production and shortening the time taken by cultured fish to attain consumer demand driven sizes. For instance, biofloc technology aims to maximize on-farm utilization of available protein sources and reduce discharge of effluents to surrounding water sources [13]. The main fish species cultured include Nile tilapia and the African catfish (**Figure 1**).

2.1 Re-circulatory aquaculture system

A re-circulatory aquaculture system comprises of a water filtration system to prevent algal growth and a water recycling system (**Figure 2**). The system uniformly distributes fish feed and other ecological parameters, allowing accessibility by all

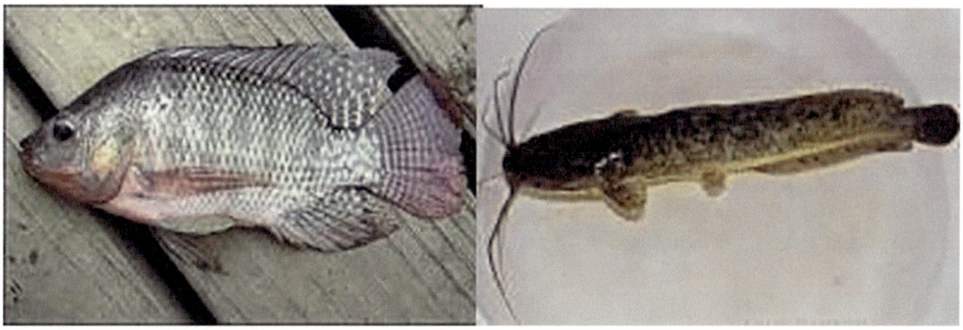

Figure 1.
Two major cultured aquaculture species in Kenya: A—Nile tilapia, Oreochromis niloticus and B—The African catfish, Clarias gariepinus.

fry hence guarantees greater success of sex reversal. In this water re-use system, optimum water quality is maintained through bio-filtration, removal of ammonia, Carbon (iv) oxide and suspended solids and re-oxygenation of water [14]. The water is re-used continuously as it is being recycled with approximately 10–15% replacement biweekly, to cater for system loses due to evaporation and cleaning of biofilters. Although the system is highly suitable for water deficient regions, it can be also used in areas which experience high levels of pollution from urban and municipal wastes as well as untreated sewage discharge into freshwater sources [15]. This makes it virtually impossible to attain 95% all male fingerlings during sex reversal conducted in nursery ponds. Availability of planktons or live feed in the nursery ponds causes a shift in preference of fry feeding from consuming hormone impregnated feeds to planktons [16]. Nevertheless, the design should take into consideration the local needs to ensure long-term sustainability in efficiency and operational costs [16].

2.2 Design of the re-circulatory aquaculture system

2.2.1 Egg incubation system

This system includes a table stand with several MacDonald jars, made from transparent plastic material, hatching trays, and a UV sterilizer. Water is drawn from the header tank into the jars through a vertical tube causing upwelling to keep the eggs suspended. Each jar overflows in a plastic hatching tray, where swim-up larvae are trapped until stocking in the larvae system. For instance, the jars have a height of 46 cm and a diameter of 16 cm with 8-liter capacity for can be used to incubate up to 20,000 eggs [17].

2.2.2 Larval rearing system

This system consists of 20 nestable tanks fitted with a center drain that pulls all the wastes into a common drain pipe to the collecting basin at the drum filter. The drum filter that is backwashed periodically is used as the mechanical filter. The system bio-filter consists of a sump that contains bio media containing nitrifying bacteria (Nitrobacter) that breaks down toxic un-ionized ammonia (NH_3), which is highly toxic to fish and known to depress the appetite of tilapia at concentrations more higher than 0.2 mg, by converting it into less toxic nitrites [18]. The concentration of

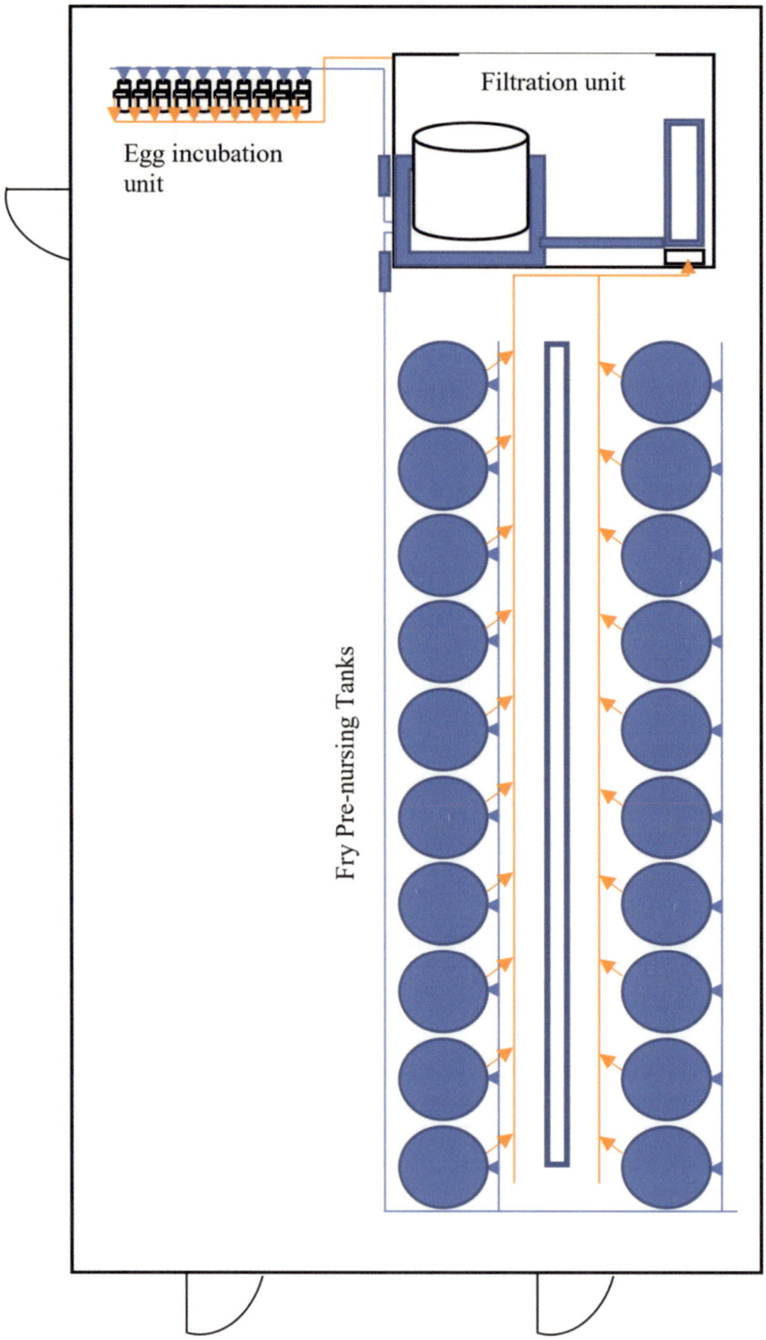

Figure 2.
Proposed sketch design plan of a recirculatory aquaculture system at the County Fish Multiplication and training Center (CFM &TC) in Kisii County, Kenya.

un-ionized ammonia in aquaculture systems can be controlled by maintaining a pH of 7.0–max. 8.75. It also contains a booster pump with an inlet and outlet that moves the water from the sump into the header tank. It is also fitted with a regenerative blower replenishes dissolved oxygen in the header tank and in the sump [19].

Water is pumped from spawning and rearing systems to cylindrical header tanks for bio-filtration and waste removal to maintain water quality by the main pump, placed after the bio-filter. In addition to bio-filters, drum filter tanks remove suspended solids and those that can settle. The drum rotates so the screen can be backwashed using high pressure water sprays to prevent clogging while the waste-water and solids are removed from the system enter the main drain. Another inlet pipe from the reservoir tank connects to the header tank to replenish the systems water [20].

To produce large quantities of fish seed, large amounts of dissolved oxygen is required for developing eggs and fry. Aeration is provided to the biofilter sump and header tank using an air pump connected to an air grid and submerged air stones respectively. The flow of air bubbles increases contact with air and thus oxygen exchange between the air and water [21]. This type of aeration also strips carbon dioxide from the water. Two regenerative air blowers are used in the system. There is one spare air blower which should be stored in a clean, cool area, together with the spare parts. From the manifold, air stones in the header tanks are connected through air hoses. Air stones used are disc stones with a diameter of 5 cm and 20 cm [22].

3. Development of fish nutrition

3.1 Alternative protein sources

Cultured fish have diverse nutritional requirements based on their trophic levels and feeding habits [23]. For instance, the highly omnivorous African catfish require high in protein content in their diets compared to exclusively herbivorous species such as the Nile Tilapia. This makes their feed more expensive than those of Nile tilapia. High cost of fish feed that accounts for up to 70% of the total production costs usually results from the inclusion of high-quality animal-based protein ingredients which are essential in promoting faster growth in cultured fish [24]. Their high-quality protein usually is responsible for highly palatability; digestibility and assimilation of fish feed into fish tissues to build up high quality and balanced amino acid (AA) profile. Besides being a relatively expensive ingredient, fishmeal, the common source of protein in fish feeds is geographically unavailable to most farmers and has many other competitive uses such as formulation of poultry and livestock feeds [25, 26]. The main sources of fish meal in Kenya are the freshwater shrimps, *Caridina niloticus*, and the discards of silver cyprinid, *Rastrineobola argentea.* However, the seasonal availability of *C. niloticus* has served to increase the overall cost of production because of competition for the use of fishmeal from other production enterprises such livestock sector, where it is mainly used as feed ingredient for poultry and other livestock [27]. Increased dependency on fish meal often leads to unsustainable exploitation of freshwater fisheries in Lake Victoria, while threatening the stability of food chains of the self-sustaining native and exotic stocks as well as diversity of Lake Victoria's highly diverse multi-species ecosystems [1, 27]. Slow growth and development of aquaculture has been linked to availability of few reputable large-scale feed mills which continues to hamper aquaculture growth, contributing to increased cost of production, in addition to decreased availability and reliability of the quality fish feed supply [24]. Some unscrupulous sellers have resorted to incorporating of low-level crude protein in fish feeds which they sell directly to unsuspecting farmers resulting to slow growth of the cultured species [24, 28].

Most semi-intensive pond-culture systems employ pond fertilization together with supplemental feeding to increase nutrient supply for fish growth [7]. It is recommended to fertilize the ponds of Nile tilapia prior to stocking of fingerlings to promote production of live feeds (Which include larger zooplankton such as daphnia and phytoplankton). However, supplemental feeding is still required as the production tends to be insufficient to meet the nutritional requirements of early stages of growth [29].

3.2 Black soldier fly (*Hermetia illucens*)

The dry matter of black soldier fly (*Hermetia illucens*) pre-pupae contains 42% crude protein and 35% fat and several micro-nutrients such as magnesium, Copper, Iron, Molybdenum, and Zinc [30]. These dietary components have been found to promote optimal growth farm animals such as chicks, swine, rainbow trout and catfish [31, 32]. Studies have shown that black soldier fly pre-pupae has been used to replace more than 25% of the fish meal in formulating the diet of rainbow trout and channel catfish, producing a feed with over 60% crude protein level. Nevertheless, growth trials using these feeds showed no significant reduction in weight gain and feed conversion efficiency [31, 32]. In addition, culture trials of Nile tilapia and channel catfish have shown no significant differences between formulated BSF pre-puppae diets and commercial diets [33]. However, to enhance feed digestibility and protein utilization, it is necessary to remove chitin from BSF larvae if using raw insect as a feedstuff for fish feeds formulation. Furthermore, studies on food safety and bacteriological considerations have shown that BFS larval activity significantly reduced *Escherichia coli* and *Salmonella enterica* in chicken manure, which could be due to anti-microbial factors they contain [34]. However, there will be need to conduct detailed bacteriological assessments and other food safety issues to ascertain the safe use of this novel feedstuff in aquaculture. The feedstuff requires less energy for processing than fish meal, and provides better management of problematic manure to reduce negative impacts on the environment because it reduces pathogens that naturally occur in manure [34, 35].

3.3 Fishmeal and fish oil

The demand for fishmeal and fish oil has doubled over the last three decades due to increased production of farmed fish [36]. However, the annual global fishmeal and fish oil production has correspondingly stagnated implying that the aquaculture industry cannot continue relying on finite stocks of fishmeal in the foreseeable future [37]. The increased use of fishmeal has sparked global interest into finding most suitable alternative feedstuffs to replace it in aquafeed production.

Although plant-based ingredients are readily affordable, they can only replace up to 3% of fishmeal in the aquafeed for farmed tilapia [38]. It is prudent to find other protein and fish oil alternatives, which can meet the nutritional requirements to yield optimal growth and production [39]. This can cause a knock-on effect to decrease over-reliance on fish meal protein and reverse the dwindling trends in freshwater fisheries [40]. However, plant-based protein has low crude protein levels. They lack certain essential amino acids and micro-nutrients, and contain high amounts of crude fiber which lowers their palatability and digestibility [41], and anti-nutritional factors, which lower their feed conversion efficiencies [42]. In addition, some feedstuffs such as soya beans require additional processing before, they are incorporated into fish feeds, to improve their nutritional quality [43, 44]. Terrestrial plant oils have shown limited ability to fully replace fish oils in aquafeeds. With exception of some oilseeds, they low levels of Omega-3 (ω3) PUFAs and completely lack long chain Omega-3 (ω3) PUFAs, but are rich in Omega-6 (ω6) and Omega-9 (ω9) fatty acids. Feeding fish exclusively on plant protein sources will result in inevitably lower levels of docosahexaenoic acid (DHA) and eicosatetraenoic acid (EPA) in their tissues which will reduce the health and nutritional benefits derived from fish, which will be detrimental to human health after fish consumption [37]. It will also predispose fish to a high incidence of cardiovascular disorders [45]. Consequently, the plant protein sources to be considered as a most suitable substitute for FO should contain high levels of ω3 poly-unsaturated fatty acids (PUFAs) (LNA) and a high ω3/ω6 ratio. This makes plant proteins have a lower nutritional advantage over fishmeal.

3.4 Chemical analysis of fish feed components

While several studies have evaluated and compared the proximate composition of locally available proteins sources such as red-worms *Eisenia foetida*, Black solder fly and bioflocs, finding an alternative protein source that can adequately substitute fishmeal in formulated fish feeds is still a high global interest [46]. Some previous studies have reported that *E. foetida* is a viable alternative to fish meal because of its high composition of protein, essential amino acids, fats and minerals which are comparable to the composition of fishmeal [47, 48]. For instance, Akidiva et al. [49], compared the proximate composition of dried red worms, *E. foetida* and fishmeal (**Figure 3**).

Nevertheless, although its proximate composition indicates it is a viable alternative for replacement of fishmeal; little information has been documented on its use in feed formulation.

3.5 Access to quality feeds

Access to quality feeds is one of the challenges faced by most aquaculture farmers who lack adequate resources to purchase the high-quality feeds [35]. To reduce the cost of feeds, previous studies have recommended a paradigm shift from overdependence of

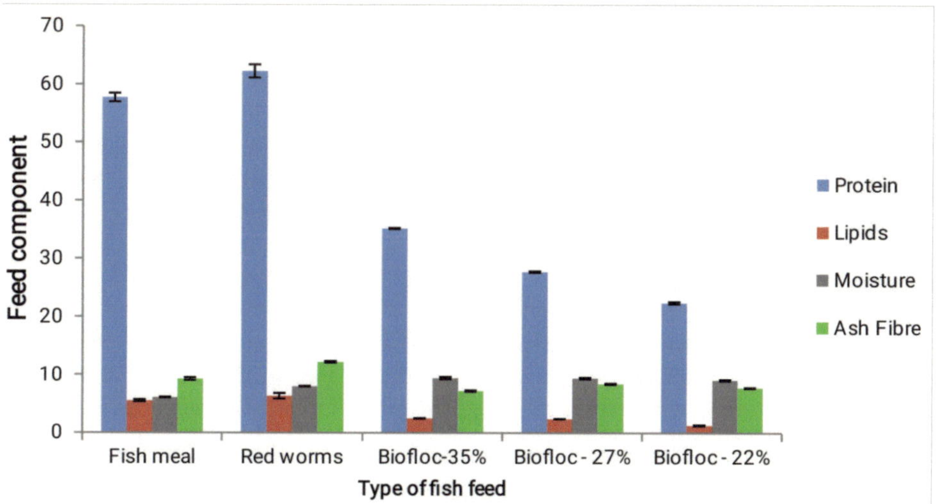

Figure 3.
Comparative chemical analysis of different components of fish feeds used in aquaculture trials. Data obtained from Akidiva et al. [49] and Zablon et al. [13].

fishmeal and fish oil towards the use of cheap and readily available alternative protein sources. Most of farmers however, lack adequate knowledge to formulate homemade feeds from locally available feedstuffs such as corn meal, wheat bran, and rice bran and cassava meal. UNGA FEEDS and Sigma Feeds are some of the major private commercial fish feed millers with extensive network of distributors in many parts of the country [24, 46]. These companies produce micro-extruded tilapia and catfish pellets that offer better pellet stability and reduced nutrient leaching into the culture water. The pellet sizes range from 0.1 mm to 5.0 mm, targeting the fish stage with specific gape size to economize consumption, while the specific protein level included in the feed target specific requirements to support optimum growth and development and reduce production cost [50].

It is prudent to note that both fry and fingerling stages require crude protein levels of >40% and >30% respectively, for muscle tissue formation which may have an important impact on later growth and maturation [51]. Therefore, the fish feeds should be formulated in such a way that they provide balanced nutrition, their protein content is sufficient to support growth and muscle development, so that the fish can attain the consumer demand driven sizes during the production cycle, and the required fatty acids and available amino acids in line with the requirements for the export market [51, 52].

4. Conclusions and recommendation

In many successful trials, BSF *Hermetia illucens* and the red worms have been extensively studied as potential feedstuffs for replacement of fish meal in aquaculture production and feed production for other livestock. In almost all cases, culture trials have shown greater success. Commercialization of BSF prepupae and red worms' production and adoption of biofloc technology can solve many agricultural and environmental problems associated with conventional aquaculture. There is need to assess whether the production and utilization of *Hermetia illucens* prepupae and redworms in commercial scale to replace fish meal would have significant positive economic and environmental impact. This study further recommends the use of recirculatory aquaculture in water scarce areas and those faced with intermittent interruptions due to prolonged droughts and pollution of surface waters.

Acknowledgements

The manuscript benefitted from technical contributions by G. Gicheru and Wilfred O. Zablon of the County Directorate of Fisheries, Kisii County Government. This however does not imply endorsement by the County Government.

Author contributions

Job Omweno conceived and conceptualized the study, wrote and supervised the writing of the manuscript with Argwings Omondi. Argwings Omondi edited, provide additional literature content, and proofread the manuscript. Authors have read and approved the final manuscript.

Funding information

This review received no funding from any institution or funding agency.

Competing interests

The authors declare that they have no known competing academic, professional and financial interests or personal relationships that could appear to influence the outcome of this paper after publication.

Availability of additional information

All sources analyzed during this review are included in the references. For supplementary material and information, all correspondences and requests should be addressed to Job Omweno.

Author details

Job O. Omweno[1,2]* and Argwings Omondi[2,3]

1 Department of Agriculture, Livestock, Fisheries, Cooperative Development and Irrigation, Kisii County Government, Kisii, Kenya

2 Department of Environment, Natural Resources and Aquatic Sciences, Kisii University, Kisii, Kenya

3 Department of Agriculture and Environmental Science, Sigalagala National Polytechnic, Kakamega, Kenya

*Address all correspondence to: omwenojob@gmail.com

References

[1] Outa NO, Yongo EO, Keyombe JLA, Ogello EO, Wanjala DN. A review on the status of some major fish species in Lake Victoria and possible conservation strategies. Lakes & Reservoirs: Research and Management. 2020;**25**(1):105-111

[2] Omweno J, Opiyo S, Omondi A, Zablon W. Natural and anthropogenic changes threatening the ecological and limnological integrity of Lake Baringo, Kenya: A review. Pan Africa Science Journal. 2021;**2**(01):103-121. DOI: 10.47787/pasj.2021.01.23

[3] Ogello OE, Outa ON, Ouma OK, Kyule ND, Munguti MJ, Obiero OK. Socio-economic consequences of imported frozen tilapia in the Kenyan aquaculture value chain: Strategies for optimizing local unexploited potential. African Journal of Food and Agricultural Nutrition Development. 2022;**22**(8):21171-21185. DOI: 10.18697/ajfand.113.21985

[4] Obwanga B, Soma K, Ingasia Ayuya O, Rurangwa E, van Wonderen D, Beekman G. Exploring enabling factors for commercializing the aquaculture sector in Kenya. 3R Kenya Research Reports. 2020;**1**:55

[5] Omweno JO, Orina PS, Albert G, Outa NO. Growth and aquaculture potential of *Tilapia jipe*, *Oreochromis jipe* and *Nile tilapia*, *Oreochromis niloticus*. International Journal of Fisheries and Aquatic Studies. 2020;**8**(3):395-399

[6] BOMOSA. Integrating BOMOSA cage fish farming systems in reservoirs, ponds and temporary water bodies in Eastern Africa. Project No. 032103. BOMOSA. 2009

[7] Munguti JM, Musa S, Orina PS, Kyule DN, Opiyo MA, Charo-Karisa H. An overview of the current status of the Kenyan fish feed industry and feed management practices, challenges and opportunities. International Journal of Fisheries and Aquatic Studies. 2014;**1**(6):128-137

[8] Ogello E. Studies on the Development of Low-cost and Stable Live Food Production Technologies for Tropical Aquaculture: A Case Study of Rotifera (Family: Brachionidae). PhD Dissertation. Japan: Nagasaki University; 2018. pp. 1-165

[9] Bostock J, McAndrew B, Richards R, Jauncey K, Telfer T, Lorenzen K, et al. Aquaculture: Global status and trends. Philosophical Transactions of the Royal Society B. 2010;**365**:2897-2912. DOI: 10.1098/rstb.2010.0170

[10] Charo-Karisa H, Gichuri M. Overview of the fish farming enterprise productivity program. In: End of Year Report Fish Farming Enterprise Productivity Program Phase I. Aquaculture Development Working Group Ministry of Fisheries Development; Nairobi, KE. 2010

[11] Ngugi CC, Bowman JR, Omolo BO. A new guide to fish farming in Kenya. Aquaculture Collaborative Research Support Program (ACRSP). 2007;**2007**:1-100

[12] Kapinga I. Characterization of Artemia from Solar Salt Works in Kenya. Ghent: Ghent University; 2012

[13] Zablon WO, Ogello EO, Getabu A, Omondi R. Biofloc system improves protein utilization efficiency and growth performance of Nile tilapia, Oreochromis niloticusfry: Experimental evidence. Aquaculture Fish and Fisheries. 2022;**1**:1-10

[14] Liti DM, Mugo RM, Munguti JM, Waidbacher H. Growth and economic performance of Nile tilapia (*Oreochromis niloticus* L.) fed on three brans (maize, wheat and rice) in fertilized ponds. Aquaculture Nutrition. 2006;**12**:239-245. DOI: 10.1111/j.1365-2095.2006.00397.x

[15] Food and Agriculture Organization of the United Nations. Small ponds make a big difference. Integrating fish with crop and livestock farming. In: Farm Management and Production Economics Service Inland Water Resources and Aquaculture Service. Rome: FAO; 2000

[16] Munguti J, Charo-Karisa H. Fish feeds and aquaculture development in Kenya. In: Samaki News: Aquaculture Development in Kenya towards Food Security, Poverty Alleviation and Wealth Creation. Journal of Food Agriculture Nutrition and Development. 2011. pp. 27-29

[17] Munguti J, Charo-Karisa H, Opiyo MA, Ogello EO, Marijani E, Nzayisenga L, et al. Nutritive value and availability of commonly used feed ingredients for farmed Nile Tilapia (*Oreochromis niloticus* L.) and African catfish (*Clarias gariepinus,* Burchell) in Kenya, Rwanda and Tanzania. African Journal of Food Agriculture Nutrition and Development. 2012. pp. 27-29

[18] Omweno JO, Getabu A, Omondi R, Orina PS. Water quality effects on growth and survival of *Oreochromis jipe* and *Oreochromis niloticus* species in aquaculture. In: Dincer S, Takci HAM, Ozdenefe MS, editors. Water Quality—New Perspectives [Working Title]. London, UK, London, UK: IntechOpen; 2022. DOI: 10.5772/intechopen.106361

[19] Musa S, Aura MC, Owiti G, Nyonje B, Orina P, Charo-Karisa H. Fish farming enterprise productivity program (FFEPP) as an impetus to *Oreochromis niloticus* (L.) farming in Western Kenya: Lessons to learn. African Journal of Agricultural Research. 2012;**7**:1324-1330. DOI: 10.5897/AJAR11.1608

[20] Ngugi CC, Manyala JO. Aquaculture extension services in Kenya. In: Aquaculture Extension Services in Sub-Saharan Africa. Rome: Food and Agriculture Organization of the United Nations; 2004. pp. 35-42

[21] Nyonje BM, Charo-Karisa H, Macharia SK, Mbugua M. Aquaculture development in Kenya: Status, potential and challenges. In: Samaki News: Aquaculture Development in Kenya towards Food Security, Poverty Alleviation and Wealth Creation. Journal of World Aquaculture Society. 2011. pp. 8-11

[22] Ogello EO. Genetic Differentiation of *Artemia franciscana* (Kellogg, 1906) in Kenyan Coastal Salt Works. Ghent: Ghent University; 2013

[23] Ogello EO, Opiyo MA. A review of the African catfish production in Kenya: Opportunities and challenges. African Journal of Food and Agricultural Nutrition Development. 2011. pp. 18-20

[24] Munguti JM, Nairuti R, Iteba JO, Obiero KO, Kyule D, Opiyo MA, et al. Nile tilapia (*Oreochromis niloticus* Linnaeus, 1758) culture in Kenya: Emerging production technologies and socio-economic impacts on local livelihoods. Aquaculture Fish and Fisheries. 2022;**2022**:1-12. DOI: 10.1002/aff2.58

[25] Kassahun A, Waidbacher H, Zollitsch W. Proximate composition of selected potential feedstuffs for small-scale aquaculture in Ethiopia. Journal of Livestock Research for Rural Development. 2012;**11**:12-28

[26] Munguti JM, Liti DM, Waidbacher H, Straif M, Zollitsch W. Proximate composition of selected

potential feedstuffs for *Nile tilapia* (*Oreochromis niloticus* Linnaeus) production in Kenya. Bodenkultur-Wien and Munchen. 2006;**57**:131

[27] Ogello EO, Mlingi FT, Nyonje BM, Charo-Karisa H, Munguti JM. Can integrated livestock-fish culture be a solution to East Africans food insecurity? A review. African Journal of Food Agriculture Nutrition and Development. 2013;**13**:8058-8076

[28] Shoko AP, Getabu A, Mwayuli G, Mgaya YD. Growth performance, yields and economic benefits of Nile Tilapia *Oreochromis niloticus* and Kales *Brassica oleracea* cultured under vegetable-fish culture integration. Tanzan Journal of Science. 2011;**37**:37-48. DOI: 10.4314%2Ftjs.v37i1

[29] Otieno MJ. Fishery Value Chain Analysis: Background Report Kenya. Rome, IT: FAO; 2011. pp. 2-10

[30] Newton GL, Booram CV, Barker RW, Hale OM. Dried Hermetia illucens larvae meal as a supplement for swine. Journal of Animal Science. 1977;**44**:395-399

[31] Newton L, Sheppard C, Watson W, Burtle G, Dove R. Using the black soldier fly, Hermetia illucens, as a value-added tool for the management of swine manure. Univ. of Georgia, College of Agric. & Environ. Sci., Dept. of Anim. & Dairy Sci. Annual Report. 2004

[32] St-HilaireS, SheppardC, TomberlinJK, Irving S, Newton L, McGuire MA, et al. Fly prepupae as a feedstuff for rainbow trout, *Oncorhynchus mykiss*. Journal of World Aquaculture Society. 2007;**38**:59-67

[33] Bondari K, Sheppard DC. Soldier fly larvae as feed in commercial fish production. Aquaculture. 1981;**24**:103-109

[34] Erickson MC, Islam M, Sheppard C, Liao J, Doyle MP. Reduction of Escherichia coli 0157:H7 and *Salmonella enterica* serovar Enteritidis in chicken manure by larvae of the black soldier fly. Journal of Food Protection. 2004;**67**:685-690

[35] Hecht T. Considerations on African aquaculture. World Aquaculture. 2000;**31**:12-19

[36] Naylor R, Hardy R, Bureau D, Chiu A, Elliott M, et al. Feeding aquaculture in an era of finite resources. PNAS. 2009;**106**:15103-15110

[37] Turchini G, Torstensen B, Ng W. Fish oil replacement in finfish nutrition. Review Aqua. 2009;**1**:10-57

[38] Tacon A, Hasan M, Metian M. Demand and supply of feed ingredients for farmed fish and curstaceans- trends and prospects. FAO Fisheries Technical Paper, 564. 2011

[39] Hertrampf J, Piedad-Pascual F. Handbook on Ingredients for Aquaculture Feeds. Netherlands: Kluwer Academic Publishers; 2000

[40] Gitonga NK, Mbugua H, Nyandati B. New approach to fish farming extension in Kenya. In: Samaki News: A Magazine of the Department of Fisheries of Kenya. Vol. 3. Nairobi, KE: Motif Creative Arts Ltd.; 2004. pp. 8-12

[41] Food and Agriculture Organization of the United Nations. The State of World Fisheries and Aquaculture 2012. Rome, Italy: FAO; 2012

[42] Krogdahl A, Penn M, Thorsen J, Refstie S, Bakke A. Important antinutrients in plant feedstuffs for aquaculture: An update on recent findings regarding responses in salmonids. Aquaculture Research. 2010;**41**:333-344

[43] Collins S, Overland M, Skrede A, Drew M. Effect of plant protein sources on growth rate in salmonids: Meta-analysis of dietary inclusion of soybean, pea and canola/rapeseed meals and protein concentrates. Aquaculture. 2013;**400**:85-100

[44] Olsen R, Hasan M. A limited supply of fishmeal: Impact on future increases in global aquaculture production. Trends in Food Science and Technology. 2012;**27**:120-128

[45] Waagbo R. Reducing production related diseases in farmed fish. In: Lie O, editor. Improving Farmed Fish Quality and Safety. UK: VS Woodhead Publishing; 2008. pp. 363-398

[46] Denny P, Kipkemboi J, Kaggwa R, Lamtane H. The potential of Fingerpond systems to increase food production from wetlands in Africa. International Journal of Ecology and Environmental Sciences. 2006;**32**:41-47

[47] Guerrero R. Earthworm culture for vermicompost and vermimeal production and for vermiceutical application in the Philippines (1978-2008): A review. Fisheries and aquatic sciences. 2009;**12**:26-38

[48] Satchell J. Earthworm Ecology: From Darwin to Vermiculture. Heidelberg; Germany: Springer nature; 2012. pp. 84-92

[49] Akidiva AA, Yasindi AW, Kitaka N. Proximate evaluation of redworms (Eisenia foetida) as an alternative protein ingredient to fish meal. International Journal of Fisheries and Aquatic Studies. 2020;**8**(4):201-205

[50] Craig S, Helfrich LA. Understanding Fish Nutrition. Petersburg, VA, US: Feeds and Feeding. Virginia Creative Extension; 2002. pp. 26-27

[51] Bolton JJ, DeClerck O, John DM. Seaweed diversity patterns in sub-Saharan Africa. In: Decker C, Griffiths CL, Prochazka K, Ras C, Whitfield A, editors. Proceedings of the Marine Biodiversity in Sub-Saharan Africa: The Known and the Unknown. Cape Town, ZA; 2003. pp. 229-241

[52] Bolton JJ, Oyieke HA, Gwada P. The seaweeds of Kenya: Checklist, history of seaweed study, coastal environment, and analysis of seaweed diversity and biogeography. South African Journal of Botany. 2007;**73**:76-88. DOI: 10.1016/j.sajb.2006.08.006

Section 4

Technology Usage in Aquaculture

Chapter 5

Bioflocs Technology in Freshwater Aquaculture: Variations in Carbon Sources and Carbon-to-Nitrogen Ratios

Solomon Melaku, Abebe Getahun, Seyoum Mengestou, Akewake Geremew and Amha Belay

Abstract

Aquaculture is one of the fastest food-producing sectors contributing half of the food fish destined for human consumption. Nevertheless, aquaculture production still needs to increase to fill the gap in supply and demand for fish, as the capture fisheries are stagnating over the years. Therefore, intensification of aquaculture production systems by increasing inputs such as feed has been devised as an alternative. On the other hand, intensive aquaculture has been associated with concerns related to environmental pollution in the past decades. Moreover, the increased cost of feed ingredients for aquaculture species has hampered the intensification of the sector. Therefore, alternative production systems such as biofloc technology were developed to mitigate the environmental impacts of intensive aquaculture and also to produce extra feed for cultured organisms. Due to their omnivorous feeding habit and tolerance to higher levels of suspended solids, freshwater finfishes have been the most cultured species in this system. The organic carbon sources used in the biofloc system are agricultural and industrial by-products which are cheap and readily available, making the technology economically feasible. C:N ratios of 10, 15, and 20 have been the most applied C:N ratios in the culture of freshwater aquaculture finfishes covered in this review.

Keywords: biofloc technology, C:N ratio, freshwater aquaculture, organic carbon sources

1. Introduction

Aquaculture is one of the fastest food-producing sectors in the world [1]. Without aquatic plants and non-food products, worldwide aquaculture production reached 80 million tons in 2016, with 54.1 million tons of finfish, 17.1 million tons of mollusks, 7.9 million tons of crustaceans, and 0.9 million tons of other aquatic animals [1]. On the other hand, world capture fisheries have stagnated over the last two decades, reaching 90.9 metric tons in 2016, of which 79.3 metric tons were from marine fisheries and 11.6 metric tons from inland fisheries [1]. According to the World Bank [2] report, the capture fisheries production is expected to remain stable at around 93 metric tons during the years 2010–2030.

Therefore, to meet the global demand for fish with relatively stable capture fisheries, world aquaculture production will need to produce an extra 36.25% and 75% of the current production by the years 2030 and 2050, respectively [1, 3]. Thus, intensification of aquaculture has emerged as a viable alternative to increase food fish production to fill this gap in supply. However, this intensification in the production systems demands increased inputs such as fish feed and medications, which in turn increases the environmental impacts of aquaculture and compromises its sustainability [4]. In order to preserve the environment and the natural resources and ensure the sustainability of the aquaculture sector, this expansion will need to take place in a sustainable way. To this end, sustainable production systems such as biofloc technology have been proposed and gained much interest from aquaculturists worldwide [5].

Biofloc technology is a relatively recent production system in aquaculture with a basic principle of manipulating C:N ratio of the feed and culture water to convert toxic nitrogenous wastes into the useful microbial protein (bioflocs) and help in improving water quality under zero-water exchange system [6–9]. To achieve this, a conglomeric aggregation of communities such as phytoplankton, bacteria, and living and dead particulate organic matter is stimulated by adding carbon source ingredients to the culture system [7]. Thus, the toxic nitrogenous wastes are taken by the microorganisms to produce single-cell protein and keep the water quality in an acceptable range for the species under culture. The consumption of biofloc by cultured animals has demonstrated several benefits such as improvement in growth rate [10] decrease of FCR, and associated costs in feed [11]. In addition to providing nutrition and water quality control, the bioflocs are also shown to contain bioactive compounds that enhance survival and defense mechanisms which act as a novel approach for health management in aquaculture by stimulating the innate immune system of cultured animals [6].

Although biofloc technology (BFT) was believed to be suitable for detritivorous species such as shrimp [12] and tilapia [13, 14] because of their filter-feeding behavior, recent research outputs are indicating that the technology can be applied with several more species [15]. Among them are the freshwater species carp [16] and catfish [17], in which promising results have been obtained at broodstock conditioning, nursery, and grow-out production stages.

The complexities of the carbon sources in biofloc technology range from agricultural by-products such as wheat bran, rice bran, sugar beet molasses, cassava meal, Sorghum meal, and tapioca flour to industrial products such as acetate, glycerol, cellulose, dextrose, and starch with their application dictated by availability, cost, and bacterial assimilation characteristics [18–20]. The type of carbon sources used also seems to affect the nutritional quality of the flocs [21] the microbial community structure [22], and the water quality parameters [23].

C:N ratio in the BFT plays a vital role in the incorporation of inorganic nitrogenous wastes into valuable bacterial cells that may act as a direct source of feed for cultured aquatic animals [7]. Usually, uptake of inorganic nitrogenous wastes takes place when the C:N ratio of the system is greater than 10 [24]. Thus, modification in the C:N ratio may result in a change from an autotrophic to a heterotrophic system [7]. The management of the C:N ratio in BFT is normally divided into the initial and formation phase, in which a C:N ratio of 12–20:1 is applied, and the maintenance phase, in which C:N ratio of 6:1 is applied, according to the total ammonia nitrogen (TAN) values. To this end, 10:1, 15:1, and 20:1 have been the most applied C:N ratios by either adjusting the feed formulation or adding of external organic carbon source [17, 25, 26].

Although BFT brings several obvious advantages discussed above, challenges related to the high demand for energy for aeration, dependence on sunlight [27], and accumulation of a large amount of suspended solids limits its commercial scale application with more aquaculture species of economic importance. Considering the limitations of intensive-fed aquaculture development in Ethiopia [28], BFT can be an alternative production system with the availability of organic carbon sources and suitable fish species like tilapia, carp, and catfish. However, knowledge gap and limited power availability may be a challenge in applying the technology in the country unless alternatives are devised by the concerned stakeholders. Therefore, the objective of this review is to document the current practices of BFT in tilapia, carp, and catfish aquaculture and to reveal the variations in carbon sources and C:N ratios.

2. Overview of bioflocs technology in aquaculture

Biofloc Technology (BFT) is an environmentally friendly aquaculture system that is considered as an efficient alternative system in which nutrients and water are continuously recycled and reused. The sustainable approach of such a system is based on the growth of microorganisms in the culture medium, benefited by the minimum or zero-water exchange [8]. The main roles of microorganisms (biofloc) are maintenance of water quality by the uptake of nitrogen compounds generating in situ microbial protein [29] and increasing culture feasibility by reducing feed conversion ratio and a decrease of feed costs [9, 30]. BFT has received a variety of applications such as single-cell protein production systems, Zero exchange autotrophic heterotrophic systems (ZEAH) [11], activated-sludge or suspended bacterial-based system [31], suspended-growth systems or microbial flocs systems [32, 33]. Moreover, BFT has been the emphasis of intensive research in the aquaculture nutrition area as a protein source in compounded diets. Such source of feed ingredient is produced in the form of "biofloc meal," mainly in bioreactors [34]. In addition, the fast spread and the large number of BFT farms worldwide induced significant research efforts on processes involved in BFT production systems.

Cultured aquatic animals in the BFT system are species that are detritivorous such as shrimp and freshwater prawns [12, 21]; Emerenciano et al. [35] and omnivorous fish such as tilapia [13] because of their filter feeding behavior and tolerance to relatively high suspended solids. Recently, Catfish [36] and carp species [37] have also been cultured in the BFT system with varying degrees of success (**Table 1**).

3. Biofloc technology in freshwater aquaculture

As discussed above, in marine aquaculture, crustaceans, mainly shrimp, have been almost the only cultured organisms under BFT system [9], while freshwater finfishes and the giant freshwater Prawn (*Macrobrachium rosenbergii*) comprise the majority of the species reared under this system (**Table 1**). The freshwater finfish species cultured under BFT system (Tilapia, carp, and catfish) are among the world's top leading aquaculture species, with a share of more than half of the total landing from aquaculture in 2016 [1]. Therefore, in what follows, more emphasis has been given to those three freshwater species in detail.

Category	Species	References
Marine	Hybrid bass	Milstein et al. [38]
	Penaeus monodon	Panjaitan [39]
	Farfantepenaeus paulensis	Emerenciano et al. [35]
	Litopenaeus vanamei	Krummenauer et al. [40]
	Farfantepenaeus brasiensis	Souza et al. [41]
	Farfantepanaeus duorarum	Emerenciano et al. [12]
	Artemia franciscana	Hoa et al. [42]
Freshwater	Mozambique tilapia	Crab et al. [29]
	Guppies (*Poecilia reticulata*)	Sreedevi and Ramasubramanian [43]
	Macrobrachim rosenbergii	Crab et al. [21]
	Nile tilapia	Choo et al. [13]
	Red tilapia	Widanarni et al. [23]
	Channel catfish	Schrader et al. [44]
	African catfish	Romano et al. [36]
	Striped catfish	Duy and Ut [45]
	Rohu (*Labeo rohita*)	Kamilya et al. [46]
	Common carp	Bakhshi et al. [37]
	Piracanjuba (*Brycon orbignyanus*)	Sgnaulin et al. [47]
	GIFT tilapia	Menaga et al. [48]

Table 1.
Summary of the list of aquaculture species cultured under BFT system.

3.1 Bioflocs technology in tilapia aquaculture

Tilapia was the first suitable species for the BFT system both at the commercial scale and laboratory level as early as 1989 when Avnimelech and his colleagues investigated the efficiency of recirculated ponds in single-cell protein production and consumption with the blue tilapia (*Oreochromis aureus*). The tried treatment in the first experiment was feeding with protein-deficient feed complemented by the daily addition of cellulose and ammonium sulfate as substrates for the production of single-cell protein. In this experiment, the growth of fish receiving most of their protein as single-cell protein was lower than those fed with the commercial protein-rich feeds and higher than that of fish grown on the protein-deficient feeds alone. The crude protein and lipid contents of fish grown on the biofloc diet were similar to those of fish grown on the commercial diet. In the second experiment, sorghum meal and ammonium sulfate were used as substrates. The results showed that the growth of fish fed with single-cell protein was similar to that of fish fed conventional protein-rich feed. Microbial integration of ammonium into the carbon-rich substrate was shown to be an efficient means of dipping the level of inorganic nitrogen in the water. Finally, Avnimelech et al. [49] concluded that tilapia could eat and utilize bacterial single-cell protein, and it can be possible to replace, at least partially, expensive protein sources with cheap carbon sources.

3.1.1 BFT in tilapia reproduction

The effect of BFT on reproductive performance of aquacultured species is one of the areas of research under investigation currently, and tilapia has been a focal point of these investigations. To this end, a biofloc-based reproductive performance study of Nile tilapia broodstock was conducted by Ekasari et al. [50]. The results of the study showed higher average body weight gain in the BFT treatment, which suggests that, although more energy was allocated for reproduction, the fish grew better in the BFT environment, whereas no significant difference in fish hepatosomatic index (HSI) level was found among treatments. Furthermore, the gonadosomatic index of female brood fish in BFT seemed to increase and reached its peak at a level of 4.01% and remained relatively constant afterward at around 3%. Egg diameter in BFT treatment was found to be insignificantly different over the experimental period, while fish fecundity was constantly higher in the BFT treatments except on day 70. This is also reflected in the total fry production during the experimental period, which was 65% higher than that of the conventional clear water system. Ekasari et al. [50] concluded that, overall, a positive effect of BFT application on Nile tilapia reproductive performance was observed in their study.

A more recent study by Gallardo-Collı et al. [51] to evaluate the reproductive performance, organ somatic indices, and body composition of the Nile tilapia cultivated at high density reusing the water from systems with biofloc technology during a grow-out period of 14 weeks showed insignificant differences in the gonadosomatic and hepatosomatic conditions either between tilapia sexes or between the different treatments groups. The results indicated that the intensive culture of *Oreochromis niloticus* in BFT system can be conducted using reused water from biofloc systems, with no adverse effects on their reproductive capacity and gonadal development.

3.1.2 BFT in the nursery rearing of tilapia

Several research activities conducted to evaluate the BFT technology in tilapia aquaculture focus on the nursery stage of the species. This is partly attributed to the fact that fingerlings of the species have the potential to grow fast and can be easily accessed compared to brood stocks and adults. To this end, in the following paragraphs, representatives of research activities on fingerlings of tilapia are presented based on chronology.

De Araújo et al. [52] evaluated the performance of Nile tilapia fingerlings cultured in biofloc technology using different densities of *Chlorella vulgaris*. In this experiment, the water quality parameters showed insignificant differences between treatments, especially TAN and NO_2-N, which were in the range acceptable for the culture of the species. The zoo technical performance parameters were not affected by the different inoculation densities of the microalgae, attaining a final mean weight of approximately 21 g for all treatments and survival rates greater than 80%. De Araújo et al. [52] concluded that the weekly inoculation densities of the microalgae *C. vulgaris* had no influence on the growth of tilapia fingerlings cultured in a biofloc system.

In the face of all problems regarding traditional tilapia food sources and production systems, the search for sustainable alternatives has been increasing. Within this context, de Sousa et al. [53] conducted research with the aim of evaluating different inclusion levels of pizzeria by-product meal (0, 20, 40, 60, 80, and 100%) in diets for Nile tilapia (*O. niloticus*) fingerlings reared under biofloc systems. Water quality parameters and the planktonic community profile were monitored throughout the feeding trial (38 days). The results indicated that the zoo technical performance of fish fed the 20% pizzeria by-product feed was statistically nonsignificant to those fed the control feed. Feed conversion ratio was also similar between these treatments and the 40% inclusion group. de Sousa et al. [53] concluded that it is possible to successfully include up to 20% of pizzeria by-product meal in diets for Nile tilapia reared in biofloc systems, and 40% inclusion of pizzeria by-product exhibited a strategic benefit to the farms that commercialize fingerlings.

Even though studies are scarce, biofloc technology can be successfully used in tilapia fingerling commercial production with some benefits. To this end, García-Ríos et al. [51] determined the effect of BFT system on the economic feasibility parameters such as productive performance and demand of feed and water in tilapia fingerlings production using carbon sources corn flour, wheat flour, sugar, and control without carbon source addition. The water quality, productive parameters, cost of consumed food, and volume of used water were determined. At the end of the growing period, the lowest weight corresponded to the systems with wheat flour as the carbon source and the highest to systems with sugar as the carbon source and control. The FCR in control was significantly higher than in the biofloc treatments. The control exhibited the lowest protein efficiency, while the maximum was recorded in systems with sugar as a carbon source. In addition, proximate tissue composition analysis showed a crude protein content of 0.0639–0.07 g/0.1 g dry weight bases, with significant differences among treatments. The survival in the stress test was similar among treatments. To produce a set of 10,000 fingerlings, the used water in BFT was 1611–2060 gal and 6314 gal in the conventional system. The mean supplied feed in BFT was 6 kg/batch, while in the control was 10.7 kg/batch. The cost of feed and carbon source was estimated on average as 7 US$/batch in BFT and of 9 US$/batch in the control. The fingerlings cultured in corn flour and sugar treatments showed a similar zoo technical performance to the control. However, the savings in feed and culture water consumption were significant.

3.1.3 BFT in grow-out culture of tilapia

The research activities range in scope from small-scale laboratory experiments to large-scale pond cultures to justify the zoo's technical and economic feasibility of the system. Azim and Little [54] evaluated BFT in the light-limited tank culture of Nile tilapia (*O. niloticus*)in a set of two biofloc treatments and one control in indoor tanks of 250 l capacity. Two BFT treatment groups were designated with 35%, and 24% crude protein diets, and a clean water control treatment without biofloc fed 35% crude protein diet. The results indicated that, fish mortality was null and net fish production was 45 times higher in the BFT treatments than in the control confirming the utilization of biofloc by fish as food. There was no difference in fish growth performance between the 35% and 24% crude protein-fed groups under the BFT system. In addition, well-being indicators in terms of fin condition, gill histology, body proximate composition, and blood hematocrit and plasma cortisol levels were compared, and no significant differences between BFT and control treatments were observed, indicating no increased fish stress due to the presence of biofloc. Despite this fact, Azim and Little [54] concluded that, in terms of commercial viability, overall fish growth and production were poor and recommended a modified system design that would allow improved feed and biofloc utilization to be proposed.

Lima et al. [55] evaluated the water quality and the growth performance of Nile tilapia cultured in bioflocs system with different stocking densities. A 128 days experiment was conducted with an initial weight of 123.0 ± 0.6 g stocked in twelve 800 L circular tanks in a completely randomized design with three densities of 15, 30, and 45 fish/m^3

and four replicates. The result showed that there was a significant effect of the different densities on the level of dissolved oxygen, with the lowest concentration of 3.97 mg/L) for the highest tested density of 45 fish/m^3. The total ammonia showed a statistical difference between the density of 15 fish/m^3 and the others. The nitrite also showed a significant difference between the density of 15 and 45 fish/m^3, but both at a directly proportional relationship with the increasing of stocking density, showing higher average concentrations of 2.56 and 3.26 mg/L (NH_3 + NH_4 and NO_2, respectively), in 45 density fish/m^3. The growth performance in the 45 fish/m^3 density showed the best results, with a yield of 16.6 kg/m^3, with a significant difference between treatments. Survival was higher than 90% for the whole three tested densities. Lima et al. [55] concluded that, bioflocs technology could be employed in intensive culture of Nile tilapia in the grow-out phase, using stocking densities up to 45 fish/m^3.

Madyod et al. [56] investigated the efficacy of dried bioflocs supplemented with immune stimulants as β-glucan and nucleotide on the mortality rate and relative percent survival (RPS) of tilapia infected with *Flavobacterium columnare*, VETSV01. The results of the study demonstrated that feeding tilapia with commercial feed in combination with dried biofloc with or without supplementation of 2 immunostimulants could lead to 100% survival rate and 100% relative percent survival rate, and it was statistically significant compared to the control group. Madyod et al. [56] conclude that biofloc product supplemented with betaglucan or nucleotide could effectively stimulate immunity against *F. columnare*, and such highly effective performance is viewed as a promising potential product to be further developed and practically employed for the aquaculture industry in the future.

Martins et al. [57] evaluated the effects of heterotrophic and mature biofloc systems on yield, water quality, slurry production, and water bacterial community composition, recovery of nutrients, and fish health in *Litopenaeus vannamei* and *O. niloticus* integrated culture through a 53 days experiment. The results showed that shrimp growth performance was unaltered, but fish cultured in the heterotrophic treatment showed better values for all growth performance variables assessed. TAN and NO_2-N were lower in the mature biofloc system, while the total slurry generated in the heterotrophic system was higher than in the mature biofloc system, resulting in greater sludge generated per animal biomass. The bacterial community range was reduced in the heterotrophic treatment, and the relative abundance of *Vibrionaceae* was reduced. The assimilation of nitrogen and phosphorus was higher in the heterotrophic treatment, and fish health was not affected by the biofloc system. Martins et al. [57] concluded that the biofloc system favored fish growth in the integrated culture system, maintaining water quality appropriate for growing organisms and healthy fish.

3.2 Bioflocs technology in catfish aquaculture

The consumption of bioflocs, and in turn, the ability to promote animal growth, is largely based on the fish's ability to collect and consume these particles. Due to this fact, suspension-feeding fish have been thought to be better adapted to consume smaller bioflocs than carnivorous species, such as catfish [36]. Nevertheless, in a series of experiments, it has been shown that catfish juveniles greatly benefited from biofloc-based systems, which may help produce better quality and more disease-resistant stock. Benefits of biofloc technology (BFT) to this carnivorous species largely depend on the carbon source [18] and the ratio to nitrogen [25]. Therefore, in the following sections, the available research on the different production stages of catfish aquaculture are presented.

3.2.1 BFT in catfish reproduction

The development of catfish aquaculture is constrained by the limited supply of good quality and quantity fingerlings [58]. Catfish fingerlings rearing, in particular, has been constrained by the seasonal spawning behavior and low reproductive success of the brood stock, and the low survival rate of larvae [59]. To this end, few studies have been conducted to evaluate the effects of BFT in the reproduction performance of the species.

Nadio [60] evaluated the effects of biofloc technology on the reproductive performance of *Clarias gariepinus* females, especially during their re-maturation period. The BFT treatments were differentiated by temperature: biofloc at 25°C (BFT + 25), biofloc at 28°C (BFT + 28), and biofloc at 31°C (BFT + 31). The results indicated that females reared in the biofloc system at 31°C achieved better reproductive performance in terms of higher eggs production per spawning (127×10^3) per kg female, shorter re-maturation period (80% of females reached maturation within 3 weeks), higher gonadal-somatic index (GSI $\geq$ 19%) as compared with the control with lower eggs production per spawning (57.3×10^3) per kg female, longer re-maturation period (20% of females reached maturity within 6 weeks) and lowest gonadal-somatic index (GSI $\leq$ 10%) respectively. On the other hand, no significant difference among the BFT treatments was observed. Nadio [60] concluded that the better reproductive performance shown by females reared in BFT system justified the application of this technology in *C. gariepinus* broodstock management.

Ekasari et al. [61] evaluated the effects of biofloc technology application on African catfish *(C. gariepinus)* broodstock reproductive performance and the quality of eggs and larvae. Biofloc and conventional clear water systems were compared for the reproductive performance of c, while the larvae produced by the brood stocks in both systems were subsequently assessed by larval starvation tolerance and growth tests. The results showed that the gonadosomatic index and fecundity of female brood stocks in both treatments were generally comparable, except on day 122 when the relative fecundity of the control brood stock was 26% lower than that of the biofloc brood stock. In addition, the embryonic development rate of eggs spawned by biofloc brood stocks was higher than the control brood stock. The survival in starvation test and growth tests were remarkably improved in the larvae produced by biofloc brood stocks. Ekasari et al. [61] concluded that rearing African catfish broodstock in biofloc systems significantly affected the embryonic development rate and the larval quality. Improvements in survival and growth were observed in the larvae reared in biofloc systems.

3.2.2 BFT in the nursery rearing of catfish

The rearing in biofloc system may be beneficial for rearing carnivorous fish larvae, especially in the early stages of culture when larvae possess feeding habits that include consumption of debris [62]. In addition, due to the high rate of cannibalistic nature, larval culture of such species might give better survival when implemented in turbid environments with low light levels [63], which could be another benefit of the biofloc system. However, tolerance of species to different concentrations of total suspended solids still needs to be investigated. TSS is the variable used to quantify the level of biofloc in the cultivation, and although Avnimelech [64] recommended values between 200 and 400 mg/L for tilapia culture, the author reported that the optimal concentrations for growing fish are not well known yet.

Poli et al. [65] conducted a 21-day experiment to evaluate the application of biofloc technology in South American catfish larvae (*Rhamdia quelen*) grown at different concentrations of biofloc. *R. quelen* larvae were grown in biofloc systems developed from the intensive culture of *O. niloticus*. Three biofloc concentrations, expressed as TSS were tested: up to 200 mg/L, between 400 and 600 mg/L, and between 800 and 1000 mg/L. In the control, the larvae were cultured in clear water from a recirculation system. The results showed that, even though the increase in TSS concentrations was not associated with the best growth of *R. quelen*, the performance of the larvae was better in the TSS level of 200 mg/L compared to 400–600 and 800–1000 mg/L. Poli et al. [65] concluded that *R. quelen* larvae could be grown in a biofloc system with TSS concentrations up to 1000 mg/L, but the best growth was registered in tanks with a lower percentage of total suspended solids which is <200 mg/L.

Hapsari [66] evaluated the effect of molasses addition on African catfish (*C. gariepinus*) fingerlings growth and feed conversion rate when the biofloc was fermented for 24 h using molasses, fish meal, and grains. The results showed that molasses treatment on the application of bioflocs showed the highest growth and the lowest feed conversion rate. FCR of African catfish in fermented biofloc was lower by almost half compared to the control and unfermented biofloc treatments. Hapsari [66] concluded that biofloc could be used as the alternative feed and that molasses treatment in fermenting biofloc can increase the nutritional values and hence increase the growth of African catfish fingerlings.

Putra et al. [67] evaluated the growth performance and feed utilization of African catfish (*C. gariepinus)* fingerlings fed a commercial diet and reared in the biofloc system enriched with probiotics where the frequency of probiotic application into the cultured system was the objective of the experiment. The results of the experiment showed that growth performance, survival, and feed utilization of African catfish were higher in the treatment with the addition of probiotics at 5-day intervals over a period of 60 days culture.

Soedibya et al. [68] determined the effect of high stocking densities on the growth performance of African catfish fingerlings in biofloc system with stocking densities of 1000 fingerlings/m^3, 1500 fingerlings/m^3), 2000 fingerings/m^3), and 2500 fingerlings/m^3). The results showed a significantly different effect against the value of hepatosomatic index, absolute growth, and daily growth rate, while specific growth rate showed insignificant difference. The treatment with the stocking density of 1500 fingerlings/m3 showed the best results than the other densities in absolute growth rate and daily growth rate. These findings demonstrate the role of biofloc technology in catfish aquaculture.

3.2.3 BFT in grow-out culture of catfish

Schrader et al. [44] determined the development and composition of phytoplankton communities and related off-flavor problems in outdoor biofloc production systems of channel catfish. In this study, water and fish flesh were analyzed for quantities of geosmin and 2-methylisoborneol as the common off-flavor compounds. The development and composition of phytoplankton in each culture tank was also observed. In addition, water and biofloc samples were assessed for the microbial sources of geosmin and 2-methylisoborneol within the culture vessels. The results of the study indicated that phytoplankton biomass, as determined by concentrations of chlorophyll a in the water, gradually increased in all culture vessels over time. In addition, a positive correlation between cumulative feed addition and chlorophyll a concentration was reported. Although geosmin and 2-methylisoborneol were present in the culture water of each tank during most of the study, levels were typically low, and only one tank yielded catfish with geosmin and 2-methylisoborneol in their muscle at levels high enough to be designated as off-flavor. A positive correlation between feed addition and 2-methylisoborneol concentrations in the water of culture tanks indicates a greater potential for 2-methylisoborneol -related off-flavor problems at high feed application rates.

Channel catfish have been cultured successfully in an outdoor BFT system. Outdoor BFT culture systems in the tropics are conducted yearly, whereas the channel catfish studies were conducted only during the growing season, and biofloc production systems were harvested and kept vacant for the winter. If an outdoor BFT culture is to be implemented by farmers in temperate areas, data gaps associated with system and fish performance over the winter must be addressed. To this end, Green [69] conducted a study to evaluate the performance of a temperate-zone channel catfish biofloc technology production system during winter. Culture waters from a recently completed biofloc production experiment that contained low and high total suspended solids were retained for the study. Three 16 m^3 tanks per water type each were stocked with market-sized channel catfish from the same experiment for a 38 weeks period. Green [69] reported that mean chlorophyll *a* concentrations were similar in both treatments during the first 55 days, after which treatments deviated and chlorophyll *a* concentration increased linearly in the low total suspended solids treatment. Ammonia from ammonium chloride spikes) added on three occasions during the experiment was transformed completely by algal uptake and nitrification. Ammonia bioconversion rate was linearly related to mean water temperature in the high total suspended solids and low solids treatments. Catfish survival through the winter was high in biofloc tanks and did not differ significantly between treatments. Net fish yield did not differ significantly between treatments. Green [69] concluded that having an active biofloc in the spring obviates the start-up time required to establish a new, fully functional biofloc and the associated TAN and nitrite spikes in winter.

More recently, Hastuti and Subandiyono [70] observed the hematological parameters of catfish (*C. gariepinus*) cultivated with a density of 1000 individuals/ m^3 using biofloc technology. With an explorative method, samples were taken from *C. gariepinus* cultivated with applications of biofloc technology. The measured variables were: total bilirubin, direct bilirubin, indirect bilirubin, and blood glucose. Calculated blood cells are red blood cells, white blood cells, hemoglobin, hematocrit, and platelets. The results showed total bilirubin and indirect bilirubin were in normal ranges, while direct bilirubin values increased by 0.3 mg/dL at week 8. According to the results, *C. gariepinus* shows a stress response with an indicator of high blood glucose from 114 to 188 mg/dL. Water quality was in optimal conditions which are in accordance with the *C. gariepinus* requirements, with a survival rate value of 96%.

3.3 Bioflocs technology in carp aquaculture

Another freshwater group of fish gaining recent attention to be cultured in the BFT system is the family Cyprinidae in which few attempts have been made to evaluate the performance of the system in the different species of the family [16, 46, 71]. This group of fishes exhibits suspension-feeding behavior and better tolerance to higher concentrations of suspended solids which are the most important attributes for the successful cultivation of a species in the BFT system [36]. Applications of BFT on the reproductive performance of carp have never been reported so far. Therefore, in the following sections, available research outputs are presented on the nursery and grow-out production cycles of different carp species.

3.3.1 BFT in the nursery rearing of Carp

The first study on BFT application on carp was undertaken by Nadjigerami et al. [16] in a 30-days experiment to investigate the effects of partial replacement of daily feeding intake with biofloc on the growth performances, digestive enzymes activity, and liver histology of the common carp *(Cyprinus carpio)* fingerlings. Two hundred and eight healthy fingerlings were randomly distributed in 12 tanks (30 L) at a density of 25.4 kg/m^3 and fed experimental treatments (100% daily feeding rate as a control, biofloc +75% daily feeding rate, biofloc +50% daily feeding rate, biofloc +25% daily feeding rate). The results indicated that the highest weight gain was observed in the fish-fed biofloc and 75% feeding rate and control, which varied significantly from those fed biofloc and 25%. The treatment with biofloc and 7% feeding rate enhanced total protease and pepsin activity compared with biofloc and 25% feeding rate and biofloc and 50% feeding rate. Insignificant difference was observed between the treatments of lipase, amylase, and alkaline phosphatase activity. In the liver, histological variations were found in the treatments, and feeding the fish with biofloc at 75% rate significantly improved hepatocellular quantification and qualification than the other treatments. Nadjigerami et al. [16] concluded that the biofloc improved growth performances, digestive enzyme activity, and liver condition of the common carp fingerlings when 25% of the daily feeding rate was replaced with one carbohydrate such as molasses in zero-water exchange system.

Sarker [72] evaluated the comparative efficacy of biofloc and feed-based common carp *(C. carpio,* L.) production systems with special reference to environmental health. The findings of the study indicated that biofloc alone was not sufficient for the growth of the test fish under a supplementary feeding regime. However, the mortality rate of the test fish was highest in biofloc alone treatment. It was clear that biofloc improved the performance of the supplementary feed both in terms of feed conversion rate and feed conversion efficiency. In spite of less absolute weight gain with feeding at 3% body weight/day because of the most promising feed conversion rate and less nutrient loading, the system demonstrated to be economically and ecologically more sustainable in the presence of bioflocs. Biofloc not only supported the test fish nutritionally but supported the planktonic productivity as well. Moreover, it also favored phosphate mineralization in the soil phase. Himaja [71] evaluated the growth performance of *Catla catla* using prepared biofloc meals incorporated into the diet with 20, 30, and 40 percent levels. The biofloc was developed in four experimental indoor cement tanks at the carbon-to-nitrogen ratio of 15:1 in the indoor tanks. Experimental diets were prepared using indoor and outdoor dry biofloc meals by replacing fish meals at different levels, while the control diet was prepared without biofloc. The results of the study revealed that *C. catla* fed with a control diet exhibited higher growth. Similarly, the growth performance of *C. catla* in 40% was more or less the same. Whereas the outdoor biofloc meal incorporated diets had better FCR than other treatments next to control and 40% feed replacement. Himaja [71] concluded that 20% indoor biofloc meal incorporated diet performed similarly to the control diet and had higher performance than that of the commercial carp diet. Hence fish meal could be replaced in the carp diet successfully by 20% of either indoor or outdoor biofloc meal.

3.3.2 BFT in the grow-out culture of carp

Unlike tilapia and catfish culture, applications of BFT in the grow-out of the different carp species are scarce, although the group constitutes potential species for the technology. Nevertheless, few attempts have been made and are presented herewith.

Sasmal et al. [73] conducted a trial of six months period to investigate the growth and production of common carp in fresh water Biofloc System in India. Three rectangular cemented tanks (5000 liter capacity) were used for this purpose. Probiotic was used for developing beneficial bacterial colonies and controlling ammonia in the confined water system. The results indicated that flocs volume ranged between 12 and 47 ml/1000 liter water sample while the average yield was recorded at 218 kg/tank after a period of 6 months from stocking, and FCR was found to be 0.9. The other important parameters recorded were an average pH value 7.7, dissolved oxygen 5.9 ppm, TDS 454 ppm, and C:N ratio 12:1. Sasmal et al. [73] concluded that the biofloc system in freshwater aquaculture improves growth performances of the common carp in almost zero-water exchange system.

4. Variations in carbon source and C:N ratios in freshwater biofloc aquaculture systems

The carbon sources applied in BFT can be classified broadly in two, that is, by-products derived from agricultural activities such as wheat bran, molasses, tapioca flour, sorghum meal, etc., and industrial products such as glycerol, acetate, glucose, and starch (**Table 2**). The addition of these carbon sources in the culture system or in the feed is aimed at maintaining a high C:N ratio, preferably above 10:1 to control nitrogenous compounds peaks. Also, a mix of plant meals can be pelletized and applied into ponds [81], or low protein diets containing high C:N ratio can also be used [15, 64]. The carbon source serves as a substrate for operating BFT systems and the production of microbial protein cells [7].

There are many considerations for the selection of carbon sources such as costs, local availability, biodegradability, and efficiency of bacteria assimilation. The organic carbon source of choice to a large degree determines the composition of the flocs produced. As an example, it was reported by Ekasari et al. [82] that, Bioflocs with glycerol as a carbon source had higher total n-6 PUFAs than that of glucose, while there was no effect of carbon source on crude protein, lipid, and total n-3 PUFAs contents of the bioflocs.

Later on, Dauda et al. [18] compared different carbon sources, that is, sucrose, glycerol, and rice bran, in a carbon-to-nitrogen ratio of 15:1 in a biofloc-based African catfish culture system. The results of the experiment indicated that glycerol significantly increased total biofloc production, and both the sucrose and glycerol treatments generally had lower nitrogenous waste levels compared to the control. Liver histopathology of fish in the rice bran biofloc treatment showed substantial vacuolation and less glycogen, while the highest was in fish from the glycerol treatment. Fish growth was not affected among the treatments, but mortality was lowest in the glycerol treatment. Dauda et al. [18] concluded that rice bran appears unsuitable for *C. gariepinus*, likely due to being a slower-releasing carbon source. Instead, they recommended glycerol based on significantly higher biofloc production and subsequently improved water quality and survival of *C. gariepinus* during their experiment.

Another study by Deng et al. [19] indicated that BFT systems with plant cellulose and plant cellulose + tapioca starch treatment groups had a higher total bacterial diversity and greater microbial richness than those with no plant cellulose treatment groups (tapioca starch alone and the conventional clear water systems).

Species	Carbon sources	C/N ratios	References
Tilapia	Cellulose and sorghum meal	15	Avnimelech et al. [49]
	Wheat flour	8.4, 11.2	Azim and little [54]
	Molasses	15	Caldini et al. [74]; Ekasari et al. [50]
	Poly-β-hydroxybutyric acid	—	Zhang et al. [75]
	Molasses	15, 30	Cavalcante et al. [76]
	Sugar, molasses, and cassava starch	10, 20	Silva et al. [77]
	Molasses	6	Alvarenga et al. [78]
	Sugar, liquid molasses, and powder molasses	15	Lima et al. [55]
	Sugar, corn flour, and wheat flour	12	García-Ríos et al. [14]
	Distillery Spent wash	10	Menaga et al. [48]
Catfish	Molasses	10, 15, 20, 25, 30	Bakar et al. [25]
	Molasses	10	Ekasari et al. [61]
	Sugar	20	Hastuti and Subandiyono [70]
	Molasses + *Bacillus* spp.	—	Putra et al. [67]
	Sucrose, glycerol, rice bran	15	Dauda et al. [18]
	Glycerol	10, 15, 20	Dauda et al. [17]
	Tapioca flour	10	Fauji et al. [79]
	Rice bran + *Bacillus* spp.	15	Romano et al. [36]
Carp	Beet molasses (24% carbon)	20	Najdegerami et al. [16]
	Boiled rice water mixed with molasses	—	Sarker [72]
	Molasses	15	Kamilya et al. [46]
	Molasses, sugar, and cornstarch	20	Bakhshi et al. [37]
	Coffee, moringa, macroalgae, and yucca	—	Castro et al. [80]

Table 2.
Summary of carbon sources and carbon to nitrogen ratios in freshwater aquaculture.

El-Husseiny et al. [20] evaluated the effect of different carbon sources on biofloc conditions and tilapia performance. Biofloc treatments with five different organic carbon simple sources (glucose and molasses) and complex sources (starch, wheat bran, and cellulose) were conducted in the presence of control (clear water). The results of the experiment showed that no significant differences were noticed among different carbon sources concerning tilapia growth performance. Complex carbon sources represented in wheat bran and cellulose showed less fluctuation in the values of ammonium and nitrite during the experimental period than the other carbon sources. The precipitated biofloc from both wheat bran and cellulose showed the highest fat content. In terms of heterotrophic bacteria production, plankton count, and biofloc nutritional content, cellulose appears to be the better choice. El-Husseiny et al. [20] concluded that, from nutritional and economic points of view, using agricultural by-products with high cellulose content as a carbon source in biofloc system is more reasonable.

The natural condition of the aquaculture system, which is rich in inorganic nitrogen, could not sustain BFT due to limitation of carbon. Thus, additional carbon is required to obtain a suitable C:N ratio for the effective formation of bioflocs complex. To this end, Bakar et al. [25] conducted an experiment on the determination of optimum carbon-to-nitrogen ratio by varying the amount of carbon introduced into the system using five different C:N ratios in remediating the aquaculture system culturing *C. gariepinus* to an acceptable water quality levels. Bioflocs density and water quality parameters were monitored throughout the treatment period. The results of the experiment showed that the highest elimination of ammonia was achieved with the formation of 92 mL/L of bioflocs concentration at an optimum carbon-to-nitrogen ratio of 15. The results showed that the application of BFT can possibly provide a sustainable and low-maintenance treatment of aquaculture systems.

Pérez-Fuentes et al. [26] also evaluated the effects of different C:N ratios (10, 12.5, 15, 17.5 and 20) on the growth performance of juvenile tilapia *(O. niloticus)* rose under biofloc cultivation using molasses as a carbon source. The results indicated that survival in all treatments with biofloc was similar and significantly higher (94.60 ± 2.03%) than in the control treatment (84.96 ± 1.53%). The 10 and 15 carbon-to-nitrogen ratio treatments had similar weight gains but not the 12.5 and 17.5 carbon-to-nitrogen treatments. Total production in the 10 ratio treatment was the highest, with slightly declining production. Water quality remained similar in all biofloc treatments, but lower concentrations of nitrogenous compounds occurred in the 10 carbon-to-nitrogen ratio treatments. Pérez-Fuentes et al. [26] concluded that a 10:1 carbon-to-nitrogen ratio provides good survival and growth of tilapia with no water exchange.

A study by Dauda et al. [17] on the effects of increasing glycerol loading rates to create carbon-to-nitrogen ratios of 0, 10, 15, and 20 on the biofloc formation, biochemical composition, and water quality, as well as the growth performance, feeding efficiency, enzyme activities, and liver glycogen levels of African catfish *(C. gariepinus)*. After 6 weeks, all fish were measured for growth; ten fishes per replicate were used for additional analysis, while ten fishes per replicate were later challenged with the bacterial pathogen, *Aeromonas hydrophila*. The results indicated that biofloc volume was significantly higher at carbon-to-nitrogen ratio of 20, but flocs biomass was significantly higher at carbon-to-nitrogen ratio 15. Dissolved oxygen was significantly lower at carbon-to-nitrogen of 20 while TAN was significantly higher in the control than the biofloc treatments. Survival, growth, and feed utilization efficiency were similar among treatments. Fish muscle cholesterol, lipid peroxidation, blood triglyceride, and blood cholesterol levels were all significantly lower in the biofloc treatments, but liver glycogen level was significantly higher in the carbon-to-nitrogen ratio of 15 treatment. Chymotrypsin activities were significantly higher in the biofloc systems while trypsin was not different among the treatments. After challenging the catfish to *A. hydrophila*, survival was significantly higher in the C:N ratio of 15 and 20 groups, which was accompanied with less histopathological liver damage compared to those in the control or C:N ratio 10 treatments. Overall, Dauda et al. [17] concluded that in a glycerol-based biofloc system, a C:N ratio of 15 led to the best balance of better water quality, nutritive value of *C. gariepinus* as well as their resistance to *A. hydrophila*.

5. Prospects and challenges of biofloc technology for aquaculture in Ethiopia

As discussed in the sections above, the BFT system proved to be a viable alternative to RAS and other conventional aquaculture systems for the major freshwater species in terms of zoo technical performances [7]. This was also partly true for the socioeconomic performances at commercial production levels, especially for tilapia aquaculture. As an illustration, Avnimelech [83] estimated that feed rations in biofloc tilapia systems could be lowered by at least 20% from conventional system levels, which can significantly reduce the cost of production. In another success story in Malawi at Chambo fisheries, from an economic perspective, results indicated a 50% feed cost reduction when compared to feeding fish on conventional 32% crude protein level feeds raised in a recirculation aquaculture system [84]. The advantages of biofloc technology include a significant reduction in the final farm-gate production cost of raising tilapias to about $1.30/kg in Malawi in 2016. A broad economic study based on data gathered at Chambo fisheries showed biofloc farms to conceivably produce tilapia at about 60% lower cost than large-scale cage culture, 34% less than RAS, and 8.5% less than green water pond farming, supposing all farms are located in or near Lake Malawi [84].

Despite this fact, using the BFT displayed some problems to cultured aquatic animals practically. Organic carbon must be supplemented to the culture water to sustain a carbon-to-nitrogen ratio of over 10. In addition, employing a system for mixing and aerating the water, which increases energy costs, is required to sustain an active BFT in suspension and to meet the oxygen demand of elevated water respiration [64]. Thus, the BFT system requires a greater consumption of electrical energy than the conventional systems [85]. Therefore, the aerator model chosen should be as efficient as possible in both oxygen transfer and power consumption [86].

The suspended solid content in BFT is typically greater than 500 mg/L, and excessive solid concentrations can clog the gills of fish or shrimp, which affects their growth and welfare [87]. In addition, if total suspended solids concentration exceed the mixing capacity of the system, solid particles settle downward and can accumulate in anaerobic soil layers or pockets of ponds. Anaerobic spots in pond bottoms can lead to the production of toxic compounds and severely hamper fish growth [85].

Knowledge gaps about BFT engineering, feeding systems and bioenergetics, cost factors, and the economics also remain to be the biggest challenge relative to conventional aquaculture systems [84]. Despite the fact that the availability of suited species and cheap carbon sources to implement the system seems a good prospect for BFT application in Ethiopia, the knowledge gap and uncertainty of electric power make the future of the technology long-standing from its implementation in the country.

6. Conclusion and recommendations

Biofloc can be a novel strategy for disease management in contrast to conventional approaches such as antibiotic, antifungal, probiotic, and prebiotic application [88]. The natural probiotic effect in BFT could act internally and/or externally against *Vibrio sp.* and ectoparasites, respectively [9, 89]. This effect is stimulated by big assemblages of microorganisms, mainly bacteria, that are considered the first trophic levels in the system. Bacteria and their produced metabolites could act similar to organic acids and might be effective biocontrol agents by maintaining host's microbial stability in the gut [90].

It can be concluded that biofloc technology holds a firm position as a potential environmentally friend and sustainable production system in freshwater aquaculture. Results from various research consulted for this review indicated that BFT application in the three major freshwater aquaculture species (tilapia, catfish, and carp) improves culture water quality hence decreasing the wastewater discharge to the environment and allowing efficient water usage. Moreover, the technology proved to be efficient in producing an extra feed for the cultured species in the form of single-cell protein, providing an opportunity to substitute up to 20% of the conventional feed by biofloc, thus implying the potential of the technology in reducing the production cost of the cultured organisms. In addition, bioflocs alone or in combination with probiotic bacteria showed promising results in enhancing the immunity of cultured freshwater species providing an alternative to chemical therapeutics that have a detrimental impact on the environment. On the other hand, the organic carbon sources used to enhance flocs formation in BFT are relatively cheaper and readily available, which makes the technology economically viable. Although various carbon sources are being used in freshwater aquaculture, molasses was found to be the most frequently applied organic carbon source in this review while C:N ratios of 10, 15, and 20 are the most frequently reported ones so far. Despite all these potentials, BFT also has its own limitations related to the higher amount of total suspended solids and energy consumption for aeration and mixing. In addition, the technology requires relatively better know-how to successfully operate the system hindering its application at the farmer's level. Therefore, it is recommended that research activities under laboratory conditions should be up-scaled on to bigger size culture setups to better understand the economic feasibility of the technology, especially in catfish and carp aquaculture. Optimizations of the levels of total suspended solids which are safe for each species based on the morphology and feeding behavior of the species needs to be dealt well. Research activities should also focus on finding alternatives to the higher power consumption such as solar systems to mitigate the challenge related to power usage. Lastly, capacity building and promotion of the technology needs to be conducted especially in developing countries where the technology is still a potential rather than a real practice.

Author details

Solomon Melaku[1*], Abebe Getahun[2], Seyoum Mengestou[2], Akewake Geremew[2] and Amha Belay[3]

1 Department of Animal Science, College of Agriculture and Natural Resource Science, Debre Berhan University, Debre Berhan, Ethiopia

2 Department of Zoological Sciences, College of Natural and Computational Sciences, Addis Ababa University, Addis Ababa, Ethiopia

3 ALGAE4ALL, LLC Latigo Cir.La Quinta, California, USA

*Address all correspondence to: solomon.melaku@aau.edu.et

References

[1] FAO. The State of World Fisheries and Aquaculture: Meeting the Sustainable Development Goals. Rome: Food and Agriculture Organization of the United Nations; 2018

[2] World Bank. Fish to 2030: Prospects for Fisheries and Aquaculture. Washington DC: The World Bank; 2013

[3] Waite R, Beveridge M, Brummett R. Improving Productivity and Environmental Performance of Aquaculture. Washington DC: World Resources Institute; 2014

[4] Dauda AB, Abdullateef A, Adenike ST, Ayoola OA. Waste production in aquaculture: Sources, components and managements in different culture systems. Aquaculture and Fisheries. 2019;**4**:81-88

[5] Bossier P, Ekasari J. Biofloc technology application in aquaculture to support sustainable development goals. Microbial Biotechnology. 2017;**10**:10121016

[6] Ahmad I, Rani A, Verma A, Maqsood M. Biofloc technology in: an emerging avenue in aquatic animal healthcare and nutrition. Aquacultural International. 2017;**25**:1215-1226

[7] Avnimelech Y. Carbon/nitrogen ratio as a control element in aquaculture systems. Aquaculture. 1999;**176**:227-235

[8] De Schryver P, Crab R, Defoirdt T, Boon N, Verstraete W. The basics of bioflocs technology: The added value for aquaculture. Aquaculture. 2008;**277**:125-137

[9] Emerenciano M, Gaxiola G, Cuzon G. Biofloc technology (BFT): A review for aquaculture application and animal food industry. In: Matovic MD, editor. Biomass Now-Cultivation and Utilization. 12th ed. Rijeka: In Tech; 2013

[10] Wasielesky W Jr, Atwood H, Stokes A, Browdy CL. Effect of natural production in a zero exchange suspended microbial floc based super-intensive culture system for white shrimp *Litopenaeus vannamei*. Aquaculture. 2006;**258**:396-403

[11] Burford MA, Thompson PJ, McIntosh RP, Bauman RH, Pearson DC. The contribution of flocculated material to shrimp (*Litopenaeus vannamei*) nutrition in a high intensity, zero-exchange system. Aquaculture. 2004;**232**:525-537

[12] Emerenciano M, Gaxiola G, Cuzon G. Biofloc technology applied to shrimp broodstock. In: Avnimelech Y, editor. Biofloc Technology – A Practical Guide Book. 2nd ed. Baton Rouge, Louisiana, USA: The World Aquaculture Society; 2012. pp. 217-230

[13] Choo HX, Caipang CM. Biofloc technology (BFT) and its application towards improved production in freshwater tilapia culture. AACL Bioflux. 2015;**8**:362-366

[14] Garcıa-Rıos L, Miranda-Baeza A, Emerenciano MG, Huerta-Rabago JA, Osuna-Amarillas P. Biofloc technology (BFT) applied to tilapia fingerlings production using different carbon sources: Emphasis on commercial applications. Aquaculture. 2019;**502**:26-31

[15] Azim ME, Little DC. The biofloc technology (BFT) in indoor tanks: Water quality, biofloc composition, and growth and welfare of Nile tilapia (*O. niloticus*). Aquaculture. 2008;**283**:29-35

[16] Najdegerami EH, Farideh B, Forouzan BL. Effects of biofloc on growth performance, digestive enzyme activities and liver histology of common carp *(Cyprinus carpio L.)* fingerlings in zero-water exchange system. Fish Physiology and Biochemistry. 2016;**42**:457-465

[17] Dauda AB, Romano N, Ebrahimi M, Teh JC, Ajadi A, Chong CM, et al. Influence of carbon/nitrogen ratios on biofloc production and biochemical composition and subsequent effects on the growth, physiological status and disease resistance of African catfish (*Clarias gariepinus*) cultured in glycerol-based biofloc system. Aquaculture. 2018;**483**:120-130

[18] Dauda AB, Romano N, Ebrahimi M, Karim M, Natrah I, Kamarudin MS, et al. Different carbon sources affected biofloc volume, water quality and the survival and physiology of African Catfish *Clarias gariepinus* fingerlings reared in intensive biofloc technology system. Fisheries Science. 2017;**83**:1037-1048

[19] Deng M, Chena J, Gou J, Hou J, Li D, He X. The effect of different carbon sources on water quality, microbial community and structure of biofloc systems. Aquaculture. 2018;**482**:103-110

[20] El-Husseiny OM, Ashraf M, Goda AS, Rania SM, Soaudy M. Complexity of carbon sources and the impact on biofloc integrity and quality in tilapia (*Oreochromis niloticus*) tanks. AACL Bioflux. 2018;**11**:846-855

[21] Crab R, Chielens B, Wille M, Bossier P, Verstraete W. The effect of different carbon sources on the nutritional value of bioflocs, a feed for *Macrobrachium rosenbergii* postlarvae. Aquaculture Research. 2010;**41**:559-567

[22] Wei Y-f, Anli W, Shao-an L. Effect of different carbon sources on microbial community structure and composition of ex-situ biofloc formation. Aquaculture. 2020;**515**:734492

[23] Widanarni R, Ekasari J, Maryam S. Evaluation of biofloc technology application on water quality and production performance of red tilapia *Oreochromis sp*. cultured at different stocking densities. Hayati Journal of Bioscience. 2012;**19**:73-80

[24] Lancelot C, Billen G. Carbon-nitrogen relationships in nutrient metabolism of coastal marine ecosystems. Advances in Aquatic Microbiology. 1985;**3**:263-321

[25] Bakar N, Nasir N, Lananan F, Hamid S, Lam S, Jusoh A. Optimization of C/N ratios for nutrient removal in aquaculture system culturing African catfish, (*Clarias gariepinus*) utilizing bioflocs technology. International Biodeterioration and Biodegradation. 2015;**102**:100-106

[26] Perez-Fuentes JA, Hernandez-Vergara MP, Perez-Rostro CI, Fogel I. C: N ratios affect nitrogen removal and production of Nile tilapia *Oreochromis niloticus* raised in a biofloc system under high density cultivation. Aquaculture. 2016;**425**:247-251

[27] Azim ME, Asaeda T. Periphyton structure, diversity and colonization. In: Azim ME, Verdegem MCJ, van Dam AA, Beveridge MCM. (editors), Periphyton – Ecology, Exploitation and Management. CABI Publishing, Wallingford; 2005. pp. 15-33

[28] Alayu Y, Eshete D, Spliethoff P. Business Opportunities Report Aquaculture No. 10 in the series written for the Ethiopian Netherlands business event 5-6 November 2015, Rijswijk, The Netherlands; 2015

[29] Crab R, Kochva M, Verstraete W, Avnimelech Y. Bio-flocs technology

application in over-wintering of tilapia. Aquacultural Engineering. 2009;**40**:105-112

[30] Hari B, Madhusoodana K, Varghese JT, Schrama JW, Verdegem MCJ. Effects of carbohydrate addition on production in extensive shrimp culture systems. Aquaculture. 2004;**241**:179-194

[31] Rakocy JE, Bailey DS, Thoman ES, Shultz RC. Intensive tank culture of tilapia with a suspended, bacterial based treatment process: New dimensions in farmed tilapia. In: Bolivar R, Mair G, Fitzsimmons K, editors. Proceedings of the Sixth International Symposium on Tilapia in Aquaculture. Manila, Philippines: Bureau of Fisheries & Aquatic Resources; 2004. pp. 584-596

[32] Ballester E, Abreu P, Cavalli R, Emerenciano M, Abreu L, Wasielesky W. Effect of practical diets with different protein levels on the performance of *Farfantepenaeus paulensis* juveniles nursed in a zero exchange suspended microbial flocs intensive system. Aquaculture Nutrition. 2010;**16**:163-172

[33] Avnimelech Y. Feeding with microbial flocs by tilapia in minimal discharge bioflocs technology ponds. Aquaculture. 2007;**264**:140-147

[34] Kuhn DD, Boardman GD, Lawrence AL, Marsh L, Flick J. Microbial floc meal as a replacement ingredient for fishmeal and soybean protein in shrimp feed. Aquaculture. 2009;**296**:5157

[35] Emerenciano MGC, Wasielesky W, Soares RB, Ballester EC, Cavalli RO, Izeppi EM. Crescimento e sobrevivêcia do camarão-rosa Farfantepenaeus paulensis na fase de berçário em meio heterotrófico. Acta Scientiarum: Biological Sciences. 2007;**29**:1-7

[36] Romano N, Dauda A, Ikhsan N, Karim M, Kamarudin M. Fermenting rice bran as a carbon source for biofloc technology improved the water quality, growth, feeding efficiencies, and biochemical composition of African catfish *Clarias gariepinus* juveniles. Aquaculture Research. 2018;**49**:3691-3701

[37] Bakhshi F, Najdegerami E, Manaffarc R, Tukmechid A, Farahe K. Use of different carbon sources for the biofloc system during the grow-out culture of common carp *(Cyprinus carpio L.)* fingerlings. Aquaculture. 2018;**484**:259-267

[38] Milstein A, Anvimelech Y, Zoran M, Joseph D. Growth performance of hybrid bass and hybrid tilapia in conventional and active suspension intensive ponds. Bamidgeh. 2001;**53**:147-157

[39] Panjaitan P. Field and Laboratory Study of *Penaeus monodon* Culture with Zero Water Exchange and Limited Water Exchange Model Using Molasses as a Carbon Source. Darwin, NT, Australia: Charles Darwin Univ; 2004

[40] Krummenauer D, Peixoto S, Cavalli RO, Poersch LH, Wasielesky W. Super intensive culture of white shrimp, *Litopenaeus vannamei* in a biofloc technology system in southern Brazil at different stocking densities. Journal of the World Aquaculture Society. 2011;**42**:726-733

[41] Souza DM, Suita SM, Romano LA, Wasielesky W, Ballester ELC. Use of molasses as a carbon source during the nursery rearing of *Farfantepenaeus brasiliensis* (Latreille, 1817) in a biofloc technology system. Aquaculture Research. 2014;**45**:270-277

[42] Hoa NV, Anh NT, Dieu DK. Use of biofloc grown at different salinities as a feed for *Artemia* in laboratory conditions (in Vietnamese). Cantho University Journal of Science Special issue: Aquaculture. 2014;**2**:150-158

[43] Sreedevi PK, Ramasubramanian V. Biocontrol of ammonia pollution in the rearing water of fish by inducing heterotrophic bacterial based food chain in the medium. Aquaculture International. 2010;**19**:789-796. DOI: 10.1007/S 10499-010-9395-7

[44] Schrader KK, Green BW, Perschbacher PW. Development of phytoplankton communities and common off-flavors in a biofloc technology system used for the culture of channel catfish (*Ictalurus punctatus*). Aquacultural Engineering. 2011;**45**:118-126

[45] Duy PQA, Ut VN. Application of biofloc technology in rearing striped catfish *Pangasianodon hypophthalmus* from juvenile to fingerling stage at different salinities. In: International Fisheries Sympossium (IFS, 2015). Penang, Malaysia; 2015

[46] Kamilya D, Debbarma M, Pal P, Kheti B, Sarkar S, Singh S. Biofloc technology application in indoor culture of Labeo rohita (Hamilton, 1822) fingerlings: The effects on inorganic nitrogen control, growth and immunity. Chemosphere. 2017;**182**:8-14

[47] Sgnaulin T, Giovanni LM, Micheli CT, Juan REG, Gustavo ARM, Emerencianoa MGC. Biofloc technology (BFT): An alternative aquaculture system for piracanjuba *Brycon orbignyanus*? Aquaculture. 2018;**485**:119-123

[48] Menaga M, Felixb S, Charulathaa M, Gopalakannana A. Effect of *in-situ* and *ex-situ* biofloc on immune response of genetically improved farmed Tilapia. Fish and Shellfish Immunology. 2019;**92**:698-705

[49] Avnimelech Y, Mokady S, Schroeder GL. Circulated ponds as efficient bioreactors for single cell protein production. Bamidgeh. 1989;**41**:58-66

[50] Ekasari J, Zairin MJ, Putri DU, Sari NP, Surawidjaja EH, Bossier P. Biofloc-based reproductive performance of Nile tilapia *Oreochromis niloticus* L. broodstock. Aquaculture Research. 2015;**46**:509-512

[51] Gallardo-Collı A, Carlos IPR, Patricia M, Vergara H. Reuse of water from biofloc technology for intensive culture of Nile tilapia (*Oreochromis niloticus*): Effects on productive performance, organosomatic indices and body composition. International Aquatic Research. 2019;**11**:43-55

[52] De Araújo M et al. The intensive culture of Nile tilapia supplemented with the microalgae *Chlorella vulgaris* in a biofloc system. Boletim do Instituto de Pesca. 2019;**45**:398

[53] De Sousa AA, Pinho SM, Rombensod AN, Giovanni LM, Emerenciano MG. Pizzeria by-product: A complementary feed source for Nile tilapia (*Oreochromis niloticus*) raised in biofloc technology? Aquaculture. 2019;**501**:359-367

[54] Little DC, Murray FJ, Azim E, Leschen W, Boyd K, Watterson A, et al. Options for producing a warm-water fish in the UK: Limits to Green growth. Trends in Food Science and Technology. 2008;**19**:255-264

[55] Lima EC, Rafael L, Wambach XF, Silva UL, Correia ES. Culture of the Nile tilapia "*Oreochromis niloticus*" in biofloc system with different stocking densities. Rev. Bras. Saúde Prod. Anim Salvador. 2015;**16**:948-957

[56] Madyod S, Suwanna M, Suwit W, Jittawat R, Rujira M, Paweera T. Effects of supplementation of dries floc as

immuno-stimulants on survival rate of tilapia infected with *Flavobacterium columnare*, VETSV01. Journal of Pharmacy and Pharmacology. 2018;**6**:526-530

[57] Martins MA, Moisés A, et al. Heterotrophic and mature biofloc systems in the integrated culture of Pacific white shrimp and Nile tilapia. Aquaculture. 2020;**514**:734517

[58] El Naggar GO, John G, Rezk MA, Elwan W, Yehia M. Effect of varying density and water level on the spawning response of African catfish Clarias gariepinus: Implications for seed production. Aquaculture. 2006;**261**:904-907

[59] Sharaf SM. Effect of GnRHa, pimozide and Ovaprim on ovulation and plasma sex steroid hormones in African catfish *Clarias gariepinus*. Theriogenology. 2012;**77**:1709-1716

[60] Nadio H. Biofloc Technology during the Re-maturation Period of the African catfish (*Clarias gariepinus*) females: Effect of Temperature and Flocs on Reproductive Performance. Indonesia: Bogor Agricultural University Bogor; 2015

[61] Ekasari J, Suprayudi MA, Wiyoto W, Hazanah RF, Lenggara GS, Sulistiani R, et al. Biofloc technology application in African catfish fingerling production: The effects on the reproductive performance of broodstock and the quality of eggs and larvae. Aquaculture. 2016;**464**:349-356

[62] Gomes LC, Golombieski JI, Gomes ARC, Baldisserotto B. Biologia dejundiá Rhamdia quelen (Teleostei, Pimelodidae). Ciênc. Rural. 2000;**30**:179-185

[63] Behr ER, Radünz-Neto J, Tronco AP, Fontana AP. Influência de difer-entes níveis de luminosidade sobre o desempenho de larvas de Jundiá (Rhamdiaquelen) (Quoy e Gaimard, 1824) (Pisces: *Pimelodidae*). Acta Science. 1999;**21**:325-330

[64] Avnimelech Y. Biofloc Technology: A Practical Guide Book. 2nd ed. Baton Rouge: World Aquaculture Society; 2012

[65] Poli MA, Rodrigo S, Alex P. The use of biofloc technology in a South American catfish (*Rhamdia quelen*) hatchery: Effect of suspended solids in the performance of larvae. Aquacultural Engineering. 2015;**66**:17-21

[66] Hapsari F. The effect of fermented and non-fermented biofloc inoculated with bacterium *Bacillus cereus* for catfish (*Clarias gariepinus*) juveniles. AACL Bioflux. 2016;**9**:334-339

[67] Putra I, Rusliadi R, Fauzi M, Usman M, Muchlisin A. Growth performance and feed utilization of African catfish *Clarias gariepinus* fed a commercial diet and reared in the biofloc system enhanced with probiotic. F1000 Research. 2017;**6**:1545-1554

[68] Soedibya P, Hary T, Emyliana L, Taufik BP, Norman AP, Taufan RH. Growth performance of catfish (*Clarias gariepenus*) cultured of high density with biofloc system.E3S. Web of Conferences. 2018;**47**:02002

[69] Green BW. Performance of a temperate-zone channel catfish biofloc technology production system during winter. Aquacultural Engineering. 2015;**64**:60-67

[70] Hastuti S, Subandiyono S. 2018 haematological parameters of the North African catfish *Clarias gariepinus* farmed using biofloc technology. AACL Bioflux. 2018;**11**:1415-1424

[71] Himaja PH. Performance of Biofloc Meal in the Diet of *Catla Catla*

(Hamilton, 1822). Nagapattinam: Tamil Nadu Fisheries University; 2016

[72] Sarker M. Comparative Efficacy of Biofloc and Feed Based Common Carp *(Cyprinus carpio,* L.) Production System with Special Reference to Environmental Health. India: West Bengal University of Animal and Fishery Sciences; 2015

[73] Sasmal S, Goutam R, Lincoln M. Studies on production of common carp (*Cyprinus carpio*) in fresh water biofloc aquaculture system. I.J.S.N. 2019;**10**:107-108

[74] Caldini NN, Cavalcante DH, Nogueira PR, Filho R, Carmoesá MV. Feeding Nile tilapia with artificial diets and dried bioflocs biomass. Acta Scientiarum. Animal Sciences Maringá. 2015;**37**:335-341

[75] Zhang N, Luo G, Tan H, Liu W, Houa Z. Growth, digestive enzyme activity and welfare of tilapia (*Oreochromis niloticus*) reared in a biofloc-based system with poly-β-hydroxybutyric as a carbon source. Aquaculture. 2016;**464**:710-717

[76] Cavalcante DH, Lima FR, Rebouças VT, Carmoesá MV. Do Nile tilapia culture under feeding restriction in bioflocs and bioflocs plus periphyton tanks. Acta Scientiarum Animal Sciences Maringá. 2017;**39**:223-228

[77] Silva UL, Dario RF, Maurício NDCP, Eudes DSC. Carbon sources and C:N ratios on water quality for Nile tilapia farming in biofloc system. Rev. Caatinga, Mossoró. 2017;**30**:1017-1027

[78] Alvarenga E, Alves G, Fernandes A, Costa G, Silva M, Teixeira E, et al. Moderate salinities enhance growth performance of Nile tilapia (*Oreochromis niloticus*) fingerlings in the biofloc system. Aquaculture Research. 2018;**2018**:1-8

[79] Fauji H, Budiardi T, Ekasari J. Growth performance and robustness of African Catfish *Clarias gariepinus* (Burchell) in biofloc-based nursery production with different stocking densities. Aquaculture Research. 2018;**49**:1339-1346

[80] Castro JM, Germán CM, Castro AE, Laura IV, Moreno LO. Weight gain comparison in *Cyprinus carpio* (Linnaeus, 1758) cultured in a biofloc system with four different carbon sources. International Journal of Fisheries and Aquatic Studies. 2018;**6**:11-15

[81] Taw N. Biofloc technology expanding at white shrimp farms. Global Advocate. 2010;**2010**:24-26

[82] Ekasari J, Crab R, Verstraete W. Primary nutritional content of bio-flocs cultured with different organic carbon sources and salinity. Hayati Journal of Bioscience. 2010;**17**:125-130

[83] Avnimelech Y. Tilapia production using biofloc technology saving water, waste recycling improves economics. Global Aquaculture Advocate. 2011;**2011**:66-69

[84] Kourie R. Large-scale biofloc tank culture of tilapia in Malawi – A technical success story. World Aquaculture Society. 2017;**2017**:25-29

[85] Pasco JJ, Jose WC, Carlos ME, Luis V. Production of Nile tilapia *Oreochromis niloticus* grown in BFT using two aeration systems. Aquaculture Research. 2018;**49**:222-231

[86] Tucker CS. Pond Aeration. Southern Regional Aquaculture Center Fact Sheet 3700. United States; 2005

[87] Luo G, Qi G, Chaohui W, Wenchang L, Dachuan S, Li L, et al. Growth, digestive activity, welfare, and

partial cost-effectiveness of genetically improved farmed tilapia *(Oreochromis niloticus)* cultured in a recirculating aquaculture system and an indoor biofloc system. Aquaculture. 2014;**422-423**:1-7

[88] De Schryver PD, Sinha AK, Kunwar PS, Baruah SK, Verstraete W, Boon N, et al. Hydroxybutyrate (PHB) increases growth performance and intestinal bacterial range-weighted richness in juvenile European sea bass, *Dicentrarchus labrax*. Applied Microbiology and Biotechnology. 2012;**86**:1535-1541

[89] Sajalia US, Atkinson NL, Desbois AP, Little DC, Murray FJ, Shinn AP. Prophylactic properties of biofloc- or Nile tilapia-conditioned water against *Vibrio parahaemolyticus* infection of white leg shrimp (*Penaeus vannamei*). Aquaculture. 2019;**498**:496-502

[90] Sinha AK, Baruah K, Bossier P. Horizon scanning: The potential use of biofloc as an anti-infective strategy in aquaculture – An overview. Aquaculture Health International. 2008;**13**:8-10

Section 5

Bivalve Culture

Chapter 6

Perspective Chapter: Health and Safety in Oyster Aquaculture

Norma Estrada

Abstract

The globalization of oyster markets has accelerated the commercial exchange of food, needing to implement strategies that contribute to ensuring the safety of food products. Among the factors that can threaten the safety of oysters are chemical contaminants (heavy metals, antibiotics, pesticides, etc.), biological (viruses, bacteria, etc.), and physical (pieces of metal, splinters, among others). These characteristics, together with the organoleptic, commercial, and nutritional ones, constitute the basic requirements that must be considered to access the various markets because they provide a high degree of confidence to the consumer. Oyster products for human consumption need a sanitary certification that guarantees the quality of their products and ensures competitive and permanent participation in the market. To achieve this, each link in the chain food industry must establish controls and activities that minimize contamination risks.

Keywords: oyster, health, safety, aquaculture, human consumption

1. Introduction

Oysters are one of the best known and most widely cultivated marine animals, which are highly valorized seafood products, and a large part of the international seafood trade recognized for their crucial role in food security and nutrition as a source of basic nutrients such as proteins, essential fats, minerals, and vitamins. Commonly farmed food oysters include the Eastern oyster (*Crassostrea virginica*), the Pacific oyster (*Crassostrea gigas*), Kumamoto oyster (*Crassostrea sesame*), Chilean flat oyster (*Ostrea chilensis*), Belon oyster (*Ostrea edulis*), the Sydney rock oyster (*Saccostrea glomerata*), Olympia oyster (*Ostrea lurid*), and the Southern mud oyster (*Ostrea angasi*) [1]. Oyster mariculture is achieving spectacular development worldwide, constituting a growing food sector with economic development opportunities for the coastal economy. World production of oysters stands out with more than 4.5 million tons, producing a yield of approximately 3.7 billion dollars, with *C. gigas* being the most widely cultured species. Prioritizing and better integrating aquaculture products in global, regional, and national food system strategies and policies should be a vital part of the necessary transformation of the agrifood systems. This trend has to be maintained or increased to maintain the current levels of consumption of oyster products as the world population continues its increase [1, 2].

The globalization of oyster markets has accelerated the commercial exchange of food, increasing the problems related to food biosecurity, with the necessity to implement strategies that contribute to ensuring the safety of food products. Aquaculture products typically pose a health risk to consumers through contamination from the environment, in which they are grown, their inherent chemical composition, cross-contamination during handling, improper processing, poor storage, distribution practices, and marketing [3]. Particular hazards are associated with the consumption of oyster products, usually defined as the physical, chemical, or biological agents present in the food or one of its properties, which can cause harm to the health of the consumer when being ingested. Expanding the trading of oyster products requires scaling up transformative changes in policy, management, innovation, and investment to achieve sustainable, inclusive, and equitable global aquaculture with inherent food biosecurity [2].

2. Food safety risks of oysters

Oyster aquaculture has long been an important food source and livelihood for millions worldwide, consumed by inhabitants of all five continents. However, if oyster food products are not handled, stored, and processed correctly, their safety may be affected due to contamination by different agents. Hazards can occur at various stages of the production chain and vary depending on the aquatic environment from which they come and postharvest handling and processing procedures. Identifying the hazards associated with aquaculture products is essential to understanding the level of risk in food safety. Investigations of disease outbreaks linked to oyster consumption have been reported in the scientific literature; however, only a few countries systematically collate and report such data through a disease surveillance system [3]. Oysters are filter feeders, so they naturally concentrate anything in the surrounding water. Oysters can be contaminated with biological (viruses, bacteria, parasites), chemicals (e.g., heavy metals, marine biotoxins), and physical agents (e.g., glass and metal fragments) [4].

2.1 Biological contamination

Oysters and many commercial bivalve species are prevalent in coastal estuaries, as well as similar shallow or drying areas, where nutrient levels are high, and the waters are sheltered. Unfortunately, such shallow, in-shore, growing waters are frequently contaminated with human and animal sewage. In the process of filter-feeding, bivalve shellfish may also concentrate and retain human pathogens derived from such sewage contamination and naturally occurring marine pathogens [5]. Biological contamination refers to microorganisms that can potentially contaminate food and harm consumers' health. These biological hazards include parasites, viruses, and pathogenic bacteria [6].

Oysters are known as a potential source of protozoan parasites such as *Toxoplasma gondii* (responsible for toxoplasmosis), *Cryptosporidium* spp. (one of the major causes of gastroenteritis in the world), and *Giardia* spp. (responsible for gastroenteritis) [7–12]. *Crassostrea belcheri* oysters can be an effective transmission vehicle for *Cryptosporidium parvum* oocytes, especially within 24–72 h of contamination, with viable oocysts present at up to 7 days postinfection. Unless consuming well-cooked oyster dishes, eating raw oysters remains a public health concern, and in general, at least 3 days of depuration in clean sea water before consumption is recommended [12]. Many reports have shown that *Toxoplasma gondii* is present in *C. virginica* and other *Crassostrea species,* being potential sources of contamination for humans and other animals [7, 13, 14]. Although *T. gondii* infections are largely asymptomatic or clinically mild in immunocompetent individuals, infection in immunocompromised patients and fetuses infected congenitally may lead to serious health consequences [15, 16]. *Cryptosporidium* and *Giardia* were detected in commercial and noncommercial oysters (*C. gigas*) and water from the Oosterschelde, the Netherlands, suggesting that consuming raw oysters may occasionally lead to cases of gastrointestinal illness [11].

Among metazoo parasites of oysters are trematodes and nematodes with zoonosis impact [17]. Foodborne illnesses appear when raw or undercooked fish products containing the parasite in its infective stage are consumed [3]. Most of these diseases are rare and cause only mild or moderate damage, but some pose serious health risks. Some metacercariae of the families Echinostomatidae (they encyst in various tissues) and Gymnophallidae (they occur without encysting between the mantle and the valve, erecting very varied responses that compromise the mantle and the valve) are of public health importance as they are potential parasites of human [18]. In Korea, an endemic zoonosis is caused by consuming raw oyster *C. gigas*, parasitized by *Gymnophallidae metacercaria* [19]. Recently Grano-Maldonado et al. [20] and Tejeda-Arenas et al. [21] reported the first incidence of the digenean *Stephanostomum* sp. (Acanthocolpidae), encapsulated and embedded in the digestive gland and mantle tissue, parasitizing *Crassostrea corteziensis* on Mexican coasts, and other digeneos (Families Hemiuridae, Fellodistomidae, and Zoogonidae) with possible implications for the health risks posed by human consumption. Although nematodes are uncommon as bivalve parasites, few Ascaridoidea and Spirurida Nematoda species could be found as larval stages without specificity for their site infection. Indeed, they frequently appear in low prevalences and infection intensities, eliciting different capsules. Some ascaridoids are potentially pathogenic to human health [17, 22]. Second and third instar larvae of *Echinocephalus crassostreai* occur in *C. gigas* from culture off the coast of Hong Kong and adjacent coasts of China [23]. Humans ingesting this nematode can cause granulomatous gastric lesions [22, 24].

Foodborne viruses are an important and emerging problem for food safety and public health, according to a report by EFSA [25]. Oysters, aquatic filter feeders, are a notorious source of foodborne viral infections because they actively concentrate viruses from contaminated water [5, 26]. Some viruses have been epidemiologically linked to disease following the consumption of oysters or other bivalves transmitted by the fecal-oral route, many of which can contaminate oyster or their harvesting areas. Illness has been related to viruses causing gastroenteritis and viruses causing hepatitis [5, 27]. *In situ* studies with bioaccumulation of a virus indicator in oysters have shown that oysters can concentrate viruses up to 99 times compared to the surrounding water [28]. Oysters are often eaten raw, creating the potential for foodborne enteric virus infections. The leading cause of viral diseases transmitted by consuming raw or undercooked oysters (although some outbreaks have been linked to cooked oysters) is enteric viruses from infected people and animals, either *via* infected handlers or by contamination of the aquatic environment with the excrement of humans or animals [29]. The pathogens most frequently involved in these outbreaks are noroviruses (NoVs; responsible for acute gastroenteritis in humans, which is particularly hazardous for immunocompromised or chronically ill persons), and adenoviruses (AdVs, often linked with respiratory illness, gastroenteritis, and neurological diseases) [3, 30–33]. Norovirus has been detected in 5 to 55% of oysters from Europe, the United States (US), and Brazil by random sampling at marketplaces, oyster farms, and environmental samples [34–37], and in 2010, NoVs outbreaks were linked to oyster consumption in the United Kingdom, Norway, France, Sweden, and Denmark [38, 39]. Ng et al. [40] reported associated outbreaks of norovirus gastroenteritis in Singapore. Le Guyader et al. [31] reported multiple noroviruses associated with an international gastroenteritis outbreak linked to oyster consumption. Internationally distributed frozen oyster meat caused numerous outbreaks of norovirus infection in Australia [41]. In December 2009, over 200 individuals reported gastrointestinal symptoms associated with oyster consumption after dining at a North Carolina restaurant [29]. Noroviruses are difficult to remove from oysters through cleansing and also stay infectious even if cleaned [42]. A difference in accumulation and persistence between different strains of NoV in a single species of shellfish has been shown [32, 43] such as the oyster *Crassostrea ariakensis* that was shown to more efficiently accumulate NoV, murine norovirus 1, and hepatitis A virus than *C. virginica* [44]. Two New Zealand outbreaks of norovirus gastroenteritis linked to commercially farmed oysters were reported [45]. Multiple NoV genotypes have been characterized by an oyster-associated outbreak of gastroenteritis [46]. In Taiwan, surveillance of AdVs and NoVs contaminants in the water and shellfish of major oyster breeding farms was reported [33]. Moreover, AdVs can persist in the environment for a longer time and are considered one of the potential human viral indicators present in fecal-contaminated waters [47].

A wide range of positivity rates for rotavirus A (RVA) has been reported in oysters from different regions from 3.3% to 57.8% in Thailand, Japan, France, Mexico, and Argentina [37, 48–53]. Rotaviruses are the most important pathogens responsible for diarrheal deaths in children under 5 years of age, with more than 128,000 deaths worldwide each year [54, 55]. In addition, rotavirus was detected in 0.3–16.7% of cases with oyster-associated gastroenteritis [27, 51]. Oyster has been considered an important carrier of RVA transmission [27, 56]. Rotavirus has been detected in farmed oysters at rates of 3.3–44.4% [51].

Hepatitis A (HAV) is the most severe virus infection linked to shellfish consumption, causing serious debilitating disease and even, occasionally, death. Any man may contract HAV after consumption of contaminated shellfish that has not been thoroughly cooked, and many HAV outbreaks worldwide have been linked to bivalve mollusk consumption and have been reviewed by several authors [5, 57–59]. The first documented shellfish-borne outbreak of "infectious hepatitis" occurred in Sweden in 1955 when 629 cases were associated with raw oyster consumption [60]. Large outbreaks of infection involving >800 patients also occurred in Australia in 1979 [61], the United States in 1986 [62], and Japan in 1991 [63]. Conaty et al. [64] reported hepatitis A in New South Wales, Australia, from the consumption of oysters. The ability of HAV to persist was demonstrated for up to 6 weeks in Eastern oysters (*C. virginica*). These results support that oyster depuration is insufficient for completely removing infectious viruses. Extended relay times (more than 4 weeks) may be required to produce virologically safe shellfish [65]. *C. ariakensis* efficiently accumulated HAV [44]. In France in 2007, 111 HAV cases linked to the consumption of raw shellfish (mainly oysters) were present in one French farm and the surrounding area [66]. Also, in the United States (2005), 39 HAV cases were epidemiologically linked to consuming raw oysters from two Louisiana harvest areas [67, 68]. HAV can persist for several weeks in oysters despite depuration techniques. This virus is also fairly resistant to heating and may remain viable in shellfish after up to 5 minutes of steaming [69]. Shellfish-associated HAV outbreaks occur globally and are likely underreported. The relatively long incubation period from the time of exposure to the onset of symptoms renders tracing and detection of a common source difficult.

Also, oysters may be vectors of hepatitis E (HEV). Infected individuals excrete HEV, which is present in wastewater and coastal waters. HEV shares morphological and biophysical characteristics with caliciviruses; however, there are significant genomic differences. Recent taxonomic proposals leave HEV without a formally assigned virus group [70]. HEV is generally mild but can be more severe for pregnant women. Song et al. [71] described the first report of the detection in oysters of HEV that may have originated from genotype 3 swine HEV in Korea. They showed a close genetic relationship with the swKOR-1 strain and the swine and human HEV isolated in the USA. Grodzki et al. [72] demonstrated that oysters might accumulate HEV experimentally in *C. gigas* and *O. edulis*; tissue distribution analysis showed that most of the viruses were concentrated in the digestive tissues. Also, they collected 286 samples, and none were contaminated with the HEV virus despite evidence that this virus is circulating in some French areas. The number of HEV viral particles discharged into the environment is too low to detect, or the virus may persist very short in pig manure and human waste. However, as shellfish is a typical food in France, this transmission route cannot be excluded from consideration, although shellfish have not yet been implicated in an HEV outbreak in France.

Oysters can also contain harmful bacteria. Vibriosis is an illness caused by some kinds of Vibrio bacteria when eating raw or undercooked oysters. *Vibrio* naturally lives in coastal water, and the oyster that contains The *Vibrio* bacteria does not make an oyster look, smell, or taste any different, which makes it hard to detect. Cooking oysters properly can kill Vibrio and other harmful germs they might contain. Most *Vibrio* infections from oysters result in mild illness, including diarrhea and vomiting. However, people with a *Vibrio vulnificus* infection can get very sick. Infections caused by ingesting *V. vulnificus* can result in gastroenteritis with associated abdominal pain, diarrhea, and vomiting but have the potential to quickly progress to primary septicemia, exhibiting blistering skin lesions or organ failure, with mortality rates for sepsis and wound infection. *V. vulnificus* is the most deadly seafood-borne pathogen [73–75]. Also, infection with *Vibrio cholerae* is very serious and debilitating [76]. Cholera outbreaks can be initiated by transmission of "epidemic" or "non-epidemic" *V. cholerae* strains from their environmental reservoir to humans through seafood or other environmentally related food or water sources [77]. "Epidemic" strains of *V. cholerae* carrying a suite of specific virulence genes cause the disease cholera, characterized by the rapid onset of profuse, watery diarrhea, which, if untreated, can lead to dehydration, circulatory collapse, and death. *V. cholerae* strains belonging to serogroup O1 were believed to be the sole etiologic agents of cholera, and the signs and symptoms of cholera are caused by cholera toxin. Strains of *V. cholerae* that do not carry the virulence factors necessary to cause epidemic cholera have been implicated as causes of diarrheal disease, wound infections, and, in susceptible hosts, septicemia [76, 77]). Epidemiologic studies and studies involving volunteers have linked the occurrence of diarrheal illness to the production of a heat-stable enterotoxin (NAG-ST) similar to that produced by enterotoxigenic *Escherichia coli* [77]. Other species are associated with gastroenteritis of varying severity, including *Vibrio parahaemolyticus* infection, which is quite commonly associated with eating undercooked oysters. Still, most cases are sporadic because not all strains of *V. parahaemolyticus* are considered pathogenic. The thermostable direct hemolysin (encoded by tdh), which is the virulence factor associated with pathogenic functions in humans and marine animals, is rare to occur in marine environmental *V. parahaemolyticus* bacteria [78–80], although pathogenic serotypes have been found in raw oysters [80, 81]. The most common clinical presentation is watery diarrhea, but other symptoms include abdominal cramps, nausea, vomiting, headache, fever, and bloody diarrhea. Sepsis due to *V. parahaemolyticus* is quite rare and occurs primarily in patients with cirrhosis and neutropenia [76, 77]. Also, *V. mimucus* was reported acute gastroenteritis in patients who had recently ingested raw oysters [82], and *Vibrio hollisae* has been recovered from patients with gastroenteritis who consumed raw seafood before their enteric illness [83].

Other bacteria, such as *Campylobacter* spp., *Salmonella* spp., *Shigella* spp., *Plesiomonas shigelloides*, *Clostridium* spp., and *E. coli*, which are commonly implicated in gastroenteritis, are only occasionally traced to seafood [76, 84]. The vast majority of *Salmonella* isolates from oysters in the United States were *Salmonella enterica* serovar Newport, a major human pathogen, confirming the human health hazard of raw oyster consumption [85, 86], and is capable of surviving within oysters for at least 2 months within a laboratory setting [87]. Shellfish are frequently contaminated by *Campylobacter* spp. presumably originating from feces from gulls feeding in the growing or relaying waters [88]. Oysters have been shown to harbor species of *Campylobacter* (primarily *C. lari*, but also *C. jejuni*, *C. coli*, and *C. upsaliensis*), a source for human infections [89, 90]. Symptoms can range from mild to serious infections in children and the elderly and permanent neurological symptoms [91]. Sharp [92] reported a case of a prosthetic hip infection caused by *C. coli* by ingesting contaminated raw oysters. Also, Shigella has been responsible for many seafood-associated outbreaks, mainly from consuming raw oysters. Shigellosis symptoms include diarrhea, which can be watery, bloody, and/or contain mucus or pus, stomach pain and cramps, vomiting, fever, and complications, are rare but include seizures in young children, toxic megacolon, bacteremia, Reiter's syndrome, and hemolytic-uremic syndrome [84, 93, 94]. Also, Clostridium species have been reported in oysters, in untreated (influent) and treated (effluent) wastewaters, and in harvest waters [95]. Toxin-producing *C. difficile* causes a wide range of clinical manifestations in the host from asymptomatic colonization to diarrhea and even death [96]. Moreover, *E. coli* occurrence in seafood is considered a sanitary case and may represent a risk to the consumers if related to diarrheagenic *E. coli*. This bacterium in seafood is related to water contamination and/or unhygienic conditions during the handling process, being the potential cause of the quality of the ice used for conservation and the food processing plants. However, the presence of non-pathogenic *E. coli* in fish and shellfish should also alert public health since enumeration of *E. coli* is the standard way to assess the level of fecal microorganisms in water and shellfish and indirectly to estimate the associated potential risk to human health from all waterborne enteric pathogens [97].

2.2 Chemical contamination

Microorganisms are not the only cause of foodborne illness. Oysters that thrive in coastal areas, estuaries, or bays may be exposed to environmental contaminants from various sources such as rivers, marine currents, urban discharges, and natural phenomena. Biotoxins and chemical compounds, such as pesticides, organochlorines, organophosphates, heavy metals, and veterinary drugs, can be incorporated and accumulated into these organisms and cause public health problems [6, 98]. The risk of acute poisoning is very low; however, long-term exposure to high levels of chemical contaminants in food may be associated with severe diseases such as neurological damage, birth defects, cancer, and death [99, 100].

Marine biotoxins are often associated with harmful algal blooms when toxins accumulate in oysters and other shellfish and cause human disease. Shellfish poisoning human syndromes are classified as diarrhetic, amnesic, neurotoxic, paralytic, and azaspiracid [101]. Most of these toxins are produced by species of naturally occurring marine algae (phytoplankton). There are approximately 5000 species of marine algae, but only 70–80 species are known to produce toxins. During filter feeding, these organisms are bioaccumulated by oysters and other shellfish and then release their toxins into their tissues. In most cases, a complex suite of toxins can be produced by a given phytoplankton species, and these can be further metabolized by the shellfish, producing, in some cases, more potent derivatives of the precursor molecules [102]. Outbreaks of intoxication in humans due to marine biotoxins are caused by ingesting contaminated shellfish and can have a wide range of symptoms linked to the specific toxic compound [103, 104]. These marine biotoxins can cause massive economic losses to the aquaculture industry due to the cautionary closure of cultivation areas [105].

Diarrhetic shellfish poisoning (DSP) is a seafood intoxication that consists of rapid-onset gastrointestinal symptoms, such as vomiting and diarrhea. Recovery usually occurs within 3 days, with or without medical treatment. The diarrhetic shellfish toxins are polyether compounds and are grouped into four structural classes: okadaic acid (OA) and its derivatives (dinophysistoxin or DTX), pectenotoxin (PTX), yessotoxin and its derivatives (YTX), and azaspiracid (AZA) [106]. The symptoms caused by the OA group, produced by dinoflagellates of the genera Dinophysis and Prorocentrum, include diarrhea, nausea, vomiting, and abdominal pain, starting 30 min to a few hours after consumption of contaminated shellfish, with complete recovery within 3 days [107]. Chronic exposure to OA, such as polyether toxins, has been identified as a tumor promoter [108, 109]. Among the other mentioned classes, PTX and YTX have not been implicated in human illness. AZAs produce a severe toxicity syndrome in humans, causing mainly gastrointestinal problems, such as cramps, vomiting, nausea, and severe diarrhea [110]. Members of the marine dinoflagellate family Amphidomataceae, including the genera *Azadinium* and *Amphidoma* [105, 111], have been recognized as producers of a unique group of lipophilic polyether phycotoxins known as azaspiracids (AZAs). Among species of *Azadinium* and *Amphidoma languida*, more than 30 AZA analogs have been described [112]. The first incidence of human shellfish-related illness identified as DSP occurred in Japan in the late 1970s; the dinoflagellate *Dinophysis fortii* was identified as the causative organism; the toxin responsible was termed dinophysistoxin (DTX-1) [113, 114]. Many outbreaks of the diarrheic toxins worldwide have been reported in commercial harvest oyster areas [105, 115–118].

Amnesic shellfish poisoning (ASP) is caused by the consumption of shellfish that have accumulated domoic acid (DA), a neurotoxic amino acid belonging to the kainoid class of compounds, produced by some strains of microalgae, such as the diatom *Pseudo-nitzschia* [119]. The clinical effects observed in many of the affected individuals included memory loss, and for this reason, the condition was termed amnesic shellfish poisoning (ASP). The neurotoxic properties of DA by oral exposure to a few mg/kg result in neuronal degeneration, necrosis in specific regions of the hippocampus, and gastrointestinal effects, while slightly higher doses cause neurological symptoms, seizures, memory impairment, limbic system degeneration, and coma [120, 121]. Domoic acid and its isomers are water-soluble and do not degrade under ambient temperatures or when exposed to light in a sterile saline solution [122]. However, it has been shown to decompose under acidic conditions (50% DA loss in 1 week at pH 3) [123]. A serious outbreak of ASP occurred in Canada in 1987 and involved 150 reported cases, 19 hospitalizations, and four deaths after consuming contaminated mussels [121]. However, there are geographical, temporal, and species variations of DA in bivalve mollusks, as observed in organisms sampled in cultivated areas of Ireland, where the toxin was found predominantly in the hepatopancreas of scallops (*Pecten maximus*), and only trace levels of DA were present in mussels (*Mytilus edulis*) and oysters (*C. gigas*) [124].

Neurotoxic shellfish poisoning (NSP) is a disease caused by the consumption of molluscan shellfish contaminated with brevetoxins (PbTx); a suite of nine structurally related ladder-like polycyclic ether neurotoxins produced by the marine dinoflagellate, *Karenia brevis* [125]. Brevetoxins comprise a group of toxins with primarily neurological and gastrointestinal effects. Rinsing, cleaning, cooking, and freezing do not destroy the toxins, which cannot be detected by taste or smell. Symptoms of NSP include nausea, vomiting, diarrhea, paresthesia, tingling, numbness of the perioral area, loss of motor control, severe muscular ache, cramps, bronchoconstriction, seizures, coma, and, in extreme cases, may lead to death [126, 127]. NSP has been reported in temperate areas worldwide, including the southeastern coast of the United States, the Gulf of Mexico, the Caribbean, and New Zealand. Oysters and other bivalves were implicated in the major outbreak of NSP in New Zealand in 1992–1993, with over 180 cases reported over several weeks. A review of this outbreak involved *Karenia mikimotoi* as the likely causative agent, but other suspect species were also present in the bloom. Although PbTx was implicated, more than one group of marine toxins and more than one algal species appear to have been involved [127]. The largest reported outbreak of NSP in the US occurred in North Carolina after *K. brevis* was carried into that region. Illness was observed in a few cases where less than 12 oysters were consumed, but the attack rate was 65% among those eating 12 oysters or more [126, 128, 129].

Paralyzing shellfish poisoning (PSP) is caused by the consumption of shellfish contaminated with highly potent neurotoxins, saxitoxin (STX), and its analogs, produced by certain species of harmful algae such as microalgae of the genera *Alexandrium*, *Gymnodinium*, and *Pyrodinium* [130, 131] and some freshwater cyanobacteria [132]. The earliest documented report of intoxication by PSP toxins occurred in Canada in 1798 [131]. Symptoms of PSP include paresthesia and numbness, first around the lips and mouth and then the face and neck, muscular weakness, a sensation of lightness and floating, ataxia, impaired motor coordination, drowsiness, incoherence, and progressively decreasing ventilator efficiency. In severe cases, toxicity results in paralysis and death. Usually, death occurs within 1–12 h post-exposure [133]. Suffocation with cardiac arrest is the common reason for death. Acute toxicity of PSP toxins exposure is well known; however, chronic deleterious effects still need to be elucidated. PSP toxins are heat stable and are not destroyed by standard cooking procedures, marinating, or freezing. Cooking can increase toxicity by converting the less toxic derivatives into more toxic forms. Thus, it is crucial to monitor and control this hazard in the growing shellfish areas [102]. The first case of PSP was recorded in 1927 near San Francisco, United States, and was caused by *Alexandrium catenella*, resulting in 106 human illnesses and six deaths [134]. The Philippines has the highest number of PSP cases reported in Asia [135], with 2124 PSP cases and 120 deaths reported from 1983 to 2002. Around 2000 human PSP cases are reported worldwide annually, with 15% fatalities [136].

Using pesticides and other chemicals in agriculture produces environmental risks through biomagnification in trophic nets and bioaccumulation in organisms destined for human consumption. Pesticides, such as organochlorines, organophosphates, and heavy metals, have relative importance since they can be captured and accumulated by oysters and another bivalve mollusk during the leak process and cause any harmful effect to the consumer if the former is not subject to an efficient purification process. Due to their physiological characteristics, bivalve mollusks possess the capacity to bioaccumulate concentrations of contaminants that exceed levels present in the surrounding environment, thus making it possible to detect even trace levels of toxic substances [98]. In farmed *C. gigas* on the Mexican coast detected, organochlorine pesticides (endosulfan, DDE, lindane) and metals (Zn, Cd, and Pb) [137]. These organochlorine pesticides are all listed among the most dangerous toxic compounds established by the Stockholm Convention in 2013. Concentrations of lipophilic organic compounds, such as DDT, in the oyster *C. virginica* increase at sexual maturity when oysters produce lipid-rich gametes [138]. Oysters also eliminate these pollutants through spawning (release of eggs into the water). With *C. virginica*, the risk to humans is, therefore, most significant at the moment of sexual maturity. Studies demonstrated that endosulfan and its metabolites possess a carcinogenic potential and produce mutagenic and genotoxic effects in human lymphocytes and liver hepatoblastoma cells [139–141]. DDE's impact on humans includes cancer development, primarily in women [142], and lindane is a possible human carcinogen. Deltamethrin (DEL), an insecticide belonging to the pyrethroid family, became the preferred choice in many agriculture-based countries in the last two decades since the implementation of restrictions on the sale of organophosphorus insecticides can be introduced into the food chain through bioaccumulation in *C. gigas* and then potentially threatens human health [143, 144].

Estuarine and coastal ecosystems are often considered vulnerable due to the complex biogeochemical processes and human disturbances through a variety of pollution. Among environmental contaminants, heavy metals in estuarine and coastal ecosystems have been of increasing concern in environmental conservation. Oysters can also be contaminated by heavy metals, which can be carried through the water of the rivers and enter the first link of the trophic chain (microalgae) to later pass to mollusks or be absorbed directly from the water column. Acute toxicity resulting from consuming contaminated food is uncommon, but chronic exposure can result in undesirable toxic effects and symptoms of heavy metal poisoning can be life-threatening, and they can cause irreversible damage. Toxicity from heavy metals depends on the type of metals and the amount taken. Some heavy metals, including arsenic (As), cadmium (Cd), chromium (Cr), lead (Pb), and mercury (Hg), are harmful to humans, even at trace concentrations [145]. Oyster and 16 seawater samples collected from the southern coast of Korea, including designated shellfish growing areas for export, showed the metal bioaccumulation ratio in oysters that was relatively high for Zn and Cd but low for Hg, Pb, As, and Cr [146]. In various oyster species, mobile cells called amebocytes accumulate complex metals in the blood. In *O. edulis and C. virginica*, some amebocytes accumulate copper (Cu), others Zn, or Cu and Zn simultaneously [147]. Other oyster species, such as *Ostrea angasi* and *C. gigas*, have only one amebocyte type, which accumulates Cu and Zn equally well [148, 149]. Such species may accumulate high levels of contaminants in some of their tissues. When these species are consumed, the metal-metallothionein complexes, enzymes of the oysters, which form complexes with the trace elements and render them harmless, are ingested and digested, releasing the metals into the consumer's body in a manner that favors the assimilation of the metals. Therefore, the levels transferred to and absorbed by the consumer may be high [150]. Long-term exposure to inorganic Ar evidence is strongest for high blood pressure, heart attacks, circulatory disease, producing tingling and loss of sensation in the limbs, and causing brain damage. Pb is a toxic heavy metal even at very low levels of exposure in humans and targets multiple organs in the body due to its systemic toxicity, which can cause neurological, cardiovascular, renal, gastrointestinal, hematological, and reproductive effects. Cd produces kidney and bone damage, and it does not degrade in the environment to less toxic products, contributing to its bioaccumulation in the kidneys and liver. Moreover, Cu can damage the liver and kidneys, and metals, such as chromium (Cr) and nickel (Ni), have been linked with cancers [151].

Moreover, pharmaceutical residues, dioxins, polycyclic aromatic hydrocarbons (PHAs), and polychlorinated biphenyls (PCBs) have been found in the marine environment, so they also could qualify as pollutants of interest in oysters [152–156]. The inappropriate use of antibiotics can harm human health by making it difficult to treat diseases due to antimicrobial resistance. Furthermore, residues present in shellfish can make the product unacceptable to consumers [98]. Chloramphenicol, the most widely used antibiotic in bivalve hatcheries, has a long half-life, is highly toxic, and can cause larval deformities and known risks to humans, in addition to favoring the development of resistance [157]. Dioxins, PAHs, PCBs, and other organic compounds are very chemically stable molecules and, therefore, difficult to destroy. They remain in the ecosystem for years; some accumulate in the trophic chain. These compounds reach the marine environment through different sources: wastewater and industrial effluents, land runoff, or atmosphere deposition. Dioxins are primarily by-products of industrial processes but can also be produced in natural processes, such as volcanic eruptions and forest fires. They can accumulate in oysters affecting egg fertilization and development [158]. Dioxins are highly toxic to humans and can cause reproductive and developmental problems, affect the immune system, interfere with hormones, and thus cause cancer [159]. Also, there are concerns over health risks due to their accumulation of PAHs, which are organic contaminants exhibiting carcinogenic toxicity [160–162]. They originated during the incomplete combustion or pyrolysis of organic material, such as coal, oil, and gasoline, open dumps, forest fire, and in coastal marine sediments due to petroleum products deliveries and fuel combustion emissions from the ships staying alongside the quays [163, 164]. Oysters tend to concentrate very high levels of PAHs, and the lipophilicity of the organic compounds affects the accumulation patterns [154]. PCBs release into the environment through spills, leaks from electrical and other equipment, and improper disposal and storage and have been detected in the whole soft tissue of oysters [153]. A high concentration of PCBs is associated with neuropsychological and neurobehavioral deficits, dementia, immune system dysfunctions, cardiovascular diseases, and cancer and can reduce fertility [165].

2.3 Physical contamination

Physical hazards in animal feed and feed ingredients are mainly foreign objects in the food that make it unsafe for consumption since they can cause suffocation or injuries to the hands, mouth, and gastrointestinal tract. These hazards are recognized mainly by consumers and commonly reported by consumers. The typical physical hazards associated with aquaculture and fishery products are glass pieces, wood splinters, thorns, stones, hooks, and metal fragments [6, 100]. Some can be found in these products, such as hooks after their capture or harvest; others may come from the facilities, equipment, and utensils, where they are processed [3]. The Food and Drug Administration (FDA) Health Hazard Evaluation Board considers that foreign objects with dimensions less than 7 mm rarely cause severe trauma to consumers, except in risk groups, such as infants and the elderly [100, 166]. In oysters, it is common the presence of hard or sharp parts, such as shells, becomes hazardous if consumers do not expect them. The recent problem in marine edible species is the presence of microplastics [167, 168]. A systematic review shows that 94.4% of all oysters globally had microplastics, with an average of 1.41 ± 0.33 per gram of soft tissue wet weight. The study showed that wild-caught oysters contained more than double the amount of microplastic than aquaculture-raised specimens. Polymer type in commercially farmed oysters (*C. gigas* and *Saccostrea glomerata*) across a broad spatial scale, covering eight sites in southern Australia, identified that 62% of the verified microplastics were vexar plastic netting, a low-density polyethylene commonly used in aquaculture production [169].

2.4 Spoiled oyster

Despite significant progress in processing, refrigeration, and transportation, millions of tons of aquatic products are lost or nutritionally compromised yearly. Seafood commodities are among the most perishable foods and rapidly produce numerous compounds associated with objectionable odors. Oysters can have a reasonably long shelf life of up to four weeks, but their taste becomes less pleasant as they age. Preferably oysters must be eaten, cooked, or processed alive; however, oysters can be eaten on the half shell, raw, smoked, boiled, baked, fried, roasted, stewed, canned, pickled, steamed, broiled, or used in various drinks. If not correctly treated after harvesting, they can soon become unfit to consume and possibly dangerous to health due to microbial growth, chemical change, breakdown by endogenous enzymes, and cross-contamination leading to food safety risks. Proper handling, processing, preservation, packaging, and storage measures are essential to extend shelf life, ensure food safety, maintain quality and nutritional attributes, and avoid loss and waste [2].

After shellfish harvest, food-handling precautions should be followed to avoid the introduction of foodborne pathogens, as would be appropriate for any raw or processed food. Proper workers' hygiene, gloves, and regular hand washing must be practiced. The deterioration of oysters is mainly attributed to the combined activities of microbiological metabolism and biochemical deteriorations, such as enzymatic decomposition and PUFA oxidation [170, 171]. The freshness of oysters is a function of bacterial activity, which directly affects flavor, odor, texture, and color. One technique used to assess the bacterial quality of oysters is the aerobic plate count (APC), which determines the number of total aerobic microbes from which individual isolates may be further identified [172]. Changes in the microbial flora of *C. gigas* during refrigerated storage showed that Vibrionaceae and Pseudomonas were predominant in freshly harvested and shucked oysters. In contrast, Pseudomonas bacteria increased dramatically after 12 days of refrigerated storage, while Vibrionaceae remained at the same level [173]. Total bacteria above 107 cfu^{-1} is not considered acceptable quality [174]. Cao et al. [173] also found other spoilage-associated bacteria, accounting for lower proportions and decreases during storage, such as the H2S-producing *Shewanella putrefaciens*, and gram-negative bacteria *Enterobacteriaceae, Moraxella*, and *Flavobacterium*. Fernandez-Piquer et al. [175] evaluated the effect of postharvest temperature on bacterial communities in live *C. gigas* using nonculture-based methods and found that members of the Proteobacteria predominated before storage, while storage altered the bacterial profile with *Psychrilyobacter* spp. predominated at 4°C, while at 15 and 30°C, members of the phylum Bacteroidetes represented the highest percentage. Microbial diversity in oysters was observed, with at least

73 different genera-related clones among all samples, using microbial culture and pyrosequencing 16S rRNA.

Temperatures of 7, 13, and 21°C, during raw *C. virginica* harvesting and storage, may allow for the multiplication of natural spoilage flora, as well as microbial pathogens such as *V. vulnificus*, thus posing a potential health threat to susceptible consumers and compromising product quality [176]. Moreover, the concentrations of microbiological groups of organisms increased with the duration and temperature of storage and were higher in fully processed oysters than in shucked meats. Total counts of bacteria, fungi, coliforms, fecal streptococci, *Aeromonas hydrophila*, and *Clostridia* were significantly higher in shucked oysters than in those stored as shellstock [177]. The bacterial spoilage of *C. gigas* and *Saccostrea glomerata*, during storage at 4°C, revealed that the majority of bacteria at day 0 represented taxa from among the Proteobacteria, Tenericutes, and Spirochaetes, while during storage, Proteobacteria became abundant with *Pseudoalteromonas* and *Vibrio* found to be dominant in both oyster species at day 7 [171]. Bacterial spoilage profiles in the gills of *C. gigas* and *C. virginica* during refrigerated storage at 4°C showed that *Psychrobacter* and *Psychromonas* (psychrotrophic genus) were represented as the most important gill spoiled bacteria, and *Arcobacter* with pathogenic potential was the dominated bacteria in all spoiled oysters [178]. Also, as oysters spoil, a slight but important reduction in pH is noted. Fresh oysters have a pH of about 6.3, but when spoiled have a pH of six or less [173, 176], although Madigan et al. [171] and Chen et al. [178] found that pH increased with the prolonged storage time and spoiled. Although shellfish may remain viable in cold storage for a couple of weeks, it is clear that spoilage can begin within 1–2 weeks. Therefore, after more than 2 weeks, live shellfish may be unsafe to eat [179].

Interventions that reduce bacterial pathogens and non-pathogens (i.e., HPP and irradiation), to some degree, can inactivate spoilage bacteria, thereby somewhat extending the shelf life of shellstock and shucked shellfish [170, 180–182]. Cold storage of shellfish as shellstock rather than as shucked product may delay spoilage somewhat [177]. Data in *C. gigas* showed that chitosan treatment extended the shelf life of oysters from 8 to 9 days to 14–15 days [173]. The effect of super-chilling storage at −1°C depurated with ozone was studied in *C. virginica*, and without ozone in *C. gigas*, could better maintain the eating quality of shelled oysters and the extended shelf life to 9 and 21 days, respectively [183, 184].

3. Hazard analysis and risk assessment

Hazard analysis identifies all possible hazards potentially created by a product, process, or application. Risk assessment is the next step after the collection of potential hazards. Risk in this context is the probability and severity of the hazard becoming a reality. Among the factors that can threaten the safety of oysters and are considered hazards are biological and chemical contaminants and spoilage products, which have been recognized for many years. Consequentially, most countries have enacted sanitary controls on the production of oysters and other bivalve mollusks. These regulations cover similar ground on the requirements for clean growing areas, the management and processing requirements for more contaminated sites, the hygiene conditions for processing and dispatch establishments, requirements for marketing documentation, etc. [5].

To perform a hazard analysis as part of developing a plan, processors must have scientific information on potential hazards associated with raw materials and products for further processing [185]. It is important to consider naturally occurring food safety hazards in the environment from which oysters are harvested. Risks to consumer health from oysters caught in unpolluted marine environments are low, provided these products are handled according to good manufacturing practices. The risks of foodborne illness associated with aquaculture-derived oysters relate to inland and coastal ecosystems with a high potential for pollution. In some parts of the world, where shellfish are consumed either raw or partially cooked, there is an increased risk of foodborne parasitic, viral, or bacterial diseases. Health risks associated with chemical contaminants are difficult to assess because many produce long-term action (chronic risk), and evaluating the health impact of contaminated shellfish consumed by humans, exposure has to be estimated from contamination levels and consumption data. Also, as with all foods, some oyster health risks are associated with consuming certain products, which may increase when the catch is mishandled after harvest. Monitoring programs are in place in numerous countries worldwide, and oyster harvesting area closures occur when some contaminants are present.

The expansion in consumption and commercialization of aquaculture products has been accompanied by a significant development in food quality and safety standards. In this regard, FAO and the World Health Organization (WHO) are collaborating to identify and assess food safety hazards linked to the consumption of novel foods to provide the basis for further work for their control [186]. To meet these food safety and quality standards and ensure consumer protection, increasingly stringent hygiene and handling measures have been adopted at national, regional, and international levels, based on the Codex Code of Practice for Fish and Fishery Products [185], and the guidance it provides to countries on the practical aspects of implementing good hygiene practices and the hazard analysis and critical control point (HACCP)-based food safety management system [185, 187]. The Codex Alimentarius Commission was created in 1963 by the Food and Agriculture Organization of the United Nations (FAO) and World Health Organization (WHO) to develop food standards, guidelines, and related texts, such as codes of practice under the Joint FAO/WHO Food Standards Program. The Codex Alimentarius, "the food code," plays a fundamental role in protecting consumers worldwide and ensuring fair practices in the food trade. The Code of Conduct for Fish and Fishery Products is the essential reference point for technical guidelines on the harvesting, processing, transporting, and selling of fishery products [185]. The main objectives of this program are to protect consumer health, ensure fair trade practices in the food trade, and promote coordination of all food standards work carried out by international governmental and nongovernmental organizations. The Codex Alimentarius demonstrates the potential hazards and defects that must be considered in aquaculture production. The code is intended to cover not only those safety hazards but also defect action points (DAPs), including the essential product quality, composition, and labeling provisions, and more, attempting to illustrate the potential hazards and defects at the various stages in the production chain.

One of the most important activities that must be performed in a processing facility as part of the food safety management system is determining if an identified hazard or defect is significant. The two primary factors determining whether a hazard or defect is significant for HACCP purposes are the probability of occurrence of an adverse health effect and the severity of the effect [185]. Carrying out a food risk assessment means estimating the probability and severity attributable to a given food hazard. This evaluation consists of five principal stages, which are resumed by Karunasagar [188]: (1) *identify and characterize hazards*: identification of biological or chemical agents capable of causing adverse health effects that may be present in a particular food or group of foods, with a qualitative or quantitative description of the severity and the duration of the adverse health effect that may result from the ingestion of the microorganism/toxin/chemical contaminants, (2) *assess consumer exposure to such hazards*: an estimate of the number of bacteria or the level of a biotoxin or chemical agent consumed through the concerned food is made, documenting the sources of contamination, frequency, concentration, and estimation of the probability and the concentration that will be consumed, (3) *characterize the risks*: the process of determining the qualitative and/or quantitative estimation, including attendant uncertainties of the probability of occurrence and the severity of the known or potential adverse health effect in a given population based on hazard identification, exposure assessment and hazard characterization, (4) *management of risk*: the process of weighing policy alternatives in the light of the results of risk assessment and if required, selecting and implementing appropriate control options including regulatory measures, and (5) *risk communication*: an interactive process of exchange of information and opinion on risk among risk assessors, risk managers and other interested parties (e.g., government agencies, industry representatives, the media, scientists, professional societies, consumer organizations, other public interest groups, and concerned individuals).

Once significant hazards and defects have been identified, consideration needs to be given to assessing their potential to be introduced or controlled at each process step. Control measures must be considered for significant hazard(s) or defect(s) associated with each step to eliminate possible occurrence or reduce it to an acceptable level. A hazard or defect may be controlled by multiple control measures [185]. For any given hazard or defect, it may be necessary to have more than one critical limit designated for each control measure. Critical limits should be established based on scientific evidence and validated by appropriate technical experts to ensure their effectiveness in controlling the hazard or defect to the determined level [185].

4. Aquatic health and biosecurity

The potential effects of harvesting and handling of products, onboard vessel handling, or in-plant production activities on the safety and suitability of oysters and their products should be considered at all times. In particular, this includes all points where contamination may exist and taking specific measures to ensure the production of a safe and wholesome product. The type of control and supervision needed will depend on the size of the operation and the nature of its activities.

As with many illnesses, prevention is the best medicine. Adequate cooking of oysters will kill the parasite and prevent infection. For those desiring raw or lightly steamed oysters, the risk of infection will still be present. Most edible bivalves, including oysters, are generally subject to purification or depuration, which places the shellfish in a clean water flow for 12 h or more. This enables the expulsion of many potentially harmful contaminants. Health certification of live oysters is now common as are monitoring and certification of grow out waters. However, depuration does not remove biotoxins produced by microalgae and other chemical compounds, and their control and impact on oyster production are generally managed by long-term monitoring programs. In severe contamination outbreaks, area closures may be necessary, and unless they can be reduced to an acceptable level by normal sorting and/or processing, no oysters should be accepted if they are known to contain parasites, undesirable microorganisms, pesticides, veterinary drugs or toxic, decomposed, or extraneous substances known to be harmful to human health. When oysters determined as unfit for human consumption are found, they should be removed and stored separately and either reworked or disposed of in a proper manner. All oysters deemed fit for human consumption should be handled properly, with particular attention being paid to time and temperature control [185].

It is generally accepted that the most effective and reliable approach to controlling the contamination of oysters is to harvest from areas with good water quality. Control of contamination through oyster processing procedures tends to be less effective, although providing a practical option for many countries, where waters may be subject to sewage contamination. Preharvest controls are the most effective means to address microbial and chemical hazards that are introduced *via* the seafood production environment. Monitoring programs vary according to hazard and the circumstances of their introduction. Monitoring approaches include measurements either from the water column directly or in the seafood species affected [102]. The current standards used to monitor the safety of shellfish and the quality of growing waters depend on the levels of *E. coli* or total fecal coliforms [5]. Historically, these standards have succeeded in reducing many types of shellfish-related bacterial outbreaks; however, it has been shown that the bacterial standards are inadequate for estimating the presence of enteric viruses and other chemicals in shellfish and growing waters [51, 189]. For instance, cases of shellfish toxins and many chemicals are monitored by state health agencies and/or those responsible for fish and wildlife on a regular basis (e.g., weekly or biweekly), and harvests and growing areas are placed under temporary closure based on these cell density thresholds until toxin testing in shellfish can be performed. However, in some cases, direct measurement of the hazard is not effective because analytical procedures are too slow or resource intensive, and measurement of indicators is more appropriate. In an effort to provide early warning, predictive models incorporating climate and ocean conditions such as rainfall, water temperature, and salinity are under development for control of hazards, including harmful algal blooms and naturally occurring pathogens such as *Vibrio* spp. [102].

The Food and Agriculture Organization of the United Nations (FAO) is recommending a food-chain approach that encompasses the whole food chain from primary production to final consumption. In such a system, the responsibility for a supply of food that is safe, healthy, and nutritious is shared along the entire food chain by all involved in the production, processing, trade, and consumption of food. Stakeholders include farmers, fishermen, processors, transport operators (raw and processed material), and consumers, as well as governments, obliged to protect public health. In order to protect public health and facilitate international food trade, the member countries of the World Trade Organization (WTO) have signed the sanitary and phytosanitary (SPS) agreement, which emphasizes the need to apply risk analysis as a basis for taking any SPS measure. Despite improvement in several countries, aquaculture governance remains problematic in others. Lack of or limited accountability by the public and private sectors, inadequate law enforcement (where regulations exist), poor planning (causing conflicts over farming sites and leading to disease outbreaks and ecosystem deterioration), and failure to address the negative environmental and public welfare impacts of some aquaculture systems result in a tarnished image and public mistrust of the industry. This is exacerbated by the lack of aquaculture-specific governance frameworks [2]. One of the most important problems faced by countries implementing biosecurity programs is the availability of government personnel to assist or oversee a number of activities that are usually considered governmental responsibilities. In many countries, a solution has been found in terrestrial and aquatic veterinary services through National Veterinary Accreditation Programs and public-private partnerships, in which the government delegates specific responsibilities to well-trained private individuals [6, 190]. For biosecurity plans to meet international standards and national or local regulations, it is wise to include procedures described in the World Organization for Animal Health (WOAH), aquatic code and manual [6, 191], and specifics in existing national or local regulations. The significance of standards set by the OIE and other international organizations, with which the OIE collaborates, is crucial for providing guidance on issues that are important to aquaculture biosecurity. It was recognized that the approach could be applied to any infectious disease, any farmed or managed aquatic species, and be implemented on any individual farm or larger contiguous areas (zones, provinces, states, countries). Furthermore, as most countries agree to adopt OIE standards in the codes and manuals, such approach would also meet most, if not all, governmental regulations [190].

At the fourth OIE Global Conference on Aquatic Animal Health (2019), a Progressive Management Pathway for Aquaculture Biosecurity (PMP-AB) was introduced by the FAO. The PMP-AB endorsed and welcomed by the tenth session of the COFI Sub-Committee on Aquaculture [192] is a ground-breaking initiative that FAO and its partners started in 2018. It is evidence-based and supported by transparent and ongoing review, adaptable to respond to the diversity of aquaculture systems, species, production scope, and objectives, and to environmental and anthropogenic changes that impact aquaculture production [193]. The approach can be applied to manage risks in any aquaculture sector, no matter the species, environment, production system, management strategy, or operation size [2]. It was developed as an extension of the progressive control pathway (PCP) approach, which has been internationally adopted to assist countries in developing systematic frameworks for planning and monitoring risk reduction strategies for the diminution, elimination, and eradication of major livestock and zoonotic diseases. The PMP/AB can guide countries toward achieving sustainable biosecurity in aquaculture and health management systems through risk-based, progressive, and collaborative processes at the regional, national, local sector, and enterprise levels. The PMP-AB consists of four stages that might lead to a sustainable and resilient national aquaculture system: (1) risk assessments, (2) biosecurity system initiated (managed in specific sectors/compartments), (3) biosecurity systems and preparedness enhanced (management system), and (4) sustainable biosecurity and health management systems established (national aquaculture system). Moving from one stage to another should meet a set of minimum requirements and a detailed implementation plan and serve as a template that may provide a degree of consistency between participating countries or regions.

5. Alternative aquaculture systems for safety farmed oysters

In the coming years, aquaculture needs to expand sustainably to fill the gap in global demand for aquatic foods, especially in food-deficit regions, and to support poverty alleviation and food security while generating new or existing sources of income and employment. This requires updating aquaculture governance by promoting improved planning, legal and institutional frameworks, and policies. FAO and partners must focus on the urgent need to develop and transfer innovative technologies and best practices to create efficient, resilient, and sustainable farms.

In the new technological age, remote inspection to ensure product safety has proven to be reliable in delivering the necessary sanitary certificates to operators.

Electronic certification systems can improve traceability throughout the supply chain, reduce delays and costs, reduce food waste by speeding up the process, combat fraudulent practices by introducing electronic authentication methods, and increase trust between trading partners. To improve current practices, Codex Alimentarius is revising its guidelines to expand official certification to include an electronic certificate. In addition, electronic food surveillance reporting portals provide an effective tool for authorities to share real-time information on actions taken when serious risks are identified and help countries respond more quickly and in a more coordinated manner to health threats. In this context, FAO is exploring possible solutions through the Digital Solutions in Support of Improved Official Food Control Services project, which focuses on strengthening national capacity to develop and implement reporting portals, in addition to conducting remote inspections, supporting distance learning on food safety management, and expanding data pools to support the ongoing development of risk categorization frameworks and other risk-based decision-making tools [2].

Another approach is the "Blue Transformation," which is committed by FAO and is a visionary strategy that aims to enhance the role of aquatic food systems in feeding the world's growing population by providing the legal, policy, and technical frameworks required to sustain growth and innovation [2, 194]. It focuses on sustainable aquaculture expansion and intensification, effective management of all fisheries, and upgraded value chains. Blue Transformation proposes a series of actions designed to support resilience in aquatic food systems and ensure fisheries and aquaculture grow sustainably while preserving aquatic ecosystem health, preventing pollution, and protecting biodiversity and social equality. Climate- and environmentally-friendly policies and practices and technological innovations are critical building blocks for the Blue Transformation. Proactive public and private partnerships are needed to improve production, reduce food loss and waste, and increase equitable access to lucrative markets. In addition, aquatic foods need to be included in national food security and nutrition strategies, and initiatives need to be taken to raise consumer awareness of their benefits to improve availability and access.

In addition, WHO promotes safe food-handling practices worldwide and ensures consistency in their application throughout the food chain from farm to table. One of WHO's priorities is to reach people who usually do not have access to food safety training despite the important role these people often play in producing safe food for the community, in which they live [98]. Efforts have been initiated to educate consumers, restaurant proprietors, and physicians about the hazards of eating oysters. In 2001, WHO launched the Five Keys to Safer Food campaign to highlight practices needed to ensure safe food preparation in small grocery businesses and the home. The concept reinforces the One Health approach, which seeks to promote an understanding of the relationships between the health of humans, animals, and the environment and the mechanisms by which noncompliance with good hygiene practices in one sector can affect other sectors. Adopting effective food safety practices in aquaculture and handling will impact overall hygiene and environmental behaviors, improving community health, protecting the environment, and reinforcing sustainable development. The Five Keys to Safer Food poster has been translated into over 90 languages and has been the starting point for numerous national and local food safety training programs. WHO has expanded the Five Keys to Safer Food program to include more groups and sectors involved in the farm-to-table chain. The core messages of the Five Keys to Safer Food are: (1) keep clean, (2) separate raw and cooked, (3) cook thoroughly, (4) keep food at safe temperatures, and (5) use safe water and raw materials.

Without a doubt, one of the strongest recommendations is one of the key messages of the Global Conference on Aquaculture 2020, which argues that "prevention is better than cure." Focusing on prevention is a sign of a maturing industry. Use of clean seed with good husbandry practices and biosecurity strategies in a less stressful and healthier aquatic environment are basic actions. Biosecurity measures implemented proactively and preventatively are much less expensive than reactionary responses to outbreaks, and they should be integrated with aquaculture development by all producing countries. Effective biosecurity, best husbandry practices, good genetics, and quality nutrition are important for producing healthy, nutritious, and resilient farmed organisms [195, 196].

6. Final remarks

Aquaculture has long been an important food source and livelihood for millions worldwide. However, if these products are not handled, stored, and processed correctly, their safety may be affected due to contamination by different agents. Sewage and animal waste contamination of oysters harvesting areas probably represent the most significant contributing factor in human cases of oyster-associated diseases. Also, oysters can cause foodborne diseases with seafood processing through inadequate operatives or systems of hygiene practices. Of all available seafood commodities, live and raw oysters are among the riskiest products consumed by humans, although cooked oysters have also been implicated. Among the seafood, hazards include bacterial and viral pathogens, parasites, marine toxins, heavy metals, and other chemical contaminants from anthropogenic sources, such as pesticides and pharmaceuticals. Outbreaks of oyster and other bivalves-associated infections have been reported for over a century. Most infectious syndromes produce self-limiting gastrointestinal symptoms, but a few can be fatal. In the last decades, the global consumption of shellfish has increased considerably, as well as the reports of outbreaks of infection.

Some hazards that have been introduced preharvest can increase following postharvest handling, whereas others may be effectively mitigated. Additional hazards may be introduced postharvest, during production, or processing, and vary considerably among seafood commodities. Oyster commercialization needs to be careful with biosecurity and disease control, which must be coupled with effective management from aquaculture production to distribution to different sectors. Thus, the application of risk analysis to the aquaculture sector has become very important. The oyster industry has agreed that the most effective way to control risks is through the implementation of programs, manuals, and procedures for good hygiene and sanitation practices, as well as sanitation standard operating procedures. Those are part of the prerequisite programs established as the basis for implementing stricter methodologies whose main objective is to guarantee food safety and quality of novel foods considering addressing the specific implications for consumer protection, public health, and trade. Thus, the application of risk analysis and the implementation of hazard analysis critical control point plans have become very important worldwide and necessary to address proper harvest, storage, and processing procedures. With the adoption of the food-chain approach for food safety, the responsibility for the supply of safe, healthy, and nutritious seafood is shared along the entire food chain from producer to consumer. For this reason, it is imperative to implement and apply safety systems, such as good practices, to prevent or reduce the risks of contamination in food, thus contributing to the maintenance of its quality and safety, providing consumers with sustainable and secure seafood.

Author details

Norma Estrada
Centro de Investigaciones Biológicas del Noroeste, Mexico

*Address all correspondence to: nestrada@cibnor.mx

References

[1] FAO. Food and Agriculture Organization of the United Nations. The State of World Fisheries and Aquaculture, Opportunities and Challenges. Roma: Sofia; 2014. p. 243. Available from: https://www.fao.org/3/i3720e/i3720e.pdf

[2] FAO. The State of World Fisheries and Aquaculture. Towards Blue Transformation. Rome, Italy: Food and Agriculture Organization of the United Nations; 2022. p. 266. Available from: https://www.fao.org/3/cc0461en/cc0461en.pdf

[3] FAO. Food and Agriculture Organization of the United Nations. Directrices para la inspección del pescado basada en los riesgos. Roma: Organización de las Naciones Unidas para la Agricultura y la Alimentación; 2009. p. 99. Available from: https://www.fao.org/3/i0468s/i0468s.pdf

[4] CAC. Prevention and Reduction of Food and Feed Contamination. Rome, Italy: Codex Alimentarius Commission; 2012. p. 180. Available from: https://www.fao.org/3/i2556e/i2556e.pdf

[5] Lees D. Viruses and bivalve shellfish. International Journal of Food Microbiology. 2000;**59**(1-2):81-116. DOI: 10.1016/s0168-1605(00)00248-8

[6] OIE. The World Organisation for Animal Health, the Office International Des Epizooties. Aquatic Animal Health Code. Paris, France: World Organization for Animal Health (OIE); 2019. p. 324

[7] Cong W, Zhang NZ, Hou JL, Wang XC, Ma JG, Zhu XQ, et al. First detection and genetic characterization of *toxoplasma gondii* in market-sold oysters in China. Infection, Genetics and Evolution. 2017;**54**:276-278. DOI: 10.1016/j.meegid.2017.07.014

[8] Graczyk TK, Girouard AS, Tamang L, Nappier SP, Schwab KJ. Recovery, bioaccumulation, and inactivation of human waterborne pathogens by the Chesapeake Bay nonnative oyster, *Crassostrea ariakensis*. Applied and Environmental Microbiology. 2006;**72**(5):3390-3395. DOI: 10.1128/AEM.72.5.3390-3395.2006

[9] Marquis ND, Bishop TJ, Record NR, Countway PD, Fernández Robledo JA. Molecular epizootiology of *toxoplasma gondii* and *Cryptosporidium parvum* in the eastern oyster (*Crassostrea virginica*) from Maine (USA). Pathogens. 2019;**8**(3):125. DOI: 10.3390/pathogens8030125

[10] Patanasatienkul T, Greenwood SJ, McClure JT, Davidson J, Gardner I, Sanchez J. Bayesian risk assessment model of human cryptosporidiosis cases following consumption of raw eastern oysters (*Crassostrea virginica*) contaminated with *cryptosporidium* oocysts in the Hillsborough River system in Prince Edward Island, Canada. Food Waterborne Parasitol. 2020;**19**:e00079. DOI: 10.1016/j.fawpar.2020.e00079

[11] Schets FM, van den Berg HH, Engels GB, Lodder WJ, de Roda Husman AM. *Cryptosporidium* and *Giardia* in commercial and non-commercial oysters (*Crassostrea gigas*) and water from the Oosterschelde, The Netherlands. International Journal of Food Microbiology. 2007;**113**(2):189-194. DOI: 10.1016/j.ijfoodmicro.2006.06.031

[12] Sutthikornchai C, Popruk S, Chumpolbanchorn K, Sukhumavasi W, Sukthana Y. Oyster is an effective

transmission vehicle for *Cryptosporidium* infection in human. Asian Pacific Journal of Tropical Medicine. 2016;**9**(6):562-566. DOI: 10.1016/j.apjtm.2016.04.018

[13] Lindsay DS, Collins MV, Mitchell SM, Wetch CN, Rosypal AC, Flick GJ, et al. Survival of *toxoplasma gondii* oocysts in eastern oysters (*Crassostrea virginica*). The Journal of Parasitology. 2004;**90**(5):1054-1057. DOI: 10.1645/GE-296R

[14] Silva CM, Silva ALP, Watanabe KFC, Chaves Bezerra NP, Bezerra DC, Gomes HM, et al. First report of detection of *Toxoplasma gondii* DNA in oysters (*Crassostrea* sp.) in the state of Maranhão. Revista Brasileira de Parasitologia Veterinária. 2020;**29**(3):e003720. DOI: 10.1590/s1984-29612020050

[15] Elsheikha HM. Congenital toxoplasmosis: Priorities for further health promotion action. Public Health. 2008;**122**(4):335-353. DOI: 10.1016/j.puhe.2007.08.009

[16] Jones JL, Dargelas V, Roberts J, Press C, Remington JS, Montoya JG. Risk factors for *toxoplasma gondii* infection in the United States. Clinical Infectious Diseases. 2009;**49**(6):878-884. DOI: 10.1086/605433

[17] Cremonte F. Enfermedades de moluscos bivalvos de interés comercial causadas por metazoos. In: Figueras A, Novoa G, editors. Enfermedades de moluscos Bivalvos de interés en acuicultura. Madrid, España: Publicaciones Científicas y Tecnológicas de la Fundación Observatorio Español de Acuicultura; 2011. p. 543

[18] Lauckner G. Diseases of Mollusca: Bivalvia. In: Kinne O, editor. Diseases of Marine Animals, Biologische Anstalt Helgoland. Vol. II. Chichester: Wiley; 1983. pp. 477-961

[19] Lee SH, Chai JY. A review of *Gymnophalloides seoi* (digenea: Gymnophallidae) and human infections in the Republic of Korea. The Korean Journal of Parasitology. 2001;**39**(2):85-118. DOI: 10.3347/kjp.2001.39.2.85

[20] Grano-Maldonado MI, Rubalcava-Ramirez F, Rodriguez-Santiago A, Garcia-Vargas F, Medina-Jasso A, Nieves-Soto M. First record of *Stephanostomum* Sp. Looss, 1899 (digenea: Acanthocolpidae) Metacercariae parasitising the pleasure oyster *Crassostrea corteziensis* (Hertlein) from the Mexican Pacific coast. Helminthologia. 2019;**56**(3):211-218. DOI: 10.2478/helm-2019-0019

[21] Tejeda-Arenas D, Medina-Jasso A, Nieves-Soto M, Grano-Maldonado MI. Parásitos metazoarios y otros epibiontes en el ostión del placer *Crassostrea corteziensis* (hertlein, 1951) en dos zonas costeras del Pacífico mexicano. The Biologist. 2021;**19**(1):65-78. DOI: 10.24039/rtb2021191883

[22] Ko RC. Experimental infection of mammals with larval *Echinocephalus sinensis* (Nematoda: Gnathostomatidae) from oysters (*Crassostrea gigas*). Canadian Journal of Zoology. 1976;**54**(4):597-609. DOI: 10.1139/z76-070

[23] Cheng TC. *Echinocephalus crassostreai* sp. nov., a larval nematode from the oyster *Crassostrea gigas* in the orient. Journal of Invertebrate Pathology. 1975;**26**(1):81-90. DOI: 10.1016/0022-2011(75)90172-x

[24] Bower SM, McGladdery SE, Price IM. Synopsis of infectious diseases and parasites of commercially exploited shellfish. Annual Review of Fish Diseases. 1994;**4**:1-199. DOI: 10.1016/0959-8030(94)90028-0

[25] EFSA. Scientific opinion on an update on the present knowledge on the

occurrence and control of foodborne viruses. EFSA Journal. 2011;**9**(7):2190. DOI: 10.2903/j.efsa.2011.2190

[26] Bellou M, Kokkinos P, Vantarakis A. Shellfish-borne viral outbreaks: A systematic review. Food and Environmental Virology. 2013;**5**(1):13-23. DOI: 10.1007/s12560-012-9097-6

[27] Iritani N, Kaida A, Abe N, Kubo H, Sekiguchi J, Yamamoto SP, et al. Detection and genetic characterization of human enteric viruses in oyster-associated gastroenteritis outbreaks between 2001 and 2012 in Osaka City, Japan. Journal of Medical Virology. 2014;**86**(12):2019-2025. DOI: 10.1002/jmv.23883

[28] Burkhardt W 3rd, Calci KR. Selective accumulation may account for shellfish-associated viral illness. Applied and Environmental Microbiology. 2000;**66**(4):1375-1378. DOI: 10.1128/AEM.66.4.1375-1378.2000

[29] Alfano-Sobsey E, Sweat D, Hall A, Breedlove F, Rodriguez R, Greene S, et al. Norovirus outbreak associated with undercooked oysters and secondary household transmission. Epidemiology and Infection. 2012;**140**(2):276-282. DOI: 10.1017/S0950268811000665

[30] Cheng PK, Wong DK, Chung TW, Lim WW. Norovirus contamination found in oysters worldwide. Journal of Medical Virology. 2005;**76**(4):593-597. DOI: 10.1002/jmv.20402

[31] Le Guyader FS, Bon F, DeMedici D, Parnaudeau S, Bertone A, Crudeli S, et al. Detection of multiple noroviruses associated with an international gastroenteritis outbreak linked to oyster consumption. Journal of Clinical Microbiology. 2006;**44**(11):3878-3882. DOI: 10.1128/JCM.01327-06

[32] Le Guyader FS, Atmar RL, Le Pendu J. Transmission of viruses through shellfish: When specific ligands come into play. Current Opinion in Virology. 2012;**2**(1):103-110. DOI: 10.1016/j.coviro.2011.10.029

[33] Nagarajan V, Chen JS, Hsu GJ, Chen HP, Chao HC, Huang SW, et al. Surveillance of adenovirus and norovirus contaminants in the water and shellfish of major oyster breeding farms and fishing ports in Taiwan. Pathogens. 2022;**11**(3):316. DOI: 10.3390/pathogens11030316

[34] Boxman IL, Tilburg JJ, Te Loeke NA, Vennema H, Jonker K, de Boer E, et al. Detection of noroviruses in shellfish in the Netherlands. International Journal of Food Microbiology. 2006;**108**(3):391-396. DOI: 10.1016/j.ijfoodmicro.2006.01.002

[35] Costantini V, Loisy F, Joens L, Le Guyader FS, Saif LJ. Human and animal enteric caliciviruses in oysters from different coastal regions of the United States. Applied and Environmental Microbiology. 2006;**72**(3):1800-1809. DOI: 10.1128/AEM.72.3.1800-1809.2006

[36] Gentry J, Vinjé J, Guadagnoli D, Lipp EK. Norovirus distribution within an estuarine environment. Applied and Environmental Microbiology. 2009;**75**(17):5474-5480. DOI: 10.1128/AEM.00111-09

[37] Rigotto C, Victoria M, Moresco V, Kolesnikovas CK, Corrêa AA, Souza DS, et al. Assessment of adenovirus, hepatitis A virus and rotavirus presence in environmental samples in Florianopolis, South Brazil. Journal of Applied Microbiology. 2010;**109**(6):1979-1987. DOI: 10.1111/j.1365-2672.2010.04827.x

[38] Baker K, Morris J, McCarthy N, Saldana L, Lowther J, Collinson A, et al. An outbreak of norovirus infection

linked to oyster consumption at a UK restaurant, February 2010. Journal of Public Health (Oxford, England). 2011;**33**(2):205-211. DOI: 10.1093/pubmed/fdq089

[39] Westrell T, Dusch V, Ethelberg S, Harris J, Hjertqvist M, Jourdan-da Silva N, et al. Norovirus outbreaks linked to oyster consumption in the United Kingdom, Norway, France, Sweden and Denmark, 2010. Euro Surveillance. 2010;**15**(12):19524

[40] Ng TL, Chan PP, Phua TH, Loh JP, Yip R, Wong C, et al. Oyster-associated outbreaks of norovirus gastroenteritis in Singapore. The Journal of Infection. 2005;**51**(5):413-418. DOI: 10.1016/j.jinf.2004.11.003

[41] Webby RJ, Carville KS, Kirk MD, Greening G, Ratcliff RM, Crerar SK, et al. Internationally distributed frozen oyster meat causing multiple outbreaks of norovirus infection in Australia. Clinical Infectious Diseases. 2007;**44**(8):1026-1031. DOI: 10.1086/512807

[42] Berg DE, Kohn MA, Farley TA, McFarland LM. Multi-state outbreaks of acute gastroenteritis traced to fecal-contaminated oysters harvested in Louisiana. The Journal of Infectious Diseases. 2000;**181**(Suppl. 2):S381-S386. DOI: 10.1086/315581

[43] Pu J, Miura T, Kazama S, Konta Y, Azraini ND, Ito E, et al. Weekly variations in norovirus genogroup II genotypes in Japanese oysters. International Journal of Food Microbiology. 2018;**284**:48-55. DOI: 10.1016/j.ijfoodmicro.2018.06.027

[44] Nappier SP, Graczyk TK, Schwab KJ. Bioaccumulation, retention, and depuration of enteric viruses by *Crassostrea virginica* and *Crassostrea ariakensis* oysters. Applied and Environmental Microbiology. 2008;**74**(22):6825-6831. DOI: 10.1128/AEM.01000-08

[45] Wall R, Dymond N, Bell A, Thornley C, Buik H, Cumming D, et al. Two New Zealand outbreaks of norovirus gastroenteritis linked to commercially farmed oysters. The New Zealand Medical Journal. 2011;**124**(1347):63-71

[46] Gallimore CI, Cheesbrough JS, Lamden K, Bingham C, Gray JJ. Multiple norovirus genotypes characterized from an oyster-associated outbreak of gastroenteritis. International Journal of Food Microbiology. 2005;**103**(3):323-330. DOI: 10.1016/j.ijfoodmicro.2005.02.003

[47] Bofill-Mas S, Albinana-Gimenez N, Clemente-Casares P, Hundesa A, Rodriguez-Manzano J, Allard A, et al. Quantification and stability of human adenoviruses and polyomavirus JCPyV in wastewater matrices. Applied and Environmental Microbiology. 2006;**72**(12):7894-7896. DOI: 10.1128/AEM.00965-06

[48] Ito E, Pu J, Miura T, Kazama S, Nishiyama M, Ito H, et al. Weekly variation of rotavirus A concentrations in sewage and oysters in Japan, 2014-2016. Pathogens. 2019;**8**(3):89. DOI: 10.3390/pathogens8030089

[49] Kittigul L, Panjangampatthana A, Rupprom K, Pombubpa K. Genetic diversity of rotavirus strains circulating in environmental water and bivalve shellfish in Thailand. International Journal of Environmental Research and Public Health. 2014;**11**(2):1299-1311. DOI: 10.3390/ijerph110201299

[50] Kuo XX, Wu QP, Wang DP, Zhang JM. Simultaneous detection of norovirus and rotavirus in oysters by multiplex RT–PCR. Food Control.

2008;**19**:722-726. DOI: 10.1016/j.foodcont.2007.07.001

[51] Le Guyader FS, Le Saux JC, Ambert-Balay K, Krol J, Serais O, Parnaudeau S, et al. Aichi virus, norovirus, astrovirus, enterovirus, and rotavirus involved in clinical cases from a French oyster-related gastroenteritis outbreak. Journal of Clinical Microbiology. 2008;**46**(12):4011-4017. DOI: 10.1128/JCM.01044-08

[52] Mozgovoj M, Miño S, Barbieri ES, Tort FL, Victoria-Montero M, Frydman C, et al. GII.4 human norovirus and G8P[1] bovine-like rotavirus in oysters (*Crassostrea gigas*) from Argentina. International Journal of Food Microbiology. 2022;**365**:109553. DOI: 10.1016/j.ijfoodmicro.2022.109553

[53] Quiroz-Santiago C, Vázquez-Salinas C, Natividad-Bonifacio I, Barrón-Romero BL, Quiñones-Ramírez EI. Rotavirus G2P[4] detection in fresh vegetables and oysters in Mexico City. Journal of Food Protection. 2014;**77**(11):1953-1959. DOI: 10.4315/0362-028X.JFP-13-426

[54] Lorestani N, Moradi A, Teimoori A, Masodi M, Khanizadeh S, Hassanpour M, et al. Molecular and serologic characterization of rotavirus from children with acute gastroenteritis in northern Iran, Gorgan. BMC Gastroenterology. 2019;**19**(1):100. DOI: 10.1186/s12876-019-1025-x

[55] Tate JE, Burton AH, Boschi-Pinto C, Steele AD, Duque J, Parashar UD, et al. 2008 estimate of worldwide rotavirus-associated mortality in children younger than 5 years before the introduction of universal rotavirus vaccination programmes: A systematic review and meta-analysis. The Lancet Infectious Diseases. 2012;**12**(2):136-141. DOI: 10.1016/S1473-3099(11)70253-5

[56] Bagordo F, Grassi T, Idolo A, Serio F, Gabutti G, De Donno A. Rotavirus occurrence in shellfish with low levels of *E. coli*. Food and Environmental Virology. 2013;**5**(3):169-175. DOI: 10.1007/s12560-013-9119-z

[57] Sánchez G, Pintó RM, Vanaclocha H, Bosch A. Molecular characterization of hepatitis a virus isolates from a transcontinental shellfish-borne outbreak. Journal of Clinical Microbiology. 2002;**40**(11):4148-4155. DOI: 10.1128/JCM.40.11.4148-4155.2002

[58] Fusco G, Aprea G, Galiero G, Guarino A, Viscardi M. *Escherichia coli*, *Salmonella* spp., Hepatitis A virus and norovirus in bivalve molluscs in Southern Italy. Veterinaria Italiana. 2013;**49**(1):55-58

[59] Fusco G, Anastasio A, Kingsley DH, Amoroso MG, Pepe T, Fratamico PM, et al. Detection of hepatitis A virus and other enteric viruses in shellfish collected in the Gulf of Naples, Italy. International Journal of Environmental Research and Public Health. 2019;**16**(14):2588. DOI: 10.3390/ijerph16142588

[60] Roos B. Hepatitepidemi, spridd genom ostron [Hepatitis epidemic transmitted by oysters]. Svenska Läkartidningen. 1956;**53**(16):989-1003

[61] Murphy AM, Grohmann GS, Christopher PJ, Lopez WA, Davey GR, Millsom RH. An Australia-wide outbreak of gastroenteritis from oysters caused by Norwalk virus. The Medical Journal of Australia. 1979;**2**(7):329-333. DOI: 10.5694/j.1326-5377.1979.tb104133.x

[62] Morse DL, Guzewich JJ, Hanrahan JP, Stricof R, Shayegani M, Deibel R, et al. Widespread outbreaks of clam- and oyster-associated gastroenteritis. Role of Norwalk virus. The New England Journal of Medicine. 1986;**314**(11):678-681. DOI: 10.1056/NEJM198603133141103

[63] Otsu R. Outbreaks of gastroenteritis caused by SRSVs from 1987 to 1992 in Kyushu, Japan: Four outbreaks associated with oyster consumption. European Journal of Epidemiology. 1999;**15**(2):175-180. DOI: 10.1023/a:1007543924543

[64] Conaty S, Bird P, Bell G, Kraa E, Grohmann G, McAnulty JM. Hepatitis A in New South Wales, Australia from consumption of oysters: The first reported outbreak. Epidemiology and Infection. 2000;**124**(1):121-130. DOI: 10.1017/s0950268899003386

[65] Kingsley DH, Richards GP. Persistence of hepatitis A virus in oysters. Journal of Food Protection. 2003;**66**(2):331-334. DOI: 10.4315/0362-028x-66.2.331

[66] Guillois-Bécel Y, Couturier E, Le SauxJC, Roque-AfonsoAM, LeGuyaderFS, Le Goas A, et al. An oyster-associated hepatitis A outbreak in France in 2007. Euro Surveillance. 2009;**14**(10):19144

[67] Bialek SR, George PA, Xia GL, Glatzer MB, Motes ML, Veazey JE, et al. Use of molecular epidemiology to confirm a multistate outbreak of hepatitis A caused by consumption of oysters. Clinical Infectious Diseases. 2007;**44**(6):838-840. DOI: 10.1086/511874

[68] Shieh YC, Khudyakov YE, Xia G, Ganova-Raeva LM, Khambaty FM, Woods JW, et al. Molecular confirmation of oysters as the vector for hepatitis A in a 2005 multistate outbreak. Journal of Food Protection. 2007;**70**(1):145-150. DOI: 10.4315/0362-028x-70.1.145

[69] CAC. Guidelines on the Application of General Principles of Food Hygiene to the Control of Viruses in Food (CAC/GL 79—2012). Rome, Italy: Codex Alimentarius Commission; 2012. p. 13. Available from: https://www.fao.org/fao-who-codexalimentarius/codex-texts/guidelines/en/

[70] Purcell RH, Emerson SU. Hepatitis E virus infection. Lancet. 2000;**355**(9203):578. DOI: 10.1016/S0140-6736(05)73231-1

[71] Song YJ, Jeong HJ, Kim YJ, Lee SW, Lee JB, Park SY, et al. Analysis of complete genome sequences of swine hepatitis E virus and possible risk factors for transmission of HEV to humans in Korea. Journal of Medical Virology. 2010;**82**(4):583-591. DOI: 10.1002/jmv.21730

[72] Grodzki M, Schaeffer J, Piquet JC, Le Saux JC, Chevé J, Ollivier J, et al. Bioaccumulation efficiency, tissue distribution, and environmental occurrence of hepatitis E virus in bivalve shellfish from France. Applied and Environmental Microbiology. 2014;**80**(14):4269-4276. DOI: 10.1128/AEM.00978-14

[73] Cazorla C, Guigon A, Noel M, Quilici ML, Lacassin F. Fatal Vibrio vulnificus infection associated with eating raw oysters, New Caledonia. Emerging Infectious Diseases. 2011;**17**(1):136-137. DOI: 10.3201/eid1701.100603

[74] Horseman MA, Surani S. A comprehensive review of *Vibrio vulnificus*: An important cause of severe sepsis and skin and soft-tissue infection. International Journal of Infectious Diseases. 2011;**15**(3):e157-e166. DOI: 10.1016/j.ijid.2010.11.003

[75] Jones MK, Oliver JD. *Vibrio vulnificus*: Disease and pathogenesis. Infection and Immunity. 2009;**77**(5):1723-1733. DOI: 10.1128/IAI.01046-08

[76] Potasman I, Paz A, Odeh M. Infectious outbreaks associated with

bivalve shellfish consumption: A worldwide perspective. Clinical Infectious Diseases. 2002;**35**(8):921-928. DOI: 10.1086/342330

[77] Morris JG Jr. Cholera and other types of vibriosis: A story of human pandemics and oysters on the half shell. Clinical Infectious Diseases. 2003;**37**(2):272-280. DOI: 10.1086/375600

[78] Deepanjali A, Kumar HS, Karunasagar I, Karunasagar I. Seasonal variation in abundance of total and pathogenic *Vibrio parahaemolyticus* bacteria in oysters along the southwest coast of India. Applied and Environmental Microbiology. 2005;**71**(7):3575-3580. DOI: 10.1128/AEM.71.7.3575-3580.2005

[79] Gutierrez West CK, Klein SL, Lovell CR. High frequency of virulence factor genes tdh, trh, and tlh in Vibrio parahaemolyticus strains isolated from a pristine estuary. Applied and Environmental Microbiology. 2013;**79**(7):2247-2252. DOI: 10.1128/AEM.03792-12

[80] McLaughlin JB, DePaola A, Bopp CA, Martinek KA, Napolilli NP, Allison CG, et al. Outbreak of *Vibrio parahaemolyticus* gastroenteritis associated with Alaskan oysters. The New England Journal of Medicine. 2005;**353**(14):1463-1470. DOI: 10.1056/NEJMoa051594

[81] Daniels NA, Ray B, Easton A, Marano N, Kahn E, McShan AL 2nd, et al. Emergence of a new *Vibrio parahaemolyticus* serotype in raw oysters: A prevention quandary. Journal of the American Medical Association. 2000;**284**(12):1541-1545. DOI: 10.1001/jama.284.12.1541

[82] Davis BR, Fanning GR, Madden JM, Steigerwalt AG, Bradford HB Jr, Smith HL Jr, et al. Characterization of biochemically atypical *vibrio cholerae* strains and designation of a new pathogenic species, *Vibrio mimicus*. Journal of Clinical Microbiology. 1981;**14**(6):631-639. DOI: 10.1128/jcm.14.6.631-639.1981

[83] Abbott SL, Janda JM. Severe gastroenteritis associated with *vibrio hollisae* infection: Report of two cases and review. Clinical Infectious Diseases. 1994;**18**(3):310-312. DOI: 10.1093/clinids/18.3.310

[84] Iwamoto M, Ayers T, Mahon BE, Swerdlow DL. Epidemiology of seafood-associated infections in the United States. Clinical Microbiology Reviews. 2010;**2**:399-411. DOI: 10.1128/CMR.00059-09

[85] Brands DA, Inman AE, Gerba CP, Maré CJ, Billington SJ, Saif LA, et al. Prevalence of Salmonella spp. in oysters in the United States. Applied and Environmental Microbiology. 2005;**71**(2):893-897. DOI: 10.1128/AEM.71.2.893-897.2005

[86] Heinitz ML, Ruble RD, Wagner DE, Tatini SR. Incidence of salmonella in fish and seafood. Journal of Food Protection. 2000;**63**(5):579-592. DOI: 10.4315/0362-028x-63.5.579

[87] Morrison CM, Armstrong AE, Evans S, Mild RM, Langdon CJ, Joens LA. Survival of *salmonella* Newport in oysters. International Journal of Food Microbiology. 2011;**148**(2):93-98. DOI: 10.1016/j.ijfoodmicro.2011.05.006

[88] Teunis P, Havelaar A, Vliegenthart J, Roessink G. Risk assessment of *Campylobacter* species in shellfish: Identifying the unknown. Water Science and Technology. 1997;**35**(11-12):29-34. DOI: 10.1016/S0273-1223(97)00230-8

[89] Jurinović L, Ječmenica B, Džafić N, Brlek Gorski D, Šimpraga B, Krstulović F, et al. First data on *campylobacter* spp. presence in shellfish in Croatia. Pathogens. 2022;**11**(8):943. DOI: 10.3390/pathogens11080943

[90] Van Doorn LJ, Verschuuren-Van Haperen A, Van Belkum A, Endtz HP, Vliegenthart JS, Vandamme P, et al. Rapid identification of diverse *Campylobacter lari* strains isolated from mussels and oysters using a reverse hybridization line probe assay. Journal of Applied Microbiology. 1998;**84**(4):545-550. DOI: 10.1046/j.1365-2672.1998.00378.x

[91] Silva J, Leite D, Fernandes M, Mena C, Gibbs PA, Teixeira P. Campylobacter spp. as a foodborne pathogen: A review. Frontiers in Microbiology. 27 Sep 2011;**2**:200. DOI: 10.3389/fmicb.2011.00200

[92] Sharp SE. Campylobacter coli prosthetic hip infection associated with ingestion of contaminated oysters. Journal of Clinical Microbiology. Oct 2009;**47**(10):3370-3371. DOI: 10.1128/JCM.00417-09

[93] Reeve G, Martin DL, Pappas J, Thompson RE, Greene KD. An outbreak of shigellosis associated with the consumption of raw oysters. The New England Journal of Medicine. 1989;**321**(4):224-227. DOI: 10.1056/NEJM198907273210404

[94] Terajima J, Tamura K, Hirose K, Izumiya H, Miyahara M, Konuma H, et al. A multi-prefectural outbreak of *shigella sonnei* infections associated with eating oysters in Japan. Microbiology and Immunology. 2004;**48**(1):49-52. DOI: 10.1111/j.1348-0421.2004.tb03486.x

[95] Montazeri N, Liu D, Janes ME. Occurrence of toxigenic *Clostridium difficile* in Louisiana oysters (*Crassostrea virginica*) and environmental waters. Fns. 2015;**6**(11):1065-1070. DOI: 10.4236/fns.2015.611110

[96] Kuijper EJ, Coignard B, Tüll P; ESCMID Study Group for Clostridium difficile; EU Member States; European Centre for Disease Prevention and Control. Emergence of clostridium difficile-associated disease in North America and Europe. Clinical Microbiology and Infection. Oct 2006;**12**(Suppl 6):2-18. DOI: 10.1111/j.1469-0691.2006.01580.x

[97] Costa RA. *Escherichia coli* in seafood: A brief overview. Advances in Bioscience and Biotechnology. 2013;**4**:450-454. DOI: 10.4236/abb.2013.43A060

[98] WHO. Cinco claves para una mayor inocuidad de los productos de acuicultura con objeto de proteger la salud pública. Geneva, Switzerland: World Health Organization; 2016. p. 40. Available from: https://apps.who.int/iris/bitstream/handle/10665/251672/9789243510316-spa.pdf?sequence=1&isAllowed=y

[99] FAO, Assessment and management of seafood safety and quality. Current practices and emerging issues, Food and Agriculture Organization of the United NationsRome, Italy. 2014; pp. 465. Available from: https://www.fao.org/3/i3215e/i3215e.pdf

[100] Pimentel-Domínguez CI, Flores-Salazar EC. Buenas Prácticas de Manejo para Productos Acuícolas y Pesqueros en Centros de Acopio. Universidad Nacional Autónoma de México. Facultad de Medicina Veterinaria y Zootecnia; 2021. p. 127

[101] Rasmussen SA, Andersen AJ, Andersen NG, Nielsen KF, Hansen PJ, Larsen TO. Chemical diversity, origin,

and analysis of phycotoxins. Journal of Natural Products. 2016;**79**(3):662-673. DOI: 10.1021/acs.jnatprod.5b01066

[102] DePaola A, Toyofuku H. Safety of food and beverages: Seafood. In: Motarjemi J, editor. Encyclopedia of Food Safety. Elsevier Science & Technology; 2014. pp. 260-267. DOI: 10.1016/b978-0-12-378612-8.00281-x

[103] Richter I, Fidler AE. Detection of marine microalgal biotoxins using bioassays based on functional expression of tunicate xenobiotic receptors in yeast. Toxicon. 2015;**95**:13-22. DOI: 10.1016/j.toxicon.2014.12.011

[104] Turner AD, Goya AB. Occurrence and profiles of lipophilic toxins in shellfish harvested from Argentina. Toxicon. 2015;**102**:32-42. DOI: 10.1016/j.toxicon.2015.05.010

[105] Karlson B, Andersen P, Arneborg L, Cembella A, Eikrem W, John U, et al. Harmful algal blooms and their effects in coastal seas of northern Europe. Harmful Algae. 2021;**102**:101989. DOI: 10.1016/j.hal.2021.101989

[106] Berti M, Milandri A. In: Schirone M, Visciano P, editors. Le biotossine marine in Igiene Degli Alimenti. Bologna: Edagricole; 2014. pp. 163-198

[107] Trainer VL, Moore L, Bill BD, Adams NG, Harrington N, Borchert J, et al. Diarrhetic shellfish toxins and other lipophilic toxins of human health concern in Washington state. Marine Drugs. 2013;**11**(6):1815-1835. DOI: 10.3390/md11061815

[108] Fujiki H, Suganuma M, Suguri H, Yoshizawa S, Takagi K, Uda N, et al. Diarrhetic shellfish toxin, dinophysistoxin-1, is a potent tumor promoter on mouse skin. Japanese Journal of Cancer Research. 1988;**79**(10):1089-1093. DOI: 10.1111/j.1349-7006.1988.tb01531.x

[109] Suganuma M, Fujiki H, Suguri H, Yoshizawa S, Hirota M, Nakayasu M, et al. Okadaic acid: An additional non-phorbol-12-tetradecanoate-13-acetate-type tumor promoter. Proceedings of the National Academy of Sciences of the United States of America. 1988;**85**(6):1768-1771. DOI: 10.1073/pnas.85.6.1768

[110] Abal P, Louzao MC, Fraga M, Vilariño N, Ferreiro S, Vieytes MR, et al. Absorption and effect of Azaspiracid-1 over the human intestinal barrier. Cellular Physiology and Biochemistry. 2017;**43**(1):136-146. DOI: 10.1159/000480331

[111] Tillmann U, Salas R, Gottschling M, Krock B, O'Driscoll D, Elbrächter M, et al. (Dinophyceae) reveals a close relationship between *Amphidoma* and *Azadinium*. Protist. 2012;**163**(5):701-719. DOI: 10.1016/j.protis.2011.10.005

[112] Hess P, Mccarron P, Krock B, Miles CO. Azaspiracids: Chemistry, biosynthesis, metabolism, and detection. In: Botana LM, editor. seafood and Freshwater Toxins. London, UK: CRC Press; 2014. pp. 799-822

[113] Yasumoto T, Oshima Y, Yamaguchi M. Occurrence of a new type of shellfish poisoning in Japan and chemical properties of the toxin. In: Taylor D, Seliger HH, editors. Toxic Dinoflagellate Blooms. Amsterdam: Elsevier; 1979. pp. 495-502

[114] Yasumoto T, Oshima Y, Sugawara W, Fukuyo Y, Oguri H, Igarishi T, et al. Identification of Dinophysis fortii as the causative organism of diarrhetic shellfish posioning. Bulletin of the Japanese Society of Scientific Fisheries. 1980;**46**:1405-1411. DOI: 10.2331/suisan.46.1405

[115] Deeds JR, Wiles K, Heideman GB 6th, White KD, Abraham A. First U.S.

report of shellfish harvesting closures due to confirmed okadaic acid in Texas gulf coast oysters. Toxicon. 2010;**55**(6):1138-1146. DOI: 10.1016/j.toxicon.2010.01.003

[116] Farrell H, Ajani P, Murray S, Baker P, Webster G, Brett S, et al. Diarrhetic shellfish toxin monitoring in commercial wild harvest bivalve shellfish in New South Wales, Australia. Toxins (Basel). 2018;**10**(11):446. DOI: 10.3390/toxins10110446

[117] Lloyd JK, Duchin JS, Borchert J, Quintana HF, Robertson A. Diarrhetic shellfish poisoning, Washington, USA, 2011. Emerging Infectious Diseases. 2013;**19**(8):1314-1316. DOI: 10.3201/eid1908.121824

[118] Pitcher GC, Krock B, Cembella AD. Accumulation of diarrhetic shellfish poisoning toxins in the oyster *Crassostrea gigas* and the mussel *Choromytilus meridionalisin* the southern Benguela ecosystem. African Journal of Marine Science. 2011;**33**(2):273-281. DOI: 10.2989/1814232x.2011.600372

[119] Zabaglo K, Chrapusta E, Bober B, Kaminski A, Adamski M, Bialczyk J. Environmental roles and biological activity of domoic acid: A review. Algal Research. 2016;**13**:94-101. DOI: 10.1016/j.algal.2015.11.020

[120] Costa LG, Giordano G, Faustman EM. Domoic acid as a developmental neurotoxin. Neurotoxicology. 2010;**31**(5):409-423. DOI: 10.1016/j.neuro.2010.05.003

[121] Jeffery B, Barlow T, Moizer K, Paul S, Boyle C. Amnesic shellfish poison. Food and Chemical Toxicology. 2004;**42**(4):545-557. DOI: 10.1016/j.fct.2003.11.010

[122] Johannessen JN. Stability of domoic acid in saline dosing solutions. Journal of AOAC International. 2000;**83**(2):411-412

[123] Quilliam MA, Sim PG, McCulloch AW, McInnes AG. High-performance liquid chromatography of domoic acid, a marine neurotoxin, with application to shellfish and plankton. International Journal of Environmental Analytical Chemistry. 1989;**36**:139-154. DOI: 10.1080/03067318908026867

[124] James KJ, Gillman M, Amandi MF, López-Rivera A, Puente PF, Lehane M, et al. Amnesic shellfish poisoning toxins in bivalve molluscs in Ireland. Toxicon. 2005;**46**(8):852-858. DOI: 10.1016/j.toxicon.2005.02.009

[125] Duagbjerg N. Phylogeny of some of the major genera of dinoflagellates based on ultrastructure and partial LSU rDNA sequence data, including the erection of three new genera of unarmored dinoflagellates. Phycologia. 2001;**39**:302-317. DOI: 10.2216/i0031-8884-39-4-302.1

[126] Morris PD, Campbell DS, Taylor TJ, Freeman JI. Clinical and epidemiological features of neurotoxic shellfish poisoning in North Carolina. American Journal of Public Health. 1991;**81**(4):471-474. DOI: 10.2105/ajph.81.4.471

[127] Watkins SM, Reich A, Fleming LE, Hammond R. Neurotoxic shellfish poisoning. Marine Drugs. 2008;**6**(3):431-455. DOI: 10.3390/md20080021

[128] Sobel J, Painter J. Illnesses caused by marine toxins. Clinical Infectious Diseases. 2005;**41**(9):1290-1296. DOI: 10.1086/496926

[129] Tester PA. An expatriate red tide bloom: Transport, distribution and persistence. Limnology and Oceanography. 1991;**36**:1053-1061. DOI: 10.4319/lo.1991.36.5.1053

[130] Band-Schmidt CJ, Durán-Riveroll LM, Bustillos-Guzmán JJ, Leyva-Valencia I, López-Cortés DJ,

Núñez-Vázquez EJ, et al. Paralytic toxin producing dinoflagellates in Latin America: Ecology and physiology. Frontiers in Marine Science. 2019;**6**:42. DOI: 10.3389/fmars.2019.00042

[131] Kao CY. Paralytic shellfish poisoning. In: Falconer IR, editor. Algal Toxins in Seafood and Drinking Water. London: Academic Press; 1993. pp. 75-86

[132] Mahmood NA, Carmichael WW. Paralytic shellfish poisons produced by the freshwater cyanobacterium *Aphanizomenon flos-aquae* NH-5. Toxicon. 1986;**24**(2):175-186. DOI: 10.1016/0041-0101(86)90120-0

[133] Rodrigue DC, Etzel RA, Hall S, de Porras E, Velasquez OH, Tauxe RV, et al. Lethal paralytic shellfish poisoning in Guatemala. The American Journal of Tropical Medicine and Hygiene. 1990;**42**(3):267-271. DOI: 10.4269/ajtmh.1990.42.267

[134] Wang DZ. Neurotoxins from marine dinoflagellates: A brief review. Marine Drugs. 2008;**6**(2):349-371. DOI: 10.3390/md20080016

[135] Azanza RV, Taylor FJ. Are *Pyrodinium* blooms in the southeast Asian region recurring and spreading? A view at the end of the millennium. Ambio. 2001;**30**(6):356-364

[136] Van Dolah FM. Marine algal toxins: Origins, health effects, and their increased occurrence. Environmental Health Perspectives. 2000;**108**(Suppl. 1):133-141. DOI: 10.1289/ehp.00108s1133

[137] Vázquez-Boucard C, Anguiano-V ega G, Mercier L, Rojas del Castillo E. Pesticide residues, heavy metals, and DNA damage in sentinel oysters Crassostrea gigas from Sinaloa and Sonora, Mexico. Journal of Toxicology and Environmental Health. Part A. 2014;**77**(4):169-176. DOI: 10.1080/15287394.2013.853223

[138] Butler PA. Residues in fish, wildlife, and estuaries; organochlorine residues in estuarine mollusks, 1965-72--National Pesticide Monitoring Program. Pesticides Monitoring Journal. 1973;**6**(4):238-362

[139] Bajpayee M, Pandey AK, Zaidi S, Musarrat J, Parmar D, Mathur N, et al. DNA damage and mutagenicity induced by endosulfan and its metabolites. Environmental and Molecular Mutagenesis. 2006;**47**(9):682-692. DOI: 10.1002/em.20255

[140] Bedor CN, Morais RJ, Cavalcanti LS, Ferreira JV, Pavão AC. Carcinogenic potential of endosulfan and its metabolites based on a quantum chemical model. Science of the Total Environment. 2010;**408**(24):6281-6284. DOI: 10.1016/j.scitotenv.2010.09.014

[141] Jamil K, Shaik AP, Mahboob M, Krishna D. Effect of organophosphorus and organochlorine pesticides (monochrotophos, chlorpyriphos, dimethoate, and endosulfan) on human lymphocytes in-vitro. Drug and Chemical Toxicology. 2004;**27**(2):133-144. DOI: 10.1081/dct-120030725

[142] London L, de GS, Wesseling C, Kisting S, Rother HA, Mergler D. Pesticide usage and health consequences for women in developing countries: Out of sight, out of mind? International Journal of Occupational and Environmental Health. 2002;**8**(1):46-59. DOI: 10.1179/oeh.2002.8.1.46

[143] Jiao Y, Liu C, Feng C, Regenstein JM, Luo Y, Tan Y, et al. Bioaccessibility and intestinal transport of deltamethrin in Pacific oyster (*Magallana gigas*) using simulated digestion/NCM460 cell models. Frontiers in Nutrition. 2021;**8**:726620. DOI: 10.3389/fnut.2021.726620

[144] Tang W, Wang D, Wang J, Wu Z, Li L, Huang M, et al. Pyrethroid pesticide residues in the global environment: An overview. Chemosphere. 2018;**191**:990-1007. DOI: 10.1016/j.chemosphere.2017.10.115

[145] Rahman Z, Singh VP. The relative impact of toxic heavy metals (THMs) (arsenic (As), cadmium (Cd), chromium (Cr)(VI), mercury (Hg), and lead (Pb)) on the total environment: An overview. Environmental Monitoring and Assessment. 2019;**191**(7):419. DOI: 10.1007/s10661-019-7528-7

[146] Mok JS, Yoo HD, Kim PH, Yoon HD, Park YC, Lee TS, et al. Bioaccumulation of heavy metals in oysters from the southern coast of Korea: Assessment of potential risk to human health. Bulletin of Environmental Contamination and Toxicology. 2015;**94**(6):749-755. DOI: 10.1007/s00128-015-1534-4

[147] Fisher WS. Antimicrobial activity of copper and zinc accumulated in eastern oyster amebocytes. Journal of Shellfish Research. 2004;**23**(2):321-351

[148] George SG, Pirie BJ, Frazier JM, Thomson JD. Interspecies differences in heavy metal detoxication in oysters. Marine Environmental Research. 1984;**14**:462-464. DOI: 10.1016/0141-1136(84)90116-8

[149] Pirie B, George S, Lytton D, Thomson J. Metal-containing blood cells of oysters: Ultrastructure, histochemistry and X-ray microanalysis. Journal of the Marine Biological Association UK. 1984;**64**(1):115-123. DOI: 10.1017/S0025315400059671

[150] Guéguen M, Amiard JC, Arnich N, Badot PM, Claisse D, Guérin T, et al. Shellfish and residual chemical contaminants: Hazards, monitoring, and health risk assessment along French coasts. Reviews of Environmental Contamination and Toxicology. 2011;**213**:55-111. DOI: 10.1007/978-1-4419-9860-6_3

[151] Mahurpawar M. Effects of heavy metals on human health. International Journal of Research—GRANTHAALAYAH. 2015;**530**:1-7. DOI: 10.29121/granthaalayah.v3.i9SE.2015.3282

[152] Fatta-Kassinos D, Meric S, Nikolaou A. Pharmaceutical residues in environmental waters and wastewater: Current state of knowledge and future research. Analytical and Bioanalytical Chemistry. 2011;**399**(1):251-275. DOI: 10.1007/s00216-010-4300-9

[153] Ferreira AM, Vale C. PCB accumulation and alterations of lipids in two length classes of the oyster *Crassostrea angulate* and of the clam *Ruditapes decussatus*. Marine Environmental Research. 1998;**45**(3):259-268. DOI: 10.1016/S0141-1136(97)00130-X

[154] Gan N, Martin L, Xu W. Impact of polycyclic aromatic hydrocarbon accumulation on oyster health. Frontiers in Physiology. 2021;**12**:734463. DOI: 10.3389/fphys.2021.734463

[155] Nakata H, Uehara K, Goto Y, Fukumura M, Shimasaki H, Takikawa K, et al. Polycyclic aromatic hydrocarbons in oysters and sediments from the Yatsushiro Sea, Japan: Comparison of potential risks among PAHs, dioxins and dioxin-like compounds in benthic organisms. Ecotoxicology and Environmental Safety. 2014;**99**:61-68. DOI: 10.1016/j.ecoenv.2013.10.005

[156] Walraven N, Laane RW. Assessing the discharge of pharmaceuticals along the Dutch coast of the North Sea. Reviews of Environmental Contamination

and Toxicology. 2009;**199**:1-18. DOI: 10.1007/978-0-387-09808-1_1

[157] Prado S, Romalde JL, Barja JL. Probióticos en cultivos larvarios de moluscos bivalvos en criadero. In: Figueras A, Novoa G, editors. Enfermedades de moluscos Bivalvos de interés en acuicultura. Madrid, España: Publicaciones Científicas y Tecnológicas de la Fundación Observatorio Español de Acuicultura; 2011. p. 543

[158] Wintermyer ML, Cooper KR. Dioxin/furan and polychlorinated biphenyl concentrations in Eastern oyster (*Crassostrea virginica*, Gmelin) tissue and the effects on egg fertilization and development. Journal of Shellfish Research. 2003;**22**:737-746

[159] White SS, Birnbaum LS. An overview of the effects of dioxins and dioxin-like compounds on vertebrates, as documented in human and ecological epidemiology. Journal of Environmental Science and Health. Part C, Environmental Carcinogenesis & Ecotoxicology Reviews. 2009;**27**(4):197-211. DOI: 10.1080/10590500903310047

[160] Gao P, da Silva E, Hou L, Denslow ND, Xiang P, Ma LQ. Human exposure to polycyclic aromatic hydrocarbons: Metabolomics perspective. Environment International. 2018;**119**:466-477. DOI: 10.1016/j.envint.2018.07.017

[161] Hong WJ, Jia H, Li YF, Sun Y, Liu X, Wang L. Polycyclic aromatic hydrocarbons (PAHs) and alkylated PAHs in the coastal seawater, surface sediment and oyster from Dalian, Northeast China. Ecotoxicology and Environmental Safety. 2016;**128**:11-20. DOI: 10.1016/j.ecoenv.2016.02.003

[162] Wang H, Huang W, Gong Y, Chen C, Zhang T, Diao X. Occurrence and potential health risks assessment of polycyclic aromatic hydrocarbons (PAHs) in different tissues of bivalves from Hainan Island, China. Food and Chemical Toxicology. 2020;**136**:111108. DOI: 10.1016/j.fct.2019.111108

[163] Boonyatumanond R, Wattayakorn G, Togo A, Takada H. Distribution and origins of polycyclic aromatic hydrocarbons (PAHs) in riverine, estuarine, and marine sediments in Thailand. Marine Pollution Bulletin. 2006;**52**(8):942-956. DOI: 10.1016/j.marpolbul.2005.12.015

[164] Soclo HH, Garrigues PH, Ewald M. Origin of polycyclic aromatic hydrocarbons (PAHs) in coastal marine sediments: Case studies in Cotonou (Benin) and Aquitaine (France) areas. Marine Pollution Bulletin. 2000;**40**:387-396. DOI: 10.1016/S0025-326X(99)00200-3

[165] Montano L, Pironti C, Pinto G, Ricciardi M, Buono A, Brogna C, et al. Polychlorinated biphenyls (PCBs) in the environment: Occupational and exposure events, effects on human health and fertility. Toxics. 2022;**10**(7):365. DOI: 10.3390/toxics10070365

[166] Huss HH, Ababouch L, Gram L. Assessment and Management of Seafood Safety and Quality FAO Fisheries Technical Paper. No. 444. Rome: FAO; 2003. 230 p

[167] Bour A, Haarr A, Keiter S, Hylland K. Environmentally relevant microplastic exposure affects sediment-dwelling bivalves. Environmental Pollution. 2018;**236**:652-660. DOI: 10.1016/j.envpol.2018.02.006

[168] Cho Y, Shim WJ, Jang M, Han GM, Hong SH. Abundance and characteristics of microplastics in market bivalves from

South Korea. Environmental Pollution. 2019;**245**:1107-1116. DOI: 10.1016/j.envpol.2018.11.091

[169] Wootton N, Sarakinis K, Varea R, Reis-Santos P, Gillanders BM. Microplastic in oysters: A review of global trends and comparison to southern Australia. Chemosphere. 2022;**307**(Pt. 4):136065. DOI: 10.1016/j.chemosphere.2022.136065

[170] Ashie IN, Smith JP, Simpson BK. Spoilage and shelf-life extension of fresh fish and shellfish. Critical Reviews in Food Science and Nutrition. 1996;**36**(1-2):87-121. DOI: 10.1080/10408399609527720

[171] Madigan TL, Bott NJ, Torok VA, Percy NJ, Carragher JF, de Barros Lopes MA, et al. A microbial spoilage profile of half shell Pacific oysters (*Crassostrea gigas*) and Sydney rock oysters (*Saccostrea glomerata*). Food Microbiology. Apr 2014;**38**:219-227. DOI: 10.1016/j.fm.2013.09.005

[172] Kingsley DH. High pressure processing of bivalve shellfish and HPP's use as a virus intervention. Food. 2014;**3**(2):336-350. DOI: 10.3390/foods3020336

[173] Cao R, Xue CH, Liu Q. Changes in microbial flora of Pacific oysters (*Crassostrea gigas*) during refrigerated storage and its shelf-life extension by chitosan. International Journal of Food Microbiology. 2009;**131**(2-3):272-276. DOI: 10.1016/j.ijfoodmicro.2009.03.004

[174] Kim YM, Park HD, Lee DS. Shelf-life characteristics of fresh oysters and ground beef as affected by bacteriocin-coated plastic packaging film. Journal of the Science of Food and Agriculture. 2002;**82**:998-1002. DOI: 10.1002/jsfa.1125

[175] Fernandez-Piquer J, Bowman JP, Ross T, Tamplin ML. Molecular analysis of the bacterial communities in the live Pacific oyster (*Crassostrea gigas*) and the influence of postharvest temperature on its structure. Journal of Applied Microbiology. 2012;**112**(6):1134-1143. DOI: 10.1111/j.1365-2672.2012.05287.x

[176] Lorca TA, Pierson MD, Flick GJ, Hackney CR. Levels of Vibrio vulnificus and organoleptic quality of raw shellstock oysters (*Crassostrea virginica*) maintained at different storage temperatures. Journal of Food Protection. 2001;**64**(11):1716-1721. DOI: 10.4315/0362-028x-64.11.1716

[177] Hood MA, Ness GE, Rodrick GE, Blake NJ. Effects of storage on microbial loads of two commercially important shellfish species, *Crassostrea virginica* and *Mercenaria campechiensis*. Applied and Environmental Microbiology. 1983;**45**(4):1221-1228. DOI: 10.1128/aem.45.4.1221-1228.1983

[178] Chen H, Wang M, Yang C, Wan X, Ding HH, Shi Y, et al. Bacterial spoilage profiles in the gills of Pacific oysters (*Crassostrea gigas*) and eastern oysters (*C. virginica*) during refrigerated storage. Food Microbiology. 2019;**82**:209-217. DOI: 10.1016/j.fm.2019.02.008

[179] Aaraas R, Hernar IJ, Vorre A, Bergslien H, Lunestad BT, Skeie S, et al. Sensory, histological, and bacteriological changes in flat oysters, *Ostrea edulis* L., during different storage conditions. Journal of Food Science. 2004;**69**:S205-S210. DOI: 10.1111/j.1365-2621.2004.tb11006.x

[180] Kingsley D. SHELLFISH (MOLLUSCS AND CRUSTACEA) | Shellfish contamination and spoilage. In: Encyclopedia of Food Microbiology. 2nd ed. 2014. pp. 389-396. DOI: 10.1016/B978-0-12-384730-0.00306-2

[181] Andrews LS, Park DL, Chen YP. Low temperature pasteurization to

reduce the risk of vibrio infections from raw shell-stock oysters. Food Additives and Contaminants. 2000;**17**(9):787-791. DOI: 10.1080/026520300415336

[182] He H, Adams RM, Farkas DF, Morrissey MT. Use of high-pressure processing for oyster shucking and shelf-life extension. Journal of Food Science. 2002;**67**:640-645. DOI: 10.1111/j.1365-2621.2002.tb10652.x

[183] Dong S, Niu Y, Wei H, Lin Y, Lu X, Yamashita T, et al. Effect of super-chilling storage on maintenance of quality and freshness of the Pacific oyster (*Crassostrea gigas*). Food Quality and Safety. 2023;7:1-9. DOI: 10.1093/fqsafe/fyad008

[184] López Hernández K, Pardío Sedas V, Rodríguez Dehaibes S, Suárez Valencia V, Rivas Mozo I, Martínez Herrera D, et al. Improved microbial safety of direct ozone-depurated shellstock eastern oysters (*Crassostrea virginica*) by superchilled storage. Frontiers in Microbiology. 2018;**9**:2802. DOI: 10.3389/fmicb.2018.02802

[185] FAO and WHO. Code of Practice for Fish and Fishery Products. Rome, Italy: Food and Agriculture Organization of the United Nations and World Health Organization; 2020. p. 372. DOI: 10.4060/cb0658en

[186] CAC, Codex Alimentarius Commission. Joint FAO/WHO Food Standards Programme. Forty-fourth Session. 2021; pp.79. Available from: https://www.fao.org/fao-who-codexalimentarius/sh-proxy/en/?lnk=1&url=https%253A%252F%252Fworkspace.fao.org%252Fsites%252Fcodex%252FMeetings%252FCX-701-44%252FFINAL%252520REPORT%252FRep21_CACe.pdf

[187] FDA. Fish and Fishery Products Hazards and Controls Guidance. Floria, USA: Food and Drug Administration; 2022. p. 553. Available from: https://www.fda.gov/media/80637/download

[188] Karunasagar I. Food safety and public health risks associated with products of aquaculture. In: Bondad-Reantaso MG, Arthur JR, Subasinghe RP, editors. Understanding and Applying Risk Analysis in Aquaculture. FAO Fisheries and Aquaculture Technical Paper. No. 519. Rome, Italy: FAO; 2008. pp. 9-25

[189] Brooks HA, Gersberg RM, Dhar AK. Detection and quantification of hepatitis A virus in seawater via real-time RT-PCR. Journal of Virological Methods. 2005;**127**(2):109-118. DOI: 10.1016/j.jviromet.2005.03.017

[190] Scarfe AD, Palić D. Aquaculture biosecurity: Practical approach to prevent, control, and eradicate diseases. In: Aquaculture Health Management. Chapter 3. 2020. pp. 75-116. DOI: 10.1016/b978-0-12-813359-0.00003-8

[191] OIE. The World Organisation for Animal Health, the Office International Des Epizooties. Manual of Diagnostic Tests for Aquatic Animals. Paris, France: World Organization for Animal Health (OIE); 2021. p. 589

[192] FAO. COFI Sub-Committee on Aquaculture 10th Session Documents. In: Report of the Tenth Session of the SubCommittee on Aquaculture. Trondheim, Norway: Food and Agriculture Organization of the United Nations; 2019. p. 66. Available from: https://www.fao.org/3/ca7417t/CA7417T.pdf

[193] FAO. Progress towards Development of the Progressive Management Pathway for Improving Aquaculture Biosecurity (PMP/AB): Highlights of 2019 Activities. FAO Fisheries and Aquaculture Circular No. 1211. Rome, Italy: Food

and Agriculture Organization of the United Nations; 2020. p. 42. Available from: https://www.fao.org/3/cb0560en/CB0560EN.pdf

[194] FAO. Blue Transformation—Roadmap 2022-2030: A Vision for FAO's Work on Aquatic Food Systems. Rome, Italy: Food and Agriculture Organization of the United Nations; 2022. p. 40. Available from: https://www.fao.org/3/cc0459en/cc0459en.pdf

[195] FAO. Blue Finance Guidance Notes. Microfinance for Small-scale Fisheries. Rome, Italy: Food and Agriculture Organization of the United Nations; 2020. p. 16. Available from: https://www.fao.org/3/ca8645en/CA8645EN.pdf

[196] FAO. Food and Agriculture Organization of the United Nations. Enfermedades transmitidas por los alimentos y su impacto socioeconómico. Rome: Organización de las Naciones Unidas para la Agricultura y la Alimentación; 2009. p. 194. Available from: https://www.fao.org/3/i0480s/i0480s.pdf

Chapter 7

Biofouling of the Mangrove Oyster (*Crassostrea tulipa*, Lamarck, 1819) Cultivation: The West African Perspective

Isaac Kofi Osei, Edward Adzesiwor Obodai and Denis Worlanyo Aheto

Abstract

Oyster, *Crassostrea tulipa* cultivation in the West African subregion is largely carried out in estuarine and mangrove ecosystems on a small scale. These coastal water bodies generally present favorable biotic and abiotic conditions that impact positively oyster propagation. Some environmental factors including coastal flooding, eutrophication, and biofouling could hamper the culture of oysters in the wild. Biofouling is the attachment of organisms to the object of interest. It is also described as unwanted living things that occupy the same ecological niche as the desired species, causing harm by contesting for available food and living space, which is crucial in the culture of oysters where the biofoulers have deleterious effect on the growth and survival of oysters. The injurious impact of biofouling could result in en masse mortalities or reduced growth rate. Interventions to mitigate the effect will result in increased cost of operation, thereby making the business less profitable. However, existing studies in West Africa Indicate that fouling organisms may have no harmful impact on *C. tulipa* cultivation. Good water quality, a well-managed culture system, and adoption of best practices in post-harvest handling will enhance the production of oysters to provide food and nutrition security, livelihoods, and employments.

Keywords: fouling organisms, climate change, physico-chemical parameters, growth rate, survival, cultch

1. Introduction

Climate change; illegal, unreported, and unregulated (IUU) fishing; and the near collapse of some capture fisheries in Africa and the world at large have necessitated the need to opt for enhanced cultivation of fish to feed the teeming world population. More crucial is the case of Africa, in that, its economies largely depend on the climate; hence, variations in climatic conditions are likely to impact negatively its productivity and lead to the eventual collapse of the economies. Therefore, policymakers and resource managers in Africa are entreated to prioritize building climate-smart finfish and shellfish productions as well as aquaculture production to promote adaptation and mitigation measures toward achieving sustainable and resilient fisheries.

Shellfish production occurs globally; however, Africa has contributed little to global productivity [1]. This could be ascribed to low interest and investment on the part of African governments and private sectors as well as researchers when it comes to the development and culture of the resource, although shellfish production has great potential to contribute to food and nutritional security, livelihoods, and employments. According to a recent regional study on the evaluation of coastal shellfisheries covering eleven (11) West African countries, more than 300,000 mt of shellfish were landed annually, with an appraised value of USD 336 million [2]. With the appropriate policy and enforcement interventions from regional and national fishery bodies, the yield of these fisheries could be optimized to meet the growing demand of fish. Aquaculture has the potential to meet the high demand of fish as indicated by FAO [1].

Oysters in general inhabit coastal marine and brackish water systems, spanning from temperate, subtropics to tropical latitudes globally [3]. The West African mangrove oyster thrives in brackish water systems (i.e., estuaries and lagoons), normally with mangrove vegetations [4–6]. The organism largely filter-feeds on phytoplankton and substrate particles [7]; hence, no cost of feeding is incurred should the species be cultured *in situ*.

In the culture of bivalves including oysters in-situ, farmers would have to conduct an investigation as to whether biofouling would hamper their production to elicit the right management approach. Quayle and Newkirk [8] describe biofouling as the attachment of marine organisms, that is plants or animals, to the object of interest (collector, cultch, or the culture species). These fouling organisms usually occupy the same ecological niche as the culture species; hence, there is a possibility of competing for living space and available food [9]. Aside from fouling organisms, there are predators and disease-causing organisms that may be deleterious to oyster production. In addition to the aforementioned groups of organisms, it has been documented widely that the growth and survival of cultivated bivalves including oysters are influenced by environmental factors such as salinity, dissolved oxygen, temperature, turbidity, pH, and bulk density of sediments [10, 11].

Biofouling could be a severe problem in oyster cultivation in the tropics, according to Angell [12]. This position appears to be corroborated by Watson and Shumway's [13] report, which indicates that biofouling on farmed mollusks could be severe and overwhelming. However, there are reports that describe the impact of fouling organisms as mere nuisance than a severe problem on oysters of the genus Crassostrea [14]. Moreover, it has been explained that biofoulers are generally stenohaline organisms unlike the Crassostrea species; hence, the impact of the fouling organisms will be neutralized when the organism is cultivated in an estuarine environment [8].

2. West African mangrove oyster species

Crassostrea tulipa (Lamarck, 1819) and *C. gasar* (Dautzenberg, 1891) are the two species referred to as the West African mangrove oyster in literature. There were concerns as to whether these species refer to the same organism or otherwise. As characteristic of oysters, morphological characteristics of individuals in a population are greatly modified by some local environmental factors despite their similar genotypic makeup [3, 8], hence making the use of morphological indices impractical to distinguish between the two species names. Lapegue et al. [15] settled the confusion with their study on the genetic analysis of the mitochondrial DNA of the two species, where it was inferred that *C. tulipa* and *C. gasar* refer to the same organism.

Moreover, on the decision of which specific name to adopt upon realization that the two species refer to the West African mangrove oyster, *C. tulipa* is chosen over *C. gasar* owing to the precedence of the former to the latter in the literature. Yankson [16] agreed with the above position by reporting a comprehensive discussion on the matter, thereby recommending the use of *C. tulipa* as the West African mangrove oyster. In that respect, *C. tulipa* will be used throughout this document as the species name of the mangrove oyster found in the West African coastal waters.

3. Biofouling

3.1 Description and types of biofoulers

Biofouling studies carried out in West Africa have identified tube-dwelling polychaetes, mussels, barnacles, sea anemones, hydroids, and tunicates as the main fouling organisms [5, 17–19]. In a recent publication [10], the following species were observed in an experimental culture of oysters in the Densu Delta, Ghana: *Fistubalanus pallidus* (barnacle), *Chaetomorpha antennina* (green alga), *Ficopomatus* sp. (tube-dwelling worm), and *Brachidontes* sp. (mussel); see **Figure 1**. *F. pallidus* was the dominant sedentary fouling organism. To the oyster farmer, the attachment of biofoulers to cultches or substrates and the cultured oysters may be of concern.

3.2 Spatial and seasonal variations in fouling organisms

The biofoulers of *C. tulipa* are largely marine in nature. This is because the oysters inhabit brackish water systems with measurable freshwater influx, optimally with a salinity range between 35 and 5‰ [10]. In view of this, the fouling organisms tend to exhibit high abundance toward the saline end of the estuarine ecosystems. Furthermore, the biofoulers tend to thrive during the dry season when there is low rainfall or inundation at the coastal areas and vice versa.

3.3 Effect of biofoulers on cultured oysters from the African perspective

The aforementioned fouling organisms are filter-feeders, suggesting the potential of competing with oysters for food resources, except for the green alga (*C. antennina*), which is an autotroph. Competition is highly probable if there is no food resource partitioning, that is, difference in food particle size selection and feeding efficiency, among the epibionts. On the other hand, green algae reduce the setting surface of oyster spat, which is a huge challenge in collecting oyster seeds for stocking as well as obstructing the flow water into and out of the cultured oysters leading to low growth rate or mortality could lead to low growth rate or mortality. Studies carried out elsewhere reported some adverse impacts of the observed biofoulers on oyster cultivation. These include mortality, physical interruption to opening and closure of shells, and reduction in growth rate [14, 20]. The most lethal observed sedentary fouling organism was the tubeworm (*Ficopomatus* sp), which could burrow into the oyster shell.

Figure 1.
A photograph of biofoulers on (a) an oyster shell cultch: alga, barnacle, tubeworm, sea anemone and (b) cultured oyster: mussel (Source: [10]).

3.4 Growth and survival of oysters on the convex and concave surfaces as well as on the top-2-collectors and bottom-2-collectors of biofouled and cleaned coconut and oyster shell cultches

Osei et al. [10] published their findings on the growth and survival of oysters on the convex and concave surfaces of biofouled and cleaned coconut shell and oyster shell cultches, where it was inferred that biofouling had no harmful effect on the growth and survival of oysters in the Densu Delta. In that study, oysters cultivated on the biofouled cultches appeared to exhibit faster mean growth rate than their counterparts on clean cultches. Nonetheless, the treatments were not significantly different except for oysters cultivated on the concave surface/underside of oyster shell cultches.

Moreover, in concurrence with the above experiment, a similar experiment to the biofouling research [10] was done on the growth and survival of oysters cultured on the top- and bottom-2-collectors of two different collectors at the Densu Delta (see the aforementioned paper for the methodology). Generally, the growth of biofouled and cleaned oysters followed a similar pattern. Panel (a) of **Figure 2** presents the growth of oysters cultured on the top-2-collectors of biofouled and cleaned coconut-shell cultches. Oysters on biofouled and cleaned cultches grew up to 4.93 ± 0.11 cm SH (shell height) and 4.79 ± 0.13 cm SH with mean growth rates of 0.77 ± 0.20 cm/month and 0.74 ± 0.21 cm/month, respectively. The treatments were not statistically significant ($F = 1.74$, $df = 4$, $p = 0.15$).

Panel (b) of **Figure 2** shows the growth of oysters cultured on the bottom-2-collectors of biofouled and cleaned coconut-shell cultches. Oysters at these positions grew up to 5.24 ± 0.08 cm SH and 5.32 ± 0.21 cm SH with mean growth rates of

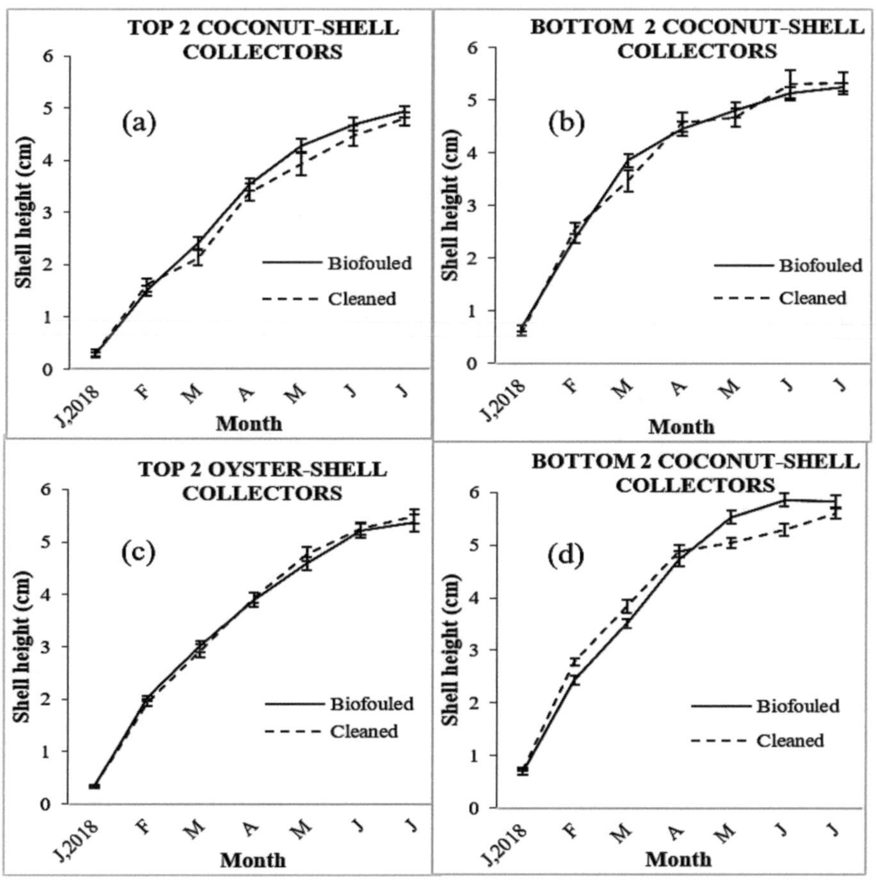

Figure 2.
Growth of Crassostrea tulipa *cultured on the top- and bottom-2-collectors of biofouled and cleaned coconut-shell and oyster-shell cultches using the suspension culture method in the Densu Delta (vertical bars indicate standard errors of means).*

0.76 ± 0.27 cm/month and 0.79 ± 0.30 cm/month, respectively. There was no significant difference between the treatments ($F = 1.74$, $df = 4$, $p = 0.15$).

The third panel (c) of **Figure 2** presents the growth of oysters cultured on the top-2-collectors of biofouled and cleaned oyster-shell cultches. Oysters at this position on the biofouled and cleaned cultches grew up to 5.36 ± 0.16 cm SH and 5.48 ± 0.13 cm SH with mean growth rates of 0.83 ± 0.21 cm/month and 0.83 ± 0.19 cm/month, respectively. The treatments were not statistically significant ($F = 1.74$, $df = 4$, $p = 0.15$).

The fourth panel (c) of **Figure 2** shows the growth of oysters cultured on the bottom-2-collectors of biofouled and cleaned oyster-shell cultches. Oysters at this position on the biofouled and cleaned cultches grew up to 5.83 ± 0.12 cm SH and 5.60 ± 0.10 cm SH with mean growth rates of 0.85 ± 0.26 cm/month and 0.81 ± 0.29 cm/month, respectively. The treatments were not statistically significant ($F = 0.90$, $df = 1$, $p = 0.35$).

The survival of biofouled and cleaned oysters cultured at the top- and bottom-2-collectors of coconut-shell and oyster-shell cultches is presented in **Figure 3**. Generally, the survival of biofouled and cleaned oysters followed a similar pattern, where it declined slowly from January to June and thereafter decreased sharply from June to July 2018. The first panel (a) of **Figure 3** illustrates the survival of oysters cultured on the top-2-collectors of biofouled and cleaned coconut-shell cultches. Survival of oysters on the biofouled and cleaned coconut-shell cultches was 59.49% and 50.90%, respectively, in July 2018. The difference in survival of the treatments was not significant ($X^2 = 0.22$, $df = 4$, $p = 0.99$). Panel (b) of the figure shows the survival of oysters cultured on the bottom-2-collectors of biofouled and cleaned coconut-shell cultches. Survival of oysters on the biofouled and cleaned cultches was 54.79% and 43.32%, respectively, in July 2018. The difference in survival of the treatments was not significant ($X^2 = 0.22$, $df = 4$, $p = 0.99$).

The third panel (c) of **Figure 3** presents the survival of oysters cultured on the top-2-collectors of biofouled and cleaned oyster-shell cultches. Survival of oysters on the biofouled and cleaned cultches was 53.95% and 48.10%, respectively, in July 2018. There was no significant difference between the treatments ($X^2 = 0.18$, $df = 4$, $p = 0.99$). Panel (d) of **Figure 3** shows the survival of oysters cultured on the bottom-2-collectors of biofouled and cleaned oyster-shell cultches. Survival of oysters on the biofouled and cleaned cultches was 49.68% and 46.8%, respectively, in July 2018. There was no statistical significance in the survival of the treatments ($X^2 = 0.06$, $df = 4$, $p = 0.99$).

Oyster growth and survival on biofouled and cleaned cultches at the top and bottom collectors showing no significant difference could be a result of a comparable community of biofoulers on the top and bottom collectors, possibly, given the shallow depth of the culture site in the Densu Delta (approximately 0.61 m high tide).

The lack of effect of biofouling on the growth of oysters on coconut-shell cultches is consistent with earlier findings [19] where the authors observed no effect of biofouling on *C. tulpa* in three different lagoons, namely Benya, Nakwa, and Jange. Elsewhere, a lack of effect of biofouling on growth and survival has been documented for *C. rhizophorae*, *C. virginica*, and *C. gigas* as reported by [21], [22], and [23], respectively. The observation of no impact of biofouling on growth and survival of oysters could be attributed to a number of factors, that is, commensalism, food-resource partitioning stimulated primary production by some biofoulers to offset the limited food resources [21, 22, 24]. It has been reported that growing oysters can tolerate a considerable degree of biofouling before becoming harmful enough to necessitate some form of control intervention [14].

A positive effect of biofouling has, however, been reported for oysters [9, 24]. The underside of suspended or floating collectors or substrates has been found to be

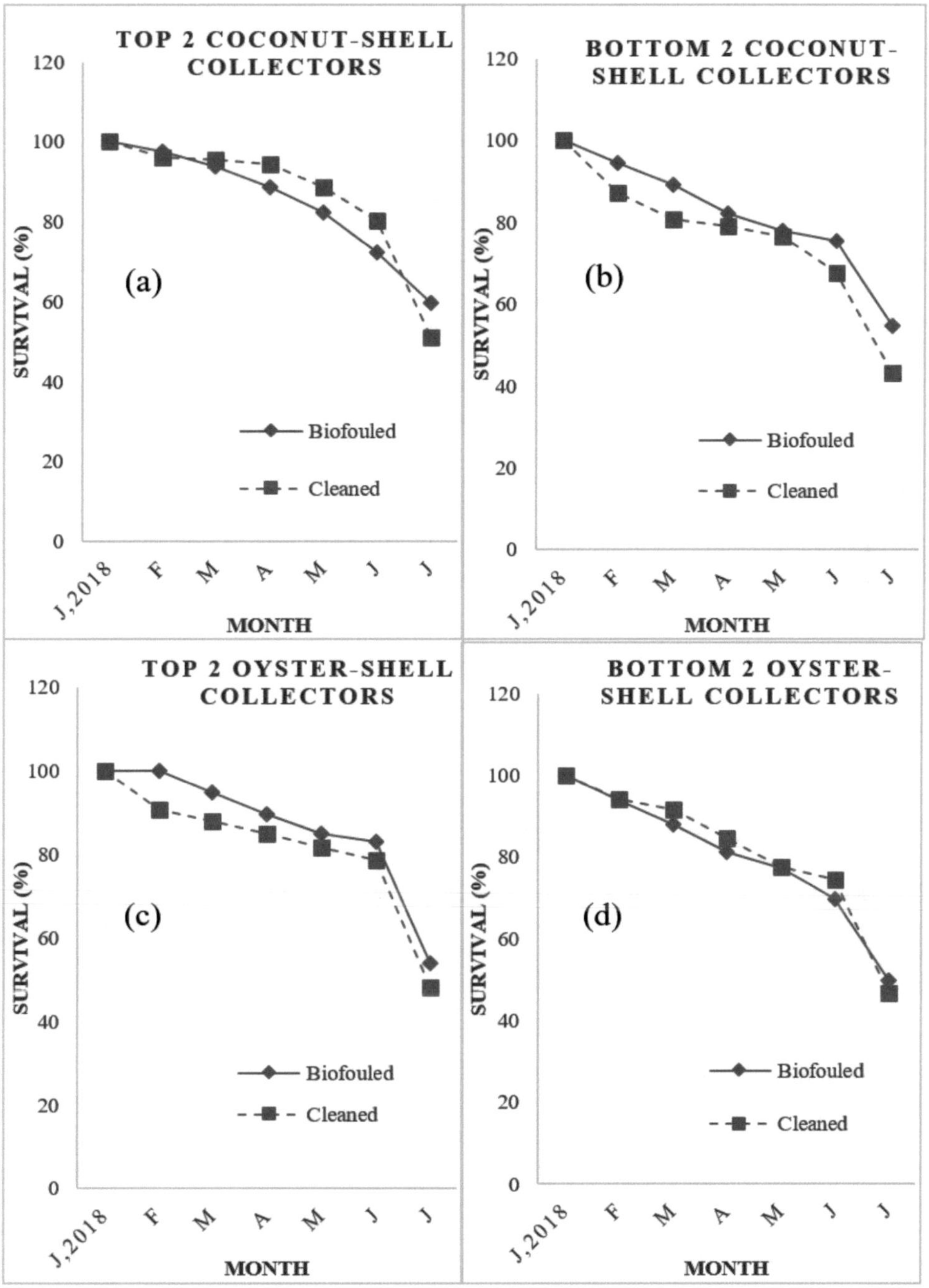

Figure 3.
Survival of Crassostrea tulipa cultured on the top- and bottom-2-collectors of biofouled and cleaned coconut-shell and oyster-shell cultches using the suspension culture method in the Densu Delta (vertical bars indicate standard errors of means).

the preferred surface for epibionts including oysters [8, 19, 25]. Tanita et al. [1961, as cited in 9] reported that the later attachment of biofoulers could stimulate shell growth in oysters, as an attempt in competing for space.

Quite a considerable number of works have reported on the devastating effect of biofouling on cultured bivalves, including oysters [11, 12]. According to Arakawa [9], biofoulers like barnacles and mussels are known to engage in severe competition with cultured oysters, resulting in reduced growth rate. Moreover, biofouling has been reported to cause decline in growth rate and mortality in oysters [11] and mussles [26, 27]. Biofouling could have financial implications on the culture, in that, it could reduce the market value especially for half-shell trading, as a result of unsightly blister shells [23] as well as increased operational cost in preventing or treating biofouling [20]. The increase in operational cost due to biofouling of oysters could be up to 30% [28].

It is rational to investigate the effects of fouling organisms on oysters *in situ* before any mass cultivation of the species. In the case of deleterious effects of epibionts, control measures must be put in place to reduce or get rid of the biofoulers. Three strategies comprising avoidance, prevention, and treatment have been described in reducing fouling organisms [29]. In most cases, farmers employ some treatment measures when the effect of biofouling is harmful, which results in increased operational cost. Efficient, cost-effective, and environmentally friendly approaches used in treating fouling organisms *in situ* include exposure to freshwater [30] and air drying [31] on small scale farms. Other methods like application of heat [32] and use of organic acids and bases [33] could be used.

4. Conclusion

There is ample evidence that fouling organisms may not have harmful impact on *C. tulipa* cultivation in the estuarine mangrove ecosystem; therefore, there is no need to implement preventive or treatment measures. However, a farmer may want to avoid, prevent, and employ treatment approaches if the target is on half-shelf trading to avoid the unsightly appearance of oyster shells, which has implications of reducing the market value of the produce.

Given the coastal degradation and biofouling in some coastal water bodies, intensive culture of *C. tulipa* will be ideal to avoid the effect of contaminants and fouling organisms.

Acknowledgements

Our sincere thanks go to the USAID/UCC Fisheries and Coastal Management Capacity Building Support Project for the award of scholarship for the study under the directorship of Professor Denis Worlanyo Aheto of the Centre for Coastal Management (CCM), Africa Centre of Excellence in Coastal Resilience (ACECoR), University of Cape Coast (UCC) for providing the enabling environment for the research special thanks go to Prof. Denis W. Aheto, Director of Centre for Coastal Management (CCM)/ African Centre of Excellence in Coastal Resilience (ACECoR) at the University of Cape Coast for offering the enabling environment for the research to come to fruition.

Conflict of interest

The authors declare no conflict of interest.

Notes/thanks/other declarations

I (Dr. Isaac Kofi Osei) would like to express my profound indebtedness to the late Prof. Emeritus Kobina Yankson, Prof. Edward Adzesiwor Obodai and Prof. Denis Worlanyo Aheto for offering professional guidance and support. Edward Adzesiwor Obodai for supervising the study, both of the Centre for Coastal Management/African Centre of Excellence in Coastal Resilience and the Department of Fisheries and Aquatic Sciences (DFAS), University of Cape Coast for their professional guidance, encouragement and support during my PhD study. I am eternally grateful to them.

Author details

Isaac Kofi Osei[1,2*], Edward Adzesiwor Obodai[1,2] and Denis Worlanyo Aheto[1,2]

1 Centre for Coastal Management (CCM), Africa Centre of Excellence in Coastal Resilience (ACECoR), University of Cape Coast, Ghana

2 Department of Fisheries and Aquatic Sciences, University of Cape Coast, Ghana

*Address all correspondence to: isaac.osei1@ucc.edu.gh

References

[1] FAO. The State of World Fisheries and Aquaculture 2022. Towards Blue Transformation. Rome: FAO; 2022. DOI: 10.4060/cc0461en

[2] Chuku EO, Effah E, Adotey J, Abrokwah S, Adade R, Okyere I, et al. Spotlighting women-led fisheries livelihoods toward sustainable coastal governance: The estuarine and mangrove ecosystem shellfisheries of West Africa. Frontiers in Marine Science. 2022;**9**:884715. DOI: 10.3389/fmars.2022.884715

[3] Gosling E. Bivalve Molluscs: Biology, Ecology and Culture. Fishing New Books, Blackwell Publishing; 2003. 443 p. DOI: 10.1002/9780470995532

[4] Adite A, Abou Y, Sossoukpê E, Fiogbé ED. The oyster farming in the coastal ecosystem of southern Benin (West Africa): Environment, growth and contribution to sustainable coastal fisheries management. International Journal of Development Research. 2013;**3**(10):087-094

[5] Osei IK, Yankson K, Obodai EA. Demographic and profitability analyses of the west African mangrove oyster. Journal of Fisheries Coastal Management. 2020;**2**:12-22. DOI: 10.5455/jfcom.20190528122752

[6] Yankson K. Fish from the Shell: Its Potential in the Quest for Adequate Protein in Ghana: An Inaugural Lecture Delivered at the University of Cape Coast. Accra, Ghana: Media Graphics & Press LTD.; 2004

[7] Adite A, Sonon SP, Gbedjissi GL. Feeding ecology of the mangrove oyster, *Crassostrea gasar* (Dautzenberg, 1891) in traditional farming at the coastal zone of Benin, West Africa. Natural Science. 2013;**5**(12):1238-1248

[8] Quayle DB, Newkirk GF. Farming Bivalve Molluscs: Methods for Study and Development. Baton Rouge, Louisiana, USA: The World Aquaculture Society and the International Development Research Centre; 1989

[9] Arakawa KY. Natural spat collecting in the Pacific oyster *Crassostrea gigas* (Thunberg). Marine Behaviour and Physiology. 1990;**17**:95-128

[10] Osei IK, Yankson K, Obodai EA. Effect of sedentary biofoulers on the growth and survival of cultured oysters (*Crassostrea tulipa*) towards its mass culture in the Densu Delta, Ghana. Aquaculture International. 2021;**29**(2):813-826. DOI: 10.1007/s10499-021-00659-9

[11] Pit JH, Southgate PC. Fouling and predation; how do they affect growth and survival of the blacklip pearl oyster, *Pinctada margaritifera*, during nursery culture? Aquaculture International. 2003;**11**(6):545-555. DOI: 10.1023/B:AQUI.0000013310.17400.97

[12] Angell CL. The Biology and Culture of Tropical Oysters, Studies and Reviews. Vol. 13. Manila, Philippines: ICLARM; 1986. DOI: 10.1073/pnas.0703993104

[13] Watson DI, Shumway SE. Shellfish safety and quality related titles. In: Shumway SE, Rodrick GE, editors. Biofouling and the Shellfish Industry. 1st ed. England: Woodhead Publishing Limited; 2009. pp. 317-337

[14] Quayle DB. Tropical Oysters: Culture and Methods. Ottawa, ON: IDRC; 1980

[15] Lapegue S, Boutet I, Leitao A, Heurtebise S, Garcia P, Thiriot-Quievreux C, et al. Trans-Atlantic distribution of a mangrove oyster species revealed by 16S mtDNA and karyological analyses. Biological Bulletin. 2002;**202**:232-242

[16] Yankson K. Certain aspects of the culture of the local mangrove oyster (*Crassostrea tulipa*) in Ghana. Oceanography. 1991;**3**:9-14

[17] Asare B. Aquaculture Potential of the West African Mangrove Oyster (*Crassostrea tulipa*): A Case Study of the Species in the Narkwa Lagoon of Ghana. Unpublished master's thesis. Ghana: Department of Fisheries and Aquatic Sciences, University of Cape Coast; 2017

[18] Chuku EO. Promoting Oyster Culture in Ghana: Strategies for Optimising Seed Collection and Growth of *Crassostrea tulipa* (Lamarck, 1819) in Coastal Water Bodies. Unpublished master's thesis. Ghana: Department of Fisheries and Aquatic Sciences, University of Cape Coast; 2019

[19] Obodai EA, Yankson K. Effects of fouling organisms on cultured oysters, *Crassostrea tulipa*, in three Ghanaian lagoons. Journal of Ghana Science Association. 2000;**2**(2):36-53

[20] Fitridge I, Dempster T, Guenther J, De Nys R. The impact and control of biofouling in marine aquaculture: A review. Biofouling. 2012;**28**(7):649-669. DOI: 10.1080/08927014.2012.700478

[21] Lodeiros C, Pico D, Prieto A, Narváez N, Guerra A. Growth and survival of the pearl oyster *Pinctada imbricata* (Röding 1758) in suspended and bottom culture in the Golfo de Cariaco, Venezuela. Aquaculture International. 2002;**10**:327-339

[22] Mallet al, Carver CE, Hardy M. The effect of floating bag management strategies on biofouling, oyster growth and biodeposition levels. Aquaculture. 2009;**287**:315-323

[23] Royer J, Ropert M, Mathieu M, Costil K. Presence of spionid worms and other epibionts in Pacific oysters (*Crassostrea gigas*) cultured in Normandy, France. Aquaculture. 2006;**253**:461-474

[24] Dalby JE, Young CM. Variable effects of ascidian competitors on oysters in a Florida epifaunal community. Journal of Experimental Marine Biology and Ecology. 1993;**167**:47-57

[25] Glasby TM, Connell SD. Orientation and position of substrata have large effects on epibiotic assemblages. Marine Ecology Progress Series. 2001;**214**:127-135

[26] Daigle R, Herbinger C. Ecological interactions between the vase tunicate (Ciona intestinalis) and the farmed blue mussel (Mytilus edulis) in Nova Scotia, Canada. Aquatic Invasions. 2009;**4**:177-187

[27] De Sa FS, Nalesso RC, Paresgue K. Fouling organisms on *Perna perna* mussels: Is it worth removing them? Brazilian Journal of Oceanography. 2007;**55**:155-161

[28] De Nys R, Steinberg P, Hodson S, Heasman MP. Evaluation of antifoulants on overcatch, other forms of biofouling and mudworms in Sydney rock oysters. Final report to FRDC Project No. 98/341. 2002. pp. 1-99

[29] Sievers M, Fitridge I, Dempster T, Keough MJ. Biofouling leads to reduced shell growth and flesh weight in the cultured mussel *Mytilus galloprovincialis*. Biofouling. 2013;**29**:97-107

[30] Forrest BM, Blakemore KA. Evaluation of treatments to reduce the spread of a marine plant pest with aquaculture transfers. Aquaculture. 2006;**257**:333-345

[31] Hillock KA, Costello MJ. Tolerance of the invasive tunicate *Styela clava* to air exposure. Biofouling. 2014;**29**:1181-1187

[32] Guenther J, Fitridge I, Misimi E. Potential antifouling strategies for marine finfish aquaculture: The effects of physical and chemical treatments on the settlement and survival of the hydroid *Ectopleura larynx*. Biofouling. 2011;**27**:1033-1042

[33] Rolheiser KC, Dunham A, Switzer SE, Pearce CM, Therriault TW. Assessment of chemical treatments for controlling *Didemnum vexillum*, other bio- fouling, and predatory sea stars in Pacific oyster aquaculture. Aquaculture. 2012;**364**:53-60